D0264338

Also by Barry Forshaw

Nordic Noir
Euro Noir
Brit Noir
Italian Cinema
American Noir

Praise for Barry Forshaw

CRITICAL ACCLAIM FOR *ITALIAN CINEMA*

'I⸱⸱⸱ ⸱n cinema is celebrated here with astute analysis in the sharply ⸱⸱⸱ ormative essays of Barry Forshaw' – **John Pitt, *New Classics***

CRITICAL ACCLAIM FOR *EURO NOIR*

'An ⸱⸱ ormative, interesting, accessible and enjoyable guide as Forshaw g⸱ ⸱es us through the crime output of a dozen nations' – ***The Times***

'E⸱ ⸱aining, illuminating, and indispensable. This is the ultimate road ⸱a⸱ for anybody interested in European crime books, film, and TV' – ***Euro But Not Trash***

'A⸱ exhilarating tour of Europe viewed through its crime fiction' – ***Guardian***

'Exer⸱⸱ ary tour of the European crime landscape… supremely readable' – ***The Independent***

i⸱ is a book for everyone and will help and expand your reading and viewing' – ***We Love This Book***

⸱⸱ all the best reference books, it made me want to read virtually e⸱⸱ry writer mentioned. And, on another note, I love the cover' – ***crimepieces.com***

' ⸱ di⸱ want to read something so drastically new, I now know where I would begin. With this book' – ***Bookwitch***

'B⸱ ⸱rry Forshaw is the master of the essential guide' – ***Shots Mag***

' ⸱his enjoyable and authoritative guide provides an invaluable c⸱ ⸱prehensive resource for anyone wishing to learn more about Eur⸱ pean Noir, to anticipate the next big success and to explore new avenues of blood-curdling entertainment' – ***Good Book Guide***

'Fascinating and well researched… refreshing and accessible' – ***The Herald***

'An entertaining guide by a real expert, with a lot of ideas for writers and film/TV to try' – **Promoting Crime Fiction**

'… a fabulous little book that is like a roadmap of European crime fiction' – **Crime Squad**

CRITICAL ACCLAIM FOR *NORDIC NOIR*

'Entertaining and informative companion… written by the person who probably knows more than anyone alive about the subject' – **The Times**

'Highly accessible guide to this popular genre' – **Daily Express**

'The perfect gift for the Scandinavian crime fiction lover in your life' – **Crime Fiction Lover**

'A comprehensive work of reference' – **Euro But Not Trash**

'Readers wanting to get into Scandinavian crime fiction should start with Forshaw's pocket guide to the genre' – **Financial Times**

'Essential (book) not only for lovers of Scandinavian crime fiction but also for anyone who appreciates and wants to expand their knowledge of the genre' – **Shots Mag**

'If you feel drowned by the tsunami that is Nordic Noir but want to know who or what is the next big thing, get this book' – **Evening Standard**

'Fascinated by Scandinavian crime dramas? Go to this handy little guide' – **News at Cinema Books**

CRITICAL ACCLAIM FOR *BRIT NOIR*

'Unsurprisingly Barry Forshaw's Brit Noir is a wonderful reference book that any self-respecting and serious connoisseur of crime fiction needs to have on their book-shelf' – **Shots Magazine**

'Brit Noir is a book to dip into but also, as I did, to read from cover to cover. I've always considered Forshaw to be an honest reviewer and the book very much reflects his personality. It made the book a stimulating and, at times, amusing read' – **Crime Pieces**

HISTORICAL NOIR

The Pocket Essential Guide
to Fiction, Film and TV

BARRY FORSHAW

POCKET ESSENTIALS

First published in 2018 by Pocket Essentials,
an imprint of Oldcastle Books Ltd,
PO Box 394, Harpenden, Herts, AL5 1XJ
www.pocketessentials.com

A CIP catalogue record for this book is available from the British Library.

ISBN
978-0-85730-135-2 (print)
978-0-85730-136-9 (epub)
978-0-85730-137-6 (kindle)
978-0-85730-138-3 (pdf)

2 4 6 8 10 9 7 5 3 1

Typeset by Avocet Typeset, Somerton, Somerset, TA11 6RT
in 9.25pt Univers Light with Myriad Pro display
Printed and bound in Great Britain by Clays Ltd, St Ives plc

For more about Crime Fiction go to crimetime.co.uk / @crimeTimeUk

Contents

1: Introduction

Critical mass is a factor in the healthy growth of the historical crime genre. After Umberto Eco's *The Name of the Rose* (1980) and the Ellis Peters Brother Cadfael novels (beginning in 1977), the genre began to awaken commercial interest among a variety of publishers. Further attention accrued when impressive writers began to enrich and expand the genre, gleaning a variety of heavyweight awards (such as Andrew Taylor with his epic *The American Boy*, which featured a youthful version of the man who invented the detective genre, Edgar Allan Poe).

Like science fiction, historical crime writing holds up a (distorting) mirror to nature: constantly finding provocative or ironic congruences with the present, but reminding us how much (and how little) the human race has changed. The reach of the genre is as wide as history itself, from Ancient Rome (with such writers as Lindsey Davis, Steven Saylor and Ruth Downie) to the Tudor period (stomping ground of multi-prize-winning CJ Sansom and SJ Parris/Stephanie Merritt) and beyond.

In my days as a CWA Ellis Peters Historical Dagger judge (often awarding prizes at intervals to the aforementioned Andrew Taylor, who supplanted CJ Sansom as default winner – to the chagrin of other worthy contenders), every other novel submitted seemed to be set in the Tudor period. At one time, Sansom seemed to have the field as his own fiefdom, with his sprawling, vivid Matthew Shardlake novels bagging multiple awards, but now he has a multitude of rivals. However, there is absolutely no underestimating the fact that Sansom's success was one of the key reasons why publishers began to spread their nets wider in the genre, principally for the kind of work he has produced – i.e. books with richer textures than authors had previously attempted in setting, period and character. After all, this is one of the most successful – and surprising – of phenomena in the entire crime fiction genre: detectives (and proto-detectives) solving crimes in earlier eras. There is now an army of historical sleuths operating from the mean streets of Ancient Rome to the Cold War era of the 1950s. Do you care that such invented detectives are ahistorical and anachronistic? Personally, I don't. After all, it is easy for readers to suspend their disbelief – just as one does when HG Wells has his protagonist climb into a machine that transports him to the far future.

I have attempted in these pages to address the phenomenon right from its inception, examining the work of such prize-winning authors as Robert Harris (whose books span the centuries) and Philip Kerr (wartime Berlin), plus Lindsey Davis, Boris Akunin, Kate Griffin, Mark Mills, Antonia Hodgson, Rory Clements, Aly Monroe, Martin Cruz Smith and SJ Parris, along with virtually every other important writer in the still-flourishing genre. And I could hardly ignore the great predecessors of the modern genre, such as Josephine Tey's *The Daughter of Time*, although I cover earlier practitioners in a preamble.

Conversations and Definitions

My conversations with many of the writers included here afforded me precious insights into why the field has admirers happily conveyed to the past both on the page and on screen – as the historical crime genre is as much about film and TV as it is about books, *Historical Noir* is also a celebration of these media.

A couple of definitions might be useful for the reader. 'Historical noir', in the context of this book, does not necessarily carry the connotation of darkness (either physical or psychological) that customarily goes with the word 'noir'; this is a generic term used for all the books I have written in this series and simply suggests 'crime'. And as for any flexibility in the word 'historical', I'm happy to channel the ground rules of the CWA's Historical Dagger (current nomenclature: the CWA Endeavour Historical Dagger). This annual award given by the Crime Writers' Association to the author of the best historical crime novel of the year was inaugurated in 1999 and in the past was presented to a novel 'with a crime theme and a historical background of any period up to 35 years before the current year' (it has now increased to 50 years). These date parameters are emblazoned on my memory from my time as a judge for the award, considering the gems of the genre with fellow judges over vinous meals at St Hilda's College by the River Cherwell in Oxford. And speaking of the most prestigious UK prize in the field, the award was known as the Ellis Peters Historical Dagger from 1999 to 2005 in honour of the influential author of the Cadfael Chronicles (written between 1977 and 1994). From 2006 to 2012–13 it became known as the Ellis Peters Historical Award, and the most recent sponsor of the award has been Endeavour Press.

As in the earlier entries in the series – *Brit Noir*, *Nordic Noir*, *American Noir* and *Euro Noir* – my aim has been to produce an accessible reader's guide to a fascinating field. I've tried to cover every major writer, often through a concentration on one or two key books (and the interview sections contain both new interviews along with several I conducted for *Crime Time*, which I edit), and exciting new talents are highlighted. However, as mentioned below, completely comprehensive international coverage is not possible in a book of this length.

Writers who tackle a variety of periods and settings (such as Imogen Robertson) presented a problem: multiple entries for such novelists under the relevant eras? In the event, I decided to combine the various eras under a single entry with principal time periods listed after these writers' names (in most cases, I made no attempt to be comprehensive to avoid the lists being unfeasibly long). In terms of globe- and era-trotting, two authors seemed to demand a separate section after all the other entries: the indefatigable duo of Andrew Taylor and Robert Goddard.

In the twenty-first century, there is a new trend for exuberant, poster-coloured, fleet-footed novels, such as those produced by the talented triumvirate of Miranda (MJ) Carter, Antonia Hodgson and Kate Griffin, stars in the new historical crime firmament. The future – and the past – is an exciting place for historical noir.

The Origins of Historical Crime Fiction

In the crime fiction field, most definitions are arbitrary; I've already talked about the fluidity of the term 'noir' – and it's not just me who adopts the edict of Lewis Carroll's Humpty Dumpty in saying 'When I use a word, it means just what I choose it to mean'. What, for instance, constitutes a 'crime' novel and what a 'thriller'? The cross-fertilisation of both genres renders such distinctions amorphous at best. And writing a book such as the one you are now holding necessitated at least a working definition of 'historical crime'; I've laid out the parameters I set for myself in the introduction above.

When I mentioned to crime writers of my acquaintance that I was following up my *Nordic*, *Brit*, *Euro* and *American Noir* with *Historical Noir*, I was asked (on more than one occasion): 'Are you including Dickens and Wilkie Collins? They had detectives in their Victorian novels!' But I pointed out that they were – at the time – contemporary novelists writing about their own period (unlike current practitioners who deal in the past), and in a book of modest proportions such as this one, these classics would not come under the spotlight. And, at this point (apropos of that remark), I should point out that this is by no means an attempt to be completely comprehensive in considering writers either of the past or of the present – there are simply too many historical crime novelists to include here, so my apologies in advance to those I've omitted.

If the prosecution and investigation of a crime (set in the historical past) are the focus of the novels considered in these pages, it is necessary to touch a few bases, as I shall attempt to do in this preamble. These include the possible anomalies I have to deal with: does the Josephine Tey classic *The Daughter of Time* from 1951 qualify, with its modern investigation of the murders of the Princes in the Tower?

Progenitors

As Bernard Knight (a man who knows his historical crime fiction) said to me, *The Daughter of Time* is just one among a few 'evolutionary sports', so it is perhaps apposite to use the inauguration of the CWA Historical Dagger in 1999 as a starting point for this study – at least in terms of the perception of the genre as something established at a fairly specific point in time.

If this introduction is the place for some concentrated namechecking, as well as Tey, one might argue that Ann Radcliffe's *The Mysteries of Udolpho* was an early progenitor of the genre, with Radcliffe setting her 1794 novel in the distant medieval period. Similarly, another early proponent of historical crime is an American writer who is now virtually forgotten: Melville Davisson Post. His *Saturday Evening Post* stories set in the nineteenth century appeared in a single-volume edition as *Uncle Abner: Master of Mysteries* in 1918. In the UK, Bow Street Runner Jasper Shrig was the creation of Jeffery Farnol at the beginning of the twentieth century, with *The Loring Mystery* a notable extended outing for his sleuth in 1925.

One writer whose reputation has been rescued (and burnished) in recent years is the novelist Georgette Heyer; her Regency romances were for many readers a guilty pleasure until her literary reputation underwent a re-evaluation in the last decade or so. Her work includes mystery and crime elements in such novels as *The Talisman Ring* (1936), and she certainly merits attention. As do such writers as Bruce Graeme and, of course, Baroness Orczy (her Scarlet Pimpernel, with his secret identity, was a precursor of Bob Kane and Bill Finger's detective Batman), while Russell Thorndike's ambiguous protagonist Dr Syn certainly utilised mystery conventions in a long-running series.

Agatha Christie made one venture into the historical crime genre with her 1944 novel *Death Comes as the End* with its Ancient Egyptian setting, while John Dickson Carr used the notion of a man from the present moving back in time to crack a mystery. Carr even co-opted the creator of *The Woman in White*, Wilkie Collins, as a sleuth in *The Hungry Goblin* in 1972. More recently, Ruth Rendell's *Anna's Book* in 1994 (published as Barbara Vine) utilised diaries from the past in which the modern-day heroine examines injustices both in history and in the present.

Many of the tropes of historical crime fiction were established by Ellis Peters and by Italian polymath Umberto Eco (two names that will appear frequently in this study), but a slew of talented writers have taken up the genre, and the individual entries that follow – divided by period and locale – will, I trust, show how it has become one of the richest and most fecund fields in crime fiction. In fact, there are so many writers now that readers cannot help but spot a rash of newly minted clichés that surface more and more frequently. For instance, we are often asked to accept that busy historical figures were able to fit in a bit of detection; for example, Oscar Wilde (in the series by Gyles Brandreth) somehow had time to solve a variety of murder mysteries between entertaining and scandalising London. But aficionados of the genre are tolerant of such things– and the most egregious cliché of all is surely necessary for the reader: the subtle imposition of a modern sensibility on a hero or heroine from the past. Common sense would suggest that, say, a totally medieval mindset from which a novel's narrative never deviated might be something of a stretch for the modern reader – Eco's *The Name of the Rose* demonstrates the author's awareness of this fact. His crime-solving monk William of Baskerville is a typical cheat in this respect, although his contemporary, psychologically aware reading of medieval events is set against canny reminders that he is very much a man of his time.

The preamble is over; it is time to climb aboard the time machine and investigate murder and mayhem set in the distant (and not so distant) past.

2: The Ancient World

LINDSEY DAVIS (Ancient Rome)

For many years Lindsey Davis has been one of the most reliable names in the realms of the historical thriller – few would argue with the proposition that she is the market leader in the 'crime in Ancient Rome' genre. Her books featuring the intelligent Roman sleuth Falco marry a great deal of authentic-seeming historical elements with storytelling nous of a rare order. *The Jupiter Myth* followed such earlier Falco novels as *Ode to a Banker*, and is just as enjoyable as its predecessors. Falco is on a holiday trip with relatives in Britain when he finds himself in familiar murderous territory: he's soon involved in a savage killing. An outlaw henchman of King Togidubnus, a crucial supporter of Rome, has been summarily dispatched and crammed head-first down a bar-room well. As usual, there's more to the incident than simply tracking down a murderer: Falco has to utilise his diplomatic skills to take the sting out of a thorny political incident. Lindsey Davis's admirers will be kept engrossed as Falco attempts to undo this particular Gordian knot. One of the key pleasures of this one for the British reader is the setting: Londinium boasts a forum and an amphitheatre, and the streets are thronging with traders and Roman criminals. The Stygian alcohol joints are dangerous places to be; prostitutes crowd the filthy streets; the law sleeps. In this pungently realised setting, Falco and his trusty friend Petronius seek the gangsters with political ambitions behind the grisly killings. One of the most trenchant concepts that Davis toys with here is the influence of the past – we are all defined by our history, and Falco's painful confrontation with this fact shows that it was ever thus. With the wharves of the River Thames joining the Colosseum as Falco's stamping grounds, *The Jupiter Myth* has a real piquancy.

Changes were rung when Lindsey Davis embarked on *Master and God*. Admittedly, she could count on a lot of reader goodwill thanks to her splendid Falco series. And the setting here is once again the ancient world, with the paranoid Roman Emperor Domitian grabbing the reins of power and styling himself 'Master and God', but Falco is nowhere to be seen – and this novel is a very different kettle of fish from customary Lindsey Davis fare. First of all, it is a love story – a distinction that may give pause to the writer's admirers: is this what we read her for? One of the two lovers here, Gaius, is a member of the Praetorian Guard and has served Rome well – he carries his facial disfigurement as a badge of service. He is drawn to Flavia, a freed woman who is hairdresser to the ladies of the imperial court. These are two fiercely self-possessed people, surviving in a dangerous world where imperial displeasure can mean sudden death. As the Emperor sinks further into the realms of mental disorder (Caligula was not alone in this respect), and as clandestine steps are taken against him, Gaius becomes aware that he has a triple choice: between Flavia, the woman he loves, the duty he has sworn to protect the Emperor, and a pressing moral imperative to bring about the death of a madman and monster who threatens the whole Roman state.

Falco remains Davis's signature character, but his adopted daughter Flavia Albia (who has her own series) is proving equally durable – and whatever Davis does is always highly accomplished.

🎙 Interview: Lindsey Davis

Nobody wanted funny romantic novels with a political slant set in the English Civil War, so by strange chance I have spent half my life mentally inhabiting the first-century Roman Empire. Well, that provided equal scope for funny romantic novels with a political slant – plus sunshine, scandal, sandals and mystery. Fair enough!

When I started writing, having *I, Claudius* on TV helped overcome publishers' fear of what was then an unfamiliar period – which I chose specifically to be original. I do feel there was intellectual snobbery about the classics, which I hope I helped overcome. The books I'm most proud of? Probably not my two crime series, though they have been wonderful to write, but my more serious standalones

– *The Course of Honour* and *Master and God*, and my huge Civil War book, *Rebels and Traitors*. All the Falcos are different in approach (by design) so it's hard to pick one out, but I am enjoying writing the Albia series in deliberate contrast. I like taking the mickey out of my own first series, and I love it when she is critical of received opinions about classical Rome. What I am aiming for is to write a good story, and for me that does involve a lot of fun. I hate the way this is sometimes viewed as inferior to misery.

I dodge any kind of question which veers dangerously towards 'influences' – as, obviously, influences are something I kick against! I love a good crime novel, contemporary or Golden Age, and I love a good historical. The glory of both genres is that they have such endless scope, though I confess that if I see the word 'medieval' I tend to reach for a gardening book... Well, I read a lot of those anyway, especially ones on pests and compost.

TOM HARPER (Byzantium Empire)

Tom Harper is the first author to write historical crime set in the Byzantium Empire as it is drawn into the early days of the crusades, filling a void in historical fiction with his novels of murder, mystery and intrigue. After growing up in West Germany, Belgium and the USA, Tom Harper studied history at Lincoln College, Oxford: as part of his degree, he focused on medieval Europe and the later Roman world. He left university wanting to write historical fiction, spent three years failing to do so while working for an actuarial firm, then was inspired by Douglas Adams' obituary to chuck in the job and focus on writing. He entered the first chapter of his first novel, *The Blighted Cliffs* (set in the Napoleonic wars and appearing under the name Edwin Thomas), for the CWA Debut Dagger and was a runner-up; the book was subsequently bought by Transworld and published by Bantam Press in June 2003. His wife is half-Greek, and it was at her suggestion that he began looking at Byzantium as a possible setting for a novel. *The Mosaic of Shadows* is the first book in his First Crusade trilogy, and is a typically accomplished novel. Someone has taken a potshot at the Emperor, someone who got very close and meant very sincerely to remove him from the throne. Demetrios the Apokalyptor is called to unravel the plot behind this attempt on the Emperor's life. It soon becomes clear that beyond simply finding the perpetrator and serving him up to the court, Demetrios has embarked upon a job that bears the responsibility of discovering a conspiracy that threatens the entire kingdom of Byzantium. Dangerous and bloody, this is a world of hidden allegiances and hungry men. Nothing is simple. Could it be the Emperor's brother lies behind a bid to claim the throne for himself? How far dare Demetrios trust Anna, the enigmatic and intriguing doctor? Harper captures the colour and excitement of the Byzantine world, in all its glory and frail stability. As an author he has a stunning ability to draw characters, entwine circumstances and keep his reader engrossed in a tightly woven storyline.

PAUL DOHERTY (Ancient Egypt)
Paul Doherty has long been one of the most reliable practitioners of the history/crime novel, and his skills are fully in evidence in *The Spies of Sobeck*, set in 1477 BC. Chief Judge Amerotke is up against dangerous forces in Ancient Egypt. Queen Hatusu is struggling to deal with the threat to her border from the neighbouring province of Nubia, with its murderous sects wreaking havoc. Her life is very much on the line, and it is up to Amerotke to save her. Transferring the tension and mystery of the modern crime novel to the ancient past is something that Doherty does better than many other writers.

Other key books: *The Mask of Ra, The Year of the Cobra* (set during the reign of Akhenaten in the fourteenth century BC).

ROSEMARY ROWE (Roman Britain)
In the crowded historical crime realm, Rowe is one of the most adroit practitioners, and her Libertus mysteries (set in a well-drawn Ancient Roman Britain) are often in the class of the two most celebrated stars of the Roman mystery field, Lindsey Davis and Steven Saylor. *The Legatus Mystery* is one of Rowe's most engrossing entries in the series: here, her resourceful protagonist Libertus has once again found his missing wife, but is prevented from enjoying the reunion by the killing of a Roman ambassador in Glevum's Imperial temple. Then things begin to get very strange indeed: the corpse vanishes, bloodstains manifest themselves mysteriously. Is the answer

connected with the elderly High Priest of Jupiter? What counts here is the brilliantly realised historical setting, with the sharply wrought plot dovetailing perfectly.

Other key books: *Murder in the Forum, The Chariots of Calyx, A Coin for the Ferryman.*

🎤 Interview: Rosemary Rowe

'Why do you choose to set your fictional Libertus crime series in Roman Britain?' readers sometimes ask, adding sympathetically, 'It must mean an awful lot of research.' Well, yes it does. And therein lies the charm. I have always been interested in social history, fascinated by museums and ancient technologies, and – as a one-time language teacher – even briefly taught non-examination Latin to some junior forms, for whom I had to make it interesting (Winnie the Pooh, rather than the Gallic Wars!). I have also been an avid reader of crime fiction, ever since I was old enough to smuggle Poirot and a torch under my bedclothes, and I was scribbling stories of one sort or another as soon as I found out what a pen was for. However, none of this is the real reason why I write crime fiction based in Roman Gloucestershire. I started because I was invited to. It was a short story, initially. After an industrial accident had interrupted my lecturing career, I had already turned to writing fiction, writing Cornish historical sagas and contributing short stories to anthologies. The editor of one of these was seeking contributions to a collection of 'classical whodunits', so I wrote a short story, based very loosely on the area where I live – making it easier to research – and deliberately set in the second century, the period of Roman occupation about which least is known, so that I was less likely to make obvious mistakes. (Commodus being 'on the throne' was also too humorous to miss.) It struck me as a useful narrative device to have an artistic 'outsider' who could interpret Roman ways, an ex-slave made a sympathetic narrator, and since I am Cornish, he was naturally a Celt. Thus Libertus was born. The editor liked the story and commented that it would make a series, so I tried a book. At this stage I had no idea that there were so many excellent practitioners already in the field, or I might have been discouraged at the start. However, knowing no better, I set to work. I'd set the period and location by this time, and I had my hero's character as well. Obviously, I was obliged to do a great deal more research to give the background for an entire book. However, the Romano-British setting is not unique in this. To write about a modern protagonist, I would have had to learn a great deal about forensic evidence, bullets, bloodstains, and laws about what my sleuths could or couldn't do, even if I was not writing a police procedural. My hero is free from all of this. When he finds a bloodstain he cannot know whether it is from a human or a hare. Fingerprints are not a giveaway. News has to be carried from point to point on foot, giving a murderer time to get away, and – given the right kind of patron, which he has – Libertus can go almost anywhere. (Making him a mosaic-maker turned out to be a useful social move, giving him access to wealthy houses, while enabling him to associate with tradesmen and the poor.) Of course, there are disadvantages as well. 'Detectives' did not exist, and authorities were more concerned with public order and financial fraud than protecting humble private individuals. An unexplained anonymous corpse in a ditch, of the kind that today sparks off a murder hunt, would merely have been dragged off for burial. So there has to be something additional – such as the threat of political embarrassment – for Libertus's patron to require him to investigate. The limitations of my hero's knowledge also limit me.

STEVEN SAYLOR (Ancient Rome)

Lindsey Davis or Steven Saylor? Many readers regard the American Saylor's Ancient Roman whodunits as the best in this particular genre. However, many others argue that Lindsey Davis's Falco (in the British author's series of Roman thrillers) is superior to Saylor's Gordianus the Finder. Frankly, though, it doesn't really matter who is the more accomplished of the duo: both scribes are exemplary in their own way, and we should be grateful that two such talented writers can deliver the goods. Saylor's Roma Sub Rosa sequence includes such titles as *Last Seen in Massilia*. A highly entertaining entry, and Gordianus's sardonic first-person narration again pulls off the clever sleight of hand of channelling a modern sensibility into a denizen of the ancient world, while always steering clear of anachronism. As a conduit to the menacing back alleys of Rome and the decadent splendours of its senatorial palaces, Gordianus is the ultimate cynical survivor. The Roman world is torn apart by a civil war, and Caesar and Pompey struggle for ascendancy. But life goes on pretty much as normal for Gordianus, who receives an anonymous message telling him that his son is dead.

Meto was playing the dangerous game of acting as a double agent for Caesar, and as Gordianus tries to discover who is behind the murder, he finds himself in the blockaded seaport of Massilia, with famine and bloodshed ever-present threats. And as he pursues what seems an impossible quest, Gordianus's only friend in the city has been chosen by the corrupt officials to die for the sins of a populace and stave off catastrophe. And then there is the young woman Gordianus has seen fall from the Sacrifice Rock outside the city... As the foregoing demonstrates, Saylor's plotting is always spot on, and the reader is constantly aware of the sights and smells of the Roman world.

Other key books: *Roman Blood*, *Arms of Nemesis*, *A Murder on the Appian Way*.

🎙 Interview: Steven Saylor

To write a novel, especially a rather long and complicated first novel, as my first, *Roman Blood*, turned out to be, I think the author has to be very deeply drawn to the people and the places he's writing about, and deeply stirred by the ideas he's exploring. That's why Ancient Rome worked as a setting for me. As a reader I'd progressed from fantasy (primarily Tolkien, but also his circle and antecedents and heirs) to science fiction, to historical fiction and spy novels, and finally to crime fiction. I've always craved pageantry and escapism on a grand scale – fantasy and science fiction give you that. But as I grew up I found those genres less satisfying, because it seemed to me that the real world and its amazing past harbour far more mystery and fascination than most writers can fabricate from whole cloth. (This struck home when I read TE Lawrence's *Seven Pillars of Wisdom* about the Bedouins, and realised it was the template for Frank Herbert's *Dune* novels set on a faraway desert planet – except that the civilisation Lawrence documented was infinitely more complex and otherworldly than anything Herbert had dreamed up.) Writing about Ancient Rome satisfies both my desire for escape into an exotic realm of imagination – the past with all its tawdriness and grandeur – and my appetite for exploring the vagaries of politics and human emotions in very realistic terms.

As for my fascination with crime fiction, that started with Sherlock Holmes. Once I started reading Holmes, I read nothing else, and I felt a great sadness and even a bit of anxiety when I closed the book on the very last of those stories. Readers today find them just as addictive as did readers a hundred years ago. The whole genre of writing that descends from Conan Doyle draws on that same addictive quality. What is it? Why is it so compelling? If we could say what fascinates us so about crime fiction, perhaps it wouldn't be quite so fascinating. I crave that quality as a reader, and as a writer – the challenge to recreate it, to play with its effects, to try to channel it in some new way is a great lure. When I write a novel I want to have all my faculties engaged at full throttle, and I find that writing a novel of ideas, with a historical setting and a murder mystery plot, suffices to keep me fully occupied. The greatest challenge is to make two things happen simultaneously at the book's climax – to reveal a solution to the mystery plot which makes perfect sense, and at the same time to bring the thematic elements of the story to a satisfying resolution. If you can pull off a further feat – to make the plot revelation and the thematic resolution reflect upon and reinforce each other – I think you've written a novel that delivers just about as much as any novel can.

RUTH DOWNIE (Ancient Rome)

Ruth Downie's anachronistic (but winning) sleuth is Gaius Petreius Ruso, an army doctor dispatched (in earlier books) to colonial Britain. In *Vita Brevis*, Ruso and his partner Tilla (who is both his Watson and the mother of his child) arrive in Rome to discover that the city's splendour is matched by corruption on a massive scale. Ruso's predecessor, Dr Kleitos, has fled the city, leaving behind a barrel bearing both a corpse and the legend 'Be careful who you trust'. Ruso's hard-won reputation is soon under threat, and he realises he must find his missing colleague – urgently. Those familiar with Downie's work will not be surprised to hear that *Vita Brevis* is crammed with pithy characterisation (notably the intuitive Ruso), mordant humour and beautifully integrated historical detail. Who cares that there were no sleuths in Ancient Rome?

Interview: Ruth Downie

I wasn't planning to write historical fiction. I was on the run from an embarrassing incident, searching for a story where none of my friends and relations could imagine I'd put them in it this time. But when we took our children to Hadrian's Wall I realised that Roman Britain was not only a safe haven – nobody can trace their ancestry back that far, whatever they tell you – it was also alive with the sort of tensions that drive a good story. The history, all written by the conquerors, was full of propaganda, muddled reporting and holes that only fiction could fill, and there were some splendid parallels with our own times.

All of the Medicus novels are driven in some way by the edgy relationship between occupier and occupied, but two books have perhaps given me the most pleasure of all of them. One is *Persona Non Grata,* where our 'barbarian' leading lady is taken to the allegedly civilised south of France – although I may be influenced by the sunlit memories of the research trips.

The other is *Tabula Rasa*, where the builders of Hadrian's Wall have to find ways of relating to the locals whose lands they are hacking apart.

Popular Roman-era fiction tends to divide between crime and military adventure, with a good spread of thrillers and political page-turners in between. All of us who write crime owe a huge debt to Lindsey Davis for making it respectable, and for paving the way for ancient-world characters who don't use quaintly ancient dialogue. I'd also like to thank the rulers of the Roman Empire for failing to create any sort of investigative police force, thus leaving the field open for a beleaguered military medic and a British woman who is caught between his world and her own.

Most of all, though, I'm obliged to Rosemary Sutcliff, whose tale combining a museum artefact with a small gap in history has entered the national consciousness. Even people who've never read *The Eagle of the Ninth* are convinced there's something mysterious about Roman Britain.

DAVID WISHART (Ancient Rome)

The streets of Caesar's Rome are becoming increasingly crowded with the cunning breed of ancient sleuths, and it's a wonder that the anachronistic detectives of Steven Saylor, Lindsey Davis and David Wishart are not stumbling over each other. But who cares? All three authors are producing work of the highest quality, shot through with sardonic wit, offbeat characterisation and highly plausible historical detail. More than his colleagues and rivals, Wishart seems to be aware that the whole Roman sleuth enterprise is a confidence trick: we know (he infers) that there were no detectives in this era, but such is his narrative skill that we completely buy the concept and enjoy the outrageously entertaining results. In *A Vote for Murder*, Wishart's canny investigator Marcus Corvinus is having a leisurely holiday with his stepdaughter and generally enjoying a bibulous time, while keeping half an eye on the Machiavellian antics involved in the pending consulate elections. But when one of the two candidates meets a violent death, Corvinus (with no reluctance) summarily ends his vacation and plunges into the murder hunt. Of course, it's too easy to assume that the rival political candidate would be behind the killing, and some labyrinthine plots are ahead before Corvinus solves the mystery in his usual fashion and brings things to a highly surprising conclusion. The varied denizens of this dangerous world are drawn with great dash, and the one-liners that Wishart specialises in are quite as sharp as anything the author has entertained us with before.

AGATHA CHRISTIE (Ancient Egypt)

Death Comes as the End (set in 2000 BC Egypt), Agatha Christie's celebrated historical crime novel, was first published in 1944 and is the sole novel by the author not to be set in her own century. What's more, Christie made this one of the first books to integrate elements of the detective story in the period-set novel, and it draws on her experiences in the field of her husband, the archaeologist Sir Max Mallowan. The setting is ancient Thebes, and the day-to-day detail of life in this era is evoked with great skill; an Egyptian family is leading a quotidian existence when the patriarch Imhotep arrives with his new concubine Nofret. Inevitably, the family is riven with jealousy and betrayal, and a series of deaths begins to occur, with the killer clearly someone in the once-peaceful household. The book was controversially received, and not all of the writer's admirers were persuaded, but it has long been a quirky favourite of Christie aficionados.

JANE FINNIS (Roman Britain)

Yorkshire resident Jane Finnis has long been one of the most reliable names in the field. Her Aurelia Marcella novels describe life in first-century Roman Britain, with the unruly province on the outskirts of the Roman Empire proving a suitable backdrop for murder and deceit. Finnis's detective figure is an innkeeper who is persuaded (against her will) to turn sleuth. The first book in the sequence, *Shadows in the Night*, features not only a cracking mystery but also a rich picture of northern Britannia with its Roman settlers and belligerent British tribesmen. The series has since shown great consistency.

Other key books: *Buried Too Deep, Danger in the Wind.*

🎙 Interview: Jane Finnis

I've been hooked on Ancient Roman history ever since as a teenager I read those two masterpieces by Robert Graves, *I Claudius* and *Claudius the God*. When I decided to try writing mysteries, I unhesitatingly chose a Roman Empire setting: Britain in the 90s AD. That was a turbulent time for the newly conquered province of Britannia, what with restless natives, an arrogant occupying army, and Roman settlers hungry for land... all making a wonderful backdrop for tales of murder and mayhem.

A bonus for me was, and still is, that I need to do plenty of historical research. Reading books, surfing the internet (caution needed here) and walking the ground the Romans walked... I love it all. Being a historian by training, I firmly believe that if I don't get the history in my mysteries right, I'm short-changing my readers. Much of my research never gets used directly in my stories (I'm not producing history textbooks), but it all helps me bring Roman Britain to life. When readers meet my characters, innkeeper Aurelia, her friends and enemies, I want them to step out of the present time into a believable past reality.

Recently, more and more writers are setting their books in the Roman era. People sometimes ask if I regard this as unwelcome competition. Quite the opposite. I'm delighted to see growing enthusiasm for my favourite period. I'm interested in other authors' Roman fiction, but I never read any of it while I'm working on my own novels. Obviously I wouldn't plagiarise consciously, but unconsciously... who knows? I prefer to play it safe.

Historical mysteries of all periods are flourishing at the moment. Sad doom-and-gloomers periodically proclaim that 'historical settings are out of fashion nowadays', but in my experience that's

> rubbish. Readers still choose them, enjoy them, and ask for more. I believe they always will.

MARGARET DOODY (Ancient Greece)

As professor of literature at the University of Notre Dame, Doody's background enabled her to write well-received studies of the novel, but she is best known for her books featuring the philosopher Aristotle as a protagonist traversing the ancient world. In *Poison in Athens* (set in 330 BC), three legal cases have Athens mesmerised. But when a man who has won a case against a wealthy patrician is found poisoned by hemlock, the sagacious Aristotle is drawn from his writing to investigate. Set in the same year, *Aristotle and the Secrets of Life* has a struggle for independence as a background.

Other key books: *Aristotle Detective*, *Aristotle and Poetic Justice*, *Mysteries of Eleusis*.

TONY HAYS (Arthurian Britain)

Hays is a journalist whose books have a convincing verisimilitude. Having written about a variety of subjects, including narcotics trafficking and Civil War history, he has also produced a series of novels utilising elements of Arthurian history. The first, *The Killing Way*, presents Arthur as a youthful warrior who is not yet on the throne. When a young woman is savagely killed and Merlin is blamed, Arthur applies for help to Malgwyn ap Cuneglas, whose knowledge of human psychology (before that term existed) is able to throw light into some dark corners.

Other key books: *The Divine Sacrifice*, *The Stolen Bride*.

ROBERT VAN GULIK (Ancient China)

Robert van Gulik demonstrated his expertise in a variety of areas, working as a successful diplomat, Orientalist and even musician. But his place in this book is justified for his much-admired Judge Dee mysteries, featuring a character that the author adopted from the eighteenth-century Chinese novel *Dee Goong An*. Books such as *The Chinese Maze Murders* (written in 1950) were conceived as something that would be of interest to Japanese and Chinese readers, but translations in other languages soon gained a considerable following for the series. These books were something of a labour of love for the Sinophile author, and frequently utilised elements from Oriental culture rather than Western writing traditions.

Other key books: *The Chinese Lake Murders*, *Murder in Canton*.

MARY REED and ERIC MAYER (Late Roman Constantinople)

The John, the Lord Chamberlain sequence of novels is the work of Mary Reed and Eric Mayer. Sometimes described as the John the Eunuch mysteries, the books focus on Emperor Justinian's Lord Chamberlain, a sixth-century Constantinople proto-sleuth. The authors specialise in persuasive and period-appropriate descriptions of their characters' behaviour.

JOHN MADDOX ROBERTS (Ancient Rome)

The books in John Maddox Roberts' SPQR series appeared between 1990 and 2010 and are set at the time of the Roman Republic. The narratives are related in the first person by Decius Caecilius Metellus, a member of the Roman Senate. Among Decius's companions are his slaves Cato, Cassandra and Hermes, and his friends, the Greek physician Asklepiodes and the slippery Titus Annius Milo, and the plots often feature well-known historical figures, including Caesar and Cleopatra.

JMC BLAIR (Arthurian Britain)

Blair's *The Excalibur Murders* posits the notion that Merlin is not so much a magician as a scholar and confidant of the king, Arthur. In this book, the fabled sword Excalibur is stolen, and Merlin has to come up with a virtually supernatural solution to the crime. More energetic than most entries in the genre, it's clear that we are not expected to take Blair's unorthodox approach to the Arthurian legends too seriously.

Other key books: *The Lancelot Murders*, *The Pendragon Murders*.

3: Medieval England and the Middle Ages

PETER TREMAYNE (Seventh-century Ireland)

Peter Tremayne's Sister Fidelma books are now something of an institution. In *The Dove of Death*, set in 670 AD, an Irish merchant ship is attacked by pirates near the Breton peninsula. Despite surrendering, the captain and a passenger (a prince) are murdered – but among those who escape death are resourceful ecclesiastical heroine Sister Fidelma and her companion, Brother Eadulf. Set ashore, they find themselves with an unenviable task: bringing to justice those who murdered the prince. She has one clue to work with: the marauding pirate vessel sported the symbol of a dove. The dangers endured by Fidelma are ratcheted up a few notches in this outing, and the result grips like a vice.

Other key books: *Absolution by Murder, Shroud for the Archbishop, Atonement of Blood.*

MICHAEL JECKS (Fourteenth-century Devon)

The Knights Templar mysteries of Michael Jecks have long been among the most accomplished in the field of historical crime fiction, with satisfyingly convoluted plotting set against some beautifully observed historical accoutrements. In *The King of Thieves*, Sir Baldwin and his friend Simon are dispatched to France with Exeter's Bishop Walter to look after the welfare of the Prince Edward on his journey to meet the French king, Charles IV. But a revenge plot has been hatched, and soon considerable danger is in the offing, with the future of the English crown in the balance. Stirring and atmospheric.

🎙 Interview: Michael Jecks

I think the medieval period chose me. I was always fascinated by the politics and violence of the Crusades, and when I started writing I was intrigued by the period immediately after the loss of Acre, during the arrest and destruction of the Templars. In England we had a weak king, Edward II, while in France the royal family was rocked by the adulterous affairs of the king's daughters-in-law, which led to the end of the Capetian dynasty and ushered in the Valois. It was a time of war, famine and plague, and gave me a huge amount of scope for a crime writer. It is difficult to select any single book of mine from a long list. My Templar series has grown to 32 titles, and, at the time of writing, a thirty-third has been commissioned. However, I made the firm decision early on that each book must be significantly different from its predecessor in plot and 'feel'. I've heard of others who have been accused of writing one book many times, and never wanted that reputation. That meant that I went from books that could be quite dark to others that were much more humorous.

I suppose two books that do stand out for me are *The Mad Monk of Gidleigh* and *The Death Ship of Dartmouth*. The former was based heavily on a local court case, and involved a lot of reference to the existing records. This was the beginning of a period in my writing when I took to actual murders from the medieval period, looking at how homicides affected other people – this was very fruitful in giving me new plot lines. I am also very pleased with *The Death Ship of Dartmouth*. This book, my twenty-first, was intended as a lighter book, with a lot of humour. However, the murder and the impact of the death were still strong aspects of the story. It was shortlisted for the CWA/Theakston Old Peculier prize in 2007, and I introduced a new character, Sir Richard de Welles, who is larger than life – more or less a mixture of James Robertson Justice and Brian Blessed. It gave me enormous pleasure to write this character, and readers seem to enjoy him just as much.

I have been very lucky to have made friends with a number of brilliant writers: Bernard Knight, Susanna Gregory, Ian Morson, Karen Maitland and CJ Sansom, among others. However, I have to admit to a strong affection for George MacDonald Fraser, who has to have been my greatest inspiration from an early age. His fabulous Flashman series showed me how an author could use actual events and people to populate a story, and then, when I started writing my own works, it was largely his *The Candlemass Road* that showed me that books need not be cosy, like Ellis Peters, but could be more gritty, more savage in their portrayal of events and people, while retaining humanity and humour.

ARIANA FRANKLIN (Medieval Cambridge)

In Ariana Franklin's *Mistress of the Art of Death*, we are in medieval Cambridge. Children are being savagely killed, and (as often in the past) the blame is being laid at the door of the Jews. And the door in question is that of the castle where the beleaguered minority is cloistered. Adelia Aguilar is one of the few women practising medicine in Henry II's reign, and she is a proto-forensic specialist, the eponymous Mistress of the Art of Death – her involvement in the tension is a foregone conclusion. Here, Ariana Franklin has come up with a fresh wrinkle in the historical crime field: a synthesis of existing elements, true, but carried off with real skill.

CANDACE ROBB (Fourteenth-century York, Thirteenth-century Scotland)

Candace Robb takes us back across the centuries to a time when life was dangerous and cheap. In *The Guilt of Innocents*, we are in fourteenth-century York: a man has drowned in the River Ouse, and it is clear that his death is no accident. Father Nicholas Ferriby has trodden on many toes as Vicar of Weston and master of a small grammar school, but his unorthodox beliefs do not make him a murderer. Robb's protagonist, the wily Owen Archer, is engaged to crack the case, and soon finds himself caught up in a maelstrom of deceit and danger. The talented Robb has demonstrated in such entertaining novels as *The Apothecary Rose* and *The King's Bishop* that her Owen Archer mysteries are solidly in the tradition of the medieval novels of Ellis Peters, full of satisfyingly convoluted plotting.

A Trust Betrayed began a series of mysteries set in Scotland at the time of Robert the Bruce. In the spring of 1297, Margaret Kerr is afraid that her merchant husband Roger has been caught up in the pending rebellion against the English. Her husband's cousin and factor, Jack Sinclair, agrees to try to locate Roger in the dangerous city of Edinburgh. When he is found murdered, Margaret undertakes to solve the mystery herself, but she quickly discovers that Scotland at war is a very dangerous place for a woman alone. Apart from the effortless conjuring of historical detail (a sine qua non of the genre), Robb is particularly acute at dealing with issues such as the place of women in this troubled society: without ever making Margaret a proto-feminist, she cannily examines attitudes to gender in the distant past while never forgetting the imperatives of a rattling yarn.

🎤 Interview: Candace Robb

A while ago I asked my good friend the historian Compton Reeves to recommend some recent articles on historiography for a lecture on writing history that I was preparing for the local arts council. He asked why I would bother with someone else's thoughts rather than speak from my heart. His response was so pertinent to my goal in setting my fiction in the past that I asked his permission to quote it, and I've done so, often.

Compton wrote: 'I think there are some among us who have empathy for those who lived in the past, and want to know more about them. History is the most humanistic of all disciplines, in that it includes all that folk in the past have done in all areas of endeavour. Doing history is an art, not a science, and it appeals to our creative instincts. Doing history also expands our specious present into whatever age and area of human history catches our fancy. To do history, then, makes us more human, for only humans among the creatures can have history. For us it is a mystical thing... Is it not of practical value to become as richly human as we are able to become? Is it not the purpose of life for each of us to grow in our individual humanity, and is not the study of past lives an exposure to the life pilgrimages of those who have gone before and can guide us?'

'Richly human' – the concept has an appealing freshness at the moment. 'Empathy' is another. We empathise with people when we glimpse their histories. My empathy for the people of Scotland who were non-combatants during the first Scottish war of independence is what motivates my Margaret Kerr series. I wondered how a community besieged would manage to maintain civil laws – or if they would. I wondered who would take the responsibility of upholding the laws. Other than the plea rolls of Edward I's army in Scotland, which are quite interesting, there is little on the subject regarding this particular war; however, information regarding other communities in similar circumstances has been helpful. I ask a basic question regarding the crimes in this series: does the end justify the means? A person is murdered because they betrayed a side in the struggles, or were perceived as threatening it. In the big picture, that may seem justified. But once we've become acquainted with the victim and the murderer that judgement can, and probably will, change, or at least move us to pause and question it. And in the case of war, whose end justifies whose means? Justice becomes quite fluid.

For the first two books in the series, *A Trust Betrayed* and *The Fire in the Flint*, I chose crimes that involved the family of my protagonist, Margaret Kerr – because as a woman her involvement in the struggle was limited (primarily to that of victim) – so that I might explore the complication of families divided in loyalties, and also to provide motivation for Margaret to move beyond the acceptable, to feel she had little to lose in risking proscription for her participation. In the third book, *A Cruel Courtship*, her focus changes to a possible crime among strangers, although family issues complicate her investigation. I enjoy exploring a society in which no one operated under the assumption that they knew all that was happening – that was impossible.

ALYS CLARE (Medieval England)

The prolific and talented Alys Clare sets most of her historical detective novels in the medieval era, and her series featuring Abbess Helewise and Josse d'Acquin have many followers. The Hawkenlye mysteries (named after Helewise's abbey) are set in twelfth-century England, and the first book in the series, *Fortune Like the Moon*, begins with the recent murder of a young nun. King Richard commissions his colleague Josse d'Acquin to investigate. All the virtues of the series are to be found in this first volume.

Other key books: *The Tavern in the Morning*, *The Chatter of the Maidens*, *A Dark Night Hidden*.

CASSANDRA CLARK (Late Fourteenth-century Europe)

Hildegard of Meaux in Cassandra Clark's atmospheric series is detective, spy and – in her day job – a nun who is slated to become an abbess. However unlikely the notion of a crime-solving nun, this picture of the life of independent women in the fourteenth century is written with authority; we are persuaded that Hildegard's wealthy order allows access to kings and potentates. Such books as *Hangman Blind* have earned for the author a dedicated readership, and the level of consistency in the series is high indeed.

Other key book: *The Red Velvet Turnshoe*.

BERNARD KNIGHT (Twelfth-century England)
Bernard Knight has no equal when it comes to marrying astute historical detail with ingenious plotting, and such books as *The Noble Outlaw* exemplify this. In twelfth-century Exeter, a school is in the process of being renovated when a mummified body is discovered in the rafters. Inevitably, it is the county coroner Sir John de Wolfe who is commissioned to investigate. In fact, it is Sir John's brother-in-law, Richard de Revelle, the founder of the school, who supplies an instant (and rather too glib) explanation, blaming a youthful rebel knight who has been reduced to sleeping rough on Dartmoor. Sir John discovers other corollary evidence against the young man, but he is never one to accept the obvious explanation, and so he digs deeper. And then a second violent murder takes the whole investigation into a critical phase. Knight has a mastery of the crucial sleight-of-hand of the genre: refracting ancient sensibilities through modern modes of speech – skills he has demonstrated throughout his considerable body of work.

🎤 **Interview: Bernard Knight**
After some 40 books of various types, I find that writing historical mysteries is the greatest challenge, especially those set in the early medieval period, such as my Crowner John series. Although the necessary research is the most satisfying part of the labour, there is much less detailed information available about the twelfth century compared with later, better-documented periods. Anachronisms have to be avoided like the plague, although often these form traps which may be hard to recognise. For example, one can hardly write that a person was 'mesmerised', as Mesmer wasn't around until the

eighteenth century. In my *The Grim Reaper* I had the priestly serial killer leave appropriate biblical references at each scene – until my fetish for accuracy led me to discover that the scriptures were not divided into 'chapters' until the thirteenth century and versification had to await the advent of printing! Probably not one reader in a million would appreciate this, but once I knew, I just couldn't use it and had to find another way round. However, anachronisms can also be in thought and speech, as it's virtually impossible for us to get into the mind of a medieval man. In this respect, I once had an academic dispute with my copyeditor when I portrayed my coroner, while viewing the execution of a young lad for a minor theft, thinking that there should be a better way of dealing with juvenile delinquents than hanging them! My editor maintained that such a thought would never have crossed the mind of someone in 1194 and that I should avoid projecting my modern attitudes back 800 years!

Dialogue is another problem and I usually include a cautionary note to the effect that it is futile to attempt a spurious 'olde worlde' style, which is sometimes seen in historical novels. In the time and place of my books, the vernacular would either have been Early Middle English – quite incomprehensible to us today – Norman French or Western Welsh (Cornish). It would be pointless to lace modern English with 'verily' or 'prithee', just as I feel that films and television dramas about the Nazis are ludicrous when they have Germans speaking among themselves in the 'Ve haff vays of making you talk' style. However, I feel that some historical writers go to the other extreme, when they have Romans saying 'The old guy has gone AWOL' or 'You kidding, pal?', which spoils any attempt to establish an authentic ambience.

There are many other problems common to all series, such as not giving away the plot of a previous book by an injudicious comment in a subsequent story – and the difficulty caused by your customers not reading the books in chronological order. This means that you have to repeat much basic information each time, at the risk of boring your regulars – although you cannot afford to leave newcomers ignorant about the running characters and the locations. There is always a lively debate when 'histmyst' authors get together about how much authenticity matters, some saying that it's only entertainment. But from the feedback that I get from readers, it seems that they relish both the recreation of a medieval atmosphere and the injection of some genuine history – perhaps a painless way of capturing what they missed in the dry tuition of long-past schooldays.

UMBERTO ECO (Fourteenth-century Italy)

It is a shame that there isn't some way I can mark Umberto Eco's entry in this study as being different from all the rest, and perhaps more significant – a gold font, perhaps? But without the Italian author and his monumental, highly influential novel *The Name of the Rose* (published in English in 1983), the whole modern notion of historical crime fiction as a distinct, marketable entity might not exist (Ellis Peters notwithstanding). For those who have never read it – and its length and challenging nature have ensured that there are plenty of people unafraid to admit that – it's difficult to remember today the force with which Eco's novel exploded on the literary scene in the 1980s. It is a groundbreaking combination of detective fiction (of which it is a prime example), historical novel (with the medieval era conjured with a lively, operatic richness), literary novel (with its peerless use of language, particularly in William Weaver's translation) and philosophical treatise (with even a religious dispute rendered fascinating – although not everyone would agree, and it was perhaps this aspect that gave the book its forbidding reputation).

Eco was a celebrated academic and chronicler of popular culture (writing on both Borges and Superman), and his novel was a harbinger of the current trend for translated fiction, not least because Weaver's remarkable translation was reviewed as enthusiastically as the novel itself at the time of the book's original release. Eco's monkish sleuth is called William of Baskerville – and if that name seems a little unlikely, it playfully suggests the book's antecedents, as well as Eco's irreverent sense of humour, which runs through the book.

Italy in the Middle Ages. William is a Franciscan monk in Italy who becomes involved when various fellow monks are murdered in a multiplicity of ways. This dangerous investigation opens up a richly detailed picture of the Middle Ages, monastic orders and the murderous religious disputes of the day. Eco is well aware that, like all historical fiction, this notion of having a modern-thinking figure amidst so much ancient theocratic intolerance is a cheat, and he reminds us at times that William is (for all his modernity of thinking) a man of his time and prone to the obscurantist thinking of the day. When his young assistant (something of a Watson figure) talks of his unprompted sexual impulses towards women, William solemnly intones the received wisdom of the day and of his religious order: that women are sent to lure men away from the path of God. It is both a joke and a reminder that such views are still held in illiberal theocratic countries throughout the world even today.

Eco was to write several other novels before his death, all of considerable interest, but none had anything remotely like the seismic impact of his masterwork.

▆ Film: THE NAME OF THE ROSE (Jean-Jacques Annaud, director)

The film of *The Name of the Rose* was directed by Jean-Jacques Annaud and appeared in 1986. It was inevitable that a movie would follow the success of Eco's novel, but admirers of the book might have wished for a less macho medieval monk than Sean Connery, who got the part of the intuitive William of Baskerville not least for his bankability. In fact, the actor does a perfectly creditable job, and the baroque production design by Dante Ferretti does full justice to the distant and mysterious world that William inhabits. The film has another great plus in the inestimable F Murray Abraham (so memorable as Salieri in Milos Forman's film of *Amadeus*), who plays the malign inquisitor with all the iciness that is his acting stock in trade. Unsurprisingly, all the philosophical and religious discourse of the novel is thrown out, leaving a focus on the basic detective mystery.

ANDREA JAPP (Fourteenth-century Normandy)

The prolific French author Andrea Japp has expertise in the field of forensic science – along with her skill at fiction – and has utilised this element in her work. But it is the authenticity of her Agnès de Souarcy series that has won her so many admirers. The novel *The Season of the Beast* is set in 1304, when the church and the king of France are engaged in a massive power struggle which will affect the future of the Knights Templar. In the bucolic regions of Normandy, youthful widow Agnès is also locked in battle, with her malignant half-brother who is determined to undermine her. When a series of monks are mutilated by an unseen nemesis, events are to lead Agnès down some strange paths. In an excellent translation by Lorenza Garcia, this was a promising harbinger for an excellent sequence.

Other key books: *The Breath of the Rose*, *The Divine Blood*.

GIULIO LEONI (Fourteenth-century Florence)

Leoni, a professor of Italian literature and history, is a resident of Rome who has also written fantasy novels under the name JP Rylan, but it is his books featuring Dante Alighieri as investigator that have cemented his reputation. In the second book in the series, *The Mosaic Crimes*, the year is 1300 and the location Florence, with the body of an artist mutilated while reclining next to an almost completed mosaic. Dante has been designated prior to the city of Florence (his magnum opus, *The Divine Comedy*, lies in the future) and his first official investigation is into this strange death. It might be argued that Leoni does not quite persuade the reader of the plausibility of Dante as a detective, but the novels are delivered with considerable panache.

Other key book: *The Kingdom of Light*.

IAN MORSON (Thirteenth-century Oxford)

Ian Morson, acclaimed for his Falconer novels, has made a speciality of medieval crime, but his fictional stamping grounds have also included Jacobean America, Ancient Egypt and Victorian England. His principal characters are William Falconer, Regent Master of Oxford; Nick Zuliani, a Venetian explorer in the thirteenth-century Mongol Empire; and Joe Malinferno and Doll Pocket, who navigate Georgian England. All of the books in whatever series are delivered in lively prose, although his popularity has faltered of late.

Key books: *Falconer and the Ritual of Death*, *Falconer's Trial*.

ELLIS PETERS (Twelfth-century Shrewsbury)

Ellis Peters (whose real name was Edith Pargeter, a name she also wrote under) first introduced readers to her brilliant medieval sleuth Brother Cadfael in *A Morbid Taste for Bones* in 1977, the inaugural novel in the long-running Cadfael Chronicles. With this book, Peters helped bring about the birth of the modern historical crime novel (and lent her name to its most prestigious prize). Over 20 books, the intuitive Benedictine monk (a former soldier who has rejected the secular world for a life of prayer) was allowed to develop as a character and as a plausible if unlikely detective figure in this far distant world. Peters brought the series to a satisfying close in 1994 with *Brother Cadfael's Penance*, which appeared the year before her death. Set in the autumn of 1145, the book has Cadfael involved once again with the son whom he fathered a year before he undertook his monastic duties. His son is kidnapped, and although the boy's mother is no longer in his life, Cadfael has maintained an interest in his offspring. He is obliged to leave the monastery despite the abbot being unwilling to let him go. What follows writes a suitably elegant and complex *finis* to an influential series. If Peters' sheer industry resulted in a daunting number of Cadfael books, it must be acknowledged that a very high level is maintained throughout.

TV: CADFAEL (various directors)

There were several elements responsible for the success of this fondly remembered television series (which ran from 1994 to 1998), but its principal ace in the hole was the impeccable casting of Derek Jacobi as the crime-solving, herb-growing titular monk. The series ran for 13 episodes over four seasons and featured strong performances from Michael Culver as Prior Robert and Julian Firth as Brother Jerome, among others. The writers Russell Lewis and Christopher Russell adapted ten of Ellis Peters' Cadfael books between them and a special set was designed in Budapest that was the closest the filmmakers could create to represent the marshes around Shrewsbury in the twelfth century. The series generally stayed close to the books, with the occasional budgetary revision, although the episode *The Pilgrim of Hate* was radically rethought for the series. Ellis Peters was given casting approval and was understandably happy with the impeccable portrayal of her character by Jacobi, not least because of the actor's careful attention to his interaction with the other protagonists. The series was wound up before it was able to tackle all of Ellis Peters' books.

EDWARD FRANKLAND (Tenth-century England)

An early entry in the historical crime stakes, Edward Frankland's deft novel *The Murders at Crossby* (1955) was set in Westmorland and focused on criminal activities among the Norse settlers. Frankland, sadly, has largely fallen from view in the twenty-first century.

ROBERT FARRINGTON (Fifteenth-century England)

Utilising as protagonist Henry Morane, a friend and associate of Richard III, Farrington created a successful (but now largely forgotten) trilogy beginning with *The Killing of Richard III*, which centred on the deaths of the Princes in the Tower. It was followed by *Tudor Agent* in which Morane is obliged to become a member of the Yorkist revolt and stop the rebel lords placing a pretender on the throne. The last book in the trilogy, *The Traitors of Bosworth*, has a Flanders setting involving a new pretender to the throne and multiple threats to the resourceful hero. Farrington incorporates modern thriller elements into his complex narratives, and his work might profitably be looked at again.

BARRY UNSWORTH (Fourteenth-century England)

His literary reputation has become slightly neglected of late, but Barry Unsworth (who died in 2012) was one of the most able practitioners of historical fiction, with 17 novels under his belt and three Booker prize nominations (he won in 1992 for the novel *Sacred Hunger*). *Morality Play* concerns itself with murder in fourteenth-century England, with a travelling troupe of players putting on religious plays – and re-enacting a local murder. As ever with Unsworth, there is a precise and capital use of language.

Film: THE RECKONING (Paul McGuigan, director)

It may be understandable, but it is a shame that Barry Unsworth's distinctive title *Morality Play* was junked in 2002 for the overfamiliar title *The Reckoning* (a moniker which has seen much service over the years). Nevertheless, Paul McGuigan's film (for all its flaws) has much to recommend it, not least the fact that it is one of the most effective marriages of the historical drama with the crime-solving narrative. The film is a British/Spanish co-production with a screenplay by Mark Mills, and was filmed on location in Spain, Wales and England. Fourteenth-century priest Nicholas (played by Paul Bettany, relatively non-anachronistic) leaves his village after being caught in a compromising sexual situation. He joins a travelling acting troupe, and soon becomes involved in a murder. The film is visceral and commanding, even if several of the actors do not successfully convey the historicity of their characters.

SARA CONWAY (Thirteenth-century England)

Sara Conway's Lord Godwin mysteries have a strong following, and a good place to start is with the second book in the series, *Daughters of Summer*, which takes place on the first day of Hexamshire's annual fair in the summer of 1221. An unpleasant merchant is poisoned and Godwin discounts the initial belief that the death was accidental. Plotting is the thing here, as much as any attention to scene setting, but Conway proves herself to be adept at both.

CAROLINE ROE (Fourteenth-century Spain)

Using her PhD research and featuring the Bishop of Girona's Jewish doctor as protagonist, Caroline Roe's historical mysteries include such novels as *Remedy for Treason*, *An Antidote for Avarice*, *Solace for a Sinner* and *Consolation for an Exile*. These assiduously detailed novels are perhaps less popular than they deserve to be.

MINETTE WALTERS (Fourteenth-century England)

Before Val McDermid comfortably assumed the role, the heir apparent to the title of the UK's Queen of Crime was Minette Walters, whose mastery of the crime fiction idiom for over two decades placed her in direct line from the twin monarchs PD James and Ruth Rendell. But then Walters (with a few barely noticed exceptions) largely disappeared from the crime fiction scene. What, readers wondered, was the reason for her abdication? Rumours abounded, and now we know that the main one was on the nail: Walters had moved in an audacious new direction, setting down a sweeping historical novel set at the time of the Black Death. Walters' shift from psychological crime to a novel about survival during the dark days of the plague allowed her to bring to bear (as she herself has said) 'the same analytical qualities to history as I did to crime'. Walters expressed the hope that readers would find *The Last Hours* 'as compelling, suspenseful and intriguing as any of my whodunnits'. Using the same orchestration of suspense and tension that distinguishes her crime fiction, Walters brings her customary psychological acuity to the genre.

SAMANTHA NORMAN (Twelfth-century England)

Samantha Norman is the daughter of the late historical writer Ariana Franklin, aka Diana Norman, and has enjoyed success as a feature writer, columnist and film critic (the profession of her father, Barry Norman, who died in 2017). She completed her mother's final novel in the Mistress of the Art of Death sequence, *The Siege Winter*, set during the civil war in twelfth-century England.

SYLVIAN HAMILTON (Medieval England)

The late Sylvian Hamilton's medieval universe has the ring of truth, in both its courtly and its ecclesiastic aspects. *The Bone-Pedlar* begins with a now famous opening line: 'In the crypt of the abbey church at Hallowdene, the monks were boiling their bishop.' Along with the cruelty of the era, the supernatural holds sway, with the holy remnants of saints (the finger of St Thomas, the tooth of St Ursula) playing key roles in the narratives. Her protagonist, Sir Richard Straccan, is a distinctive figure in a now crowded world.

🎙 **Interview: Sylvian Hamilton**

Richard Straccan, the hero of my *Bone-Pedlar* series, owes his existence to my fascination with the Interdict, that peculiar six-year period when England was cut off from the benefits and protection of the Holy Church, and Bad King John was excommunicated for defying the will of the Pope. People were deprived of the mass and the sacraments, the church bells that regulated their day's work were silenced, crucifixes were veiled in the churches, bishops scurried into exile to escape royal wrath, and even the dead suffered, denied burial in holy ground. I wondered how much, how directly, it affected ordinary people – how everyday life went on in a time of such crisis. Much as it had in the Blitz, I thought: people making the best of things with a mixture of grumbling and wry humour. It's no good saying people don't change as centuries pass – they do – but so English a trait, I felt, would have been evident as far back as the Norman Conquest. Most historical novels are very serious, have you noticed? There is seldom any humour (with the glorious exception of Patrick O'Brian's Jack Aubrey series). That has never seemed natural to me. The often misunderstood English propensity to see the funny side even of disasters probably exasperated foreigners as much in the thirteenth century as it does in the twenty-first.

OK, I had the time and place for my first novel: England during the Interdict. Now I needed a hero. What could he do that hadn't been done already? There are umpteen historical lead characters: monks, nuns, troubadours, surgeons, thieves, knights, even vampires! What could mine be that would be different? Just then I had the good luck to discover James Bentley's book *Restless Bones*, a most enjoyable history of holy relics. The importance of relics to the people of the Middle Ages made them enormously valuable. They were bought, sold, traded and frequently stolen, by kings and princes, bishops and abbots. They changed hands for vast sums of money, and were faked with enthusiasm. Just the sort of occupation for Straccan – it could lead him into dozens of 'iffy' situations and so it did, first in *The Bone-Pedlar* and afterwards in *The Pendragon Banner* and *The Gleemaiden*. As for the magic – black and white in my books – my excuse is that *they* believed in it. Spells, charms and superstitions ruled the lives of medieval men and women, and never more so than during those six years when the church turned its back on England.

SUSANNA GREGORY (Medieval Britain)

Elizabeth Cruwys, better known by her writing name of Susanna Gregory, became interested in the history of the city where she grew up, Bristol – notably its great medieval period and the struggles to succeed Henry I (the monarch in the Geoffrey Mappestone novels, written by 'Simon Beaufort', aka Gregory and her husband, Beau Riffenburgh). She is also fascinated by the turbulent period of the Black Death, the era covered in her Matthew Bartholomew novels. Other books feature Thomas Chaloner, a reluctant spy in seventeenth-century London. After a police career, Gregory undertook postgraduate studies at the University of Durham before earning a PhD at Cambridge. Research in medieval history and architecture (particularly the castles of Britain) and the archaeology and history of the College of Michaelhouse in Cambridge supplied the background for her Matthew Bartholomew series. Gregory is also a member of the Medieval Murderers, a group of writers who give talks and presentations at literary festivals, as well as writing books together. The first Sir Geoffrey Mappestone mystery, *Murder in the Holy City*, is a good starting point for those new to the writer.

Interview: Susanna Gregory

Some years ago, Mike Jecks invited Bernard Knight, Ian Morson, Philip Gooden and me to join forces and form a group called the Medieval Murderers. This entails wearing rather striking T-shirts designed by Mike's wife, and getting together to 'perform' at festivals and bookshops. At these events, we're often asked what first inspired us to write historical fiction, and how we go about our research. We all have different answers, with replies ranging from a misguided impression that writing fiction was an easy way to make lots of money (we have all now learned it is not), to thinking we could do better than Jeffrey Archer. I'd like to say that I started to write because I'd always wanted to be a novelist, or that I felt some inner calling. But the truth of the matter is that my husband went to Canada for a month, and I found myself with lots of free time and no particularly pressing work to do. Also, my Cambridge college at the time was a hotbed of politics and insurrection, and it occurred to me that such antics had probably gone on in exactly the same way 600 years ago – the medieval chroniclers certainly wrote about all manner of unsavoury dealings and nefarious plots. Writing historical fiction is a lot of fun. The research involved in producing medieval mysteries is exciting and absorbing, and it seems that however much I do, there's always masses more to learn. Writing can be lonely, stressful (where deadlines are concerned) and occasionally tedious (reading the same manuscript for the tenth time). But what other occupation allows you to explore past worlds and then make stories up about them? To all budding writers, I have just one piece of advice: go for it!

KATE SEDLEY (Fifteenth-century England)

Kate Sedley is the writing name of Bristol-born Brenda Margaret Lilian Honeyman Clarke. Her speciality is the now thriving field of the medieval murder mystery – a genre to which she has contributed many novels. Her series features the monk Roger the Chapman, who has left the monastery cell for the life of the road as a peddler (a 'chapman'). A signature novel is the twentieth in the series, *The Midsummer Crown*.

4: Tudor England and the Sixteenth Century

RORY CLEMENTS (Tudor England)

Rory Clements' *Revenger* was the surprise winner of the 2010 Ellis Peters Historical Crime Fiction Dagger, in the face of stiff competition from the likes of the all-conquering CJ Sansom. This second book to feature the Elizabethan, highly intuitive 'intelligencer' John Shakespeare (the less famous brother of the playwright) effortlessly captures all the ever-present menace but also all the excitement of living in capricious times when a misplaced word can get you dispatched to the Tower. John Shakespeare is a strongly realised character and the perfect pilot for the reader in this distant world; however familiar we think it is, there is still much that is strange to modern readers, and Clements brings it to life with great skill. It is a novel that revels in the sights and smells of Tudor England – both exhilaratingly readable and full of well-researched historical detail.

Another early outing for Shakespeare is *Prince*, which reminds us again that the author is one of the most reliable in the genre. In the spring of 1593, the plague prowls England, along with serious political unrest, and bomb attacks on the Dutch immigrant community have a powerful effect on John Shakespeare's already turbulent life. Similarly pertinent, since we live in an era of religious fundamentalists brainwashed into carrying out suicide missions, is the compellingly readable *The Heretics* – the target of the relentless Catholic assassins here is no less than Queen Elizabeth I. This is the fifth novel by Clements to feature Shakespeare, and, in terms of its comprehensive narrative grip, it is easily the equal of its distinguished predecessors. The real strength of the series is definitely Clements' protagonist – John Shakespeare is one of the great historical sleuths.

🎤 Interview: Rory Clements

If you write crime thrillers, the period you choose for your books is every bit as important as the place, the plot and the characters. My Tom Wilde series is set in the 1930s; my John Shakespeare novels are set in the late sixteenth century. What do these two periods have in common? They were both times when England (Britain in the 1930s, of course) faced the threat of deadly intrigue and the likelihood of armed invasion. For me, the Elizabethan England of John Shakespeare, with its endless conspiracies and the spy network of Sir Francis Walsingham, was a brilliant canvas for a crime thriller. So was 1930s Cambridge with its notoriety as the breeding ground for a generation of spies. I read many crime novels, histories and biographies, but I deliberately avoid reading other thrillers from my chosen periods. That said, I do love Philip Kerr's Bernie Gunther series: a great character in a great setting. Of my own books, my favourite is always my last and my most daunting is always the next. One of the joys of historical noir is the absence of twenty-first-century technology. Let's face it, Richard Hannay lost in the Highlands isn't going to work today – he'd just get on his mobile and sort everything out.

KATE ELLIS (Tudor England, Post-World War One)

While she has tackled a variety of genres, Kate Ellis is perhaps most celebrated for her archaeological mysteries featuring Wesley Peterson, along with a series set in a town based on York (renamed Eborby) with Detective Inspector Joe Plantagenet investigating the links between the past and the present. Her interest in history has also found an outlet in her novel *The Devil's Priest*, which is set in her native city of Liverpool when it was an insignificant port in the sixteenth century, in the period when Henry VIII was undertaking the dissolution of the monasteries. Katheryn, the abbess of the local convent, investigates the killing of a young nun. Ellis brings to life a Liverpool that not even the city's inhabitants will recognise.

🎤 Interview: Kate Ellis

I'm probably best known for my Wesley Peterson novels in which a historical mystery (usually uncovered by Wesley's old friend, archaeologist Dr Neil Watson) is combined with a parallel modern police investigation. I have used a different period in each book in the series, ranging from the Viking age to World War Two, because the past (with its unexpected similarities to the present) has always fascinated me. My first ever crime novel was called *The Devil's Priest*, set in Tudor Liverpool. And now I've returned to writing purely historical crime in my new trilogy set in 1919 and featuring Inspector Albert Lincoln. I feel my latest two novels are suitable representatives of my work. The first novel in my Albert Lincoln trilogy, *A High Mortality of Doves*, is about a small Derbyshire village, reeling from the loss of its men in World War One, which has to face yet more horror when a bizarre series of murders rocks its new-found peace. Then *The Mermaid's Scream*, featuring DI Wesley Peterson, involves the murder of a Devon heiress in the nineteenth century (inspired by a real case) which runs beside a contemporary investigation into the murder of a reclusive author's biographer.

Historical crime is one of my favourite genres and I particularly enjoy the work of CJ Sansom, Andrew Taylor, LC Tyler, Susanna Gregory, Peter Lovesey, Lindsey Davis and James Runcie (to name but a few). For a writer of historical crime there is the huge pleasure of immersing oneself in research – something I confess I love. LP Hartley famously said that 'the past is another country; they do things differently there', and historical fiction transports us to other times with manners and preoccupations so different from our own. Who can resist? The Black Death of 1348 was one of the most grim and dramatic events in British history, killing almost half the population and changing society for ever. So I could hardly resist including a mystery from these momentous times in my novel *The Plague Maiden*. When I began writing crime fiction, I was torn between writing about my principal interest, history, and creating the sort of contemporary crime novel that I so enjoy reading. But then I hit on a simple solution: I combined both. And in each of my books I interweave mysteries from the past and the present.

CJ SANSOM (Tudor England, Spanish Civil War)

CJ Sansom is the gold standard for historical crime fiction. A variety of writers elbow for position at the top of the tree, but for many aficionados one name has maintained an unassailable pole position for some considerable time: the British novelist CJ Sansom, a man who shuns the limelight of publicity. His lengthy, energetic and fastidiously organised novels featuring the canny hunchbacked lawyer Matthew Shardlake are catnip to those who seek something a little more challenging in the field, and it's not difficult to see why. A great many of Sansom's books (among which number *Dissolution*, *Sovereign*, *Dark Fire* and *Revelation*) are genuinely epic in their scale, and the verisimilitude with which Tudor England is evoked by the author makes most other writing in the genre seem footling. Taking one example: at over 600 pages, *Heartstone* is one of Sansom's most imposing books, but after a slowish start (something frequently attempted by Sansom – like many good writers, he often demands a certain patience from his readers), the customary comprehensive grip is rigorously maintained. The invasion of France mounted by Henry VIII has been a disaster, and, in retaliation, an imposing French fleet is making preparations to cross the Channel. At Portsmouth, the English navy is readying itself for the battle of its life, and at Henry's autocratic direction, a massive militia army is being raised. England, reeling under the debasing of its currency to pay for the war, is suffering crippling inflation and economic meltdown. (If the thought of Britain's involvement in controversial foreign wars while suffering an economic crisis might remind the reader of a few more recent parallels, there is little doubt that this is exactly what CJ Sansom intends.) Against this tumultuous backdrop, the lawyer Matthew Shardlake is presented with a difficult case via an elderly servant of Queen Catherine Parr, one that will plunge him into the labyrinthine toils of the King's Court of Wards. Shardlake's job is to look into wrongs that have been done to the young ward Hugh Curteys by a Hampshire landowner, and – as is customary with most cases involving Shardlake – violent death is soon on the agenda, as the threat of war lours. Sansom admirers will know exactly what to expect here, and all the usual pleasures afforded by this talented writer are satisfyingly on offer. In terms of reach and achievement, *Heartstone* provides something streets ahead of most of the writer's contemporaries.

A change was in store with *Winter in Madrid*. It's always a risky strategy for an author to change horses midstream. After all, if you've enjoyed the kind of critical (and commercial) success that

Sansom had with his elegantly written Tudor-era crime novels, why test the loyalty of your readership by abandoning this fertile ground and delivering a literary saga set in Spain at the end of the Civil War? Sansom, however, rapidly established that he is as much a master of this era as he is of Henry VIII's England. The 1940s. Harry Brett is a damaged ex-public schoolboy recovering from the horrors of Dunkirk. After meeting some genteel Whitehall spymasters, he finds himself reluctantly dispatched to the turbulent city of Madrid, where the inhabitants are starving. Hitler is moving inexorably over Europe, and Harry has been commissioned to ingratiate himself with an old acquaintance, Sandy Forsyth, who is engaged in various suspect transactions in Spain. Simultaneously, Sandy's lover Barbara Clare (who has worked as a nurse for the Red Cross) has her own clandestine agenda: she is engaged in a search for her ex-lover, the charismatic Bernie Piper. Bernie is introduced to the reader in a grim prologue, fighting – and seemingly dying – for the Communist International Brigade. But Barbara believes that he is still alive, and she hooks up with some very dangerous people to track him down.

While all of this may suggest literary espionage in the le Carré vein, that's not quite what we get here. Sansom deploys a fractured time scheme, moving (sometimes jarringly) between past and present: we are back in Harry's loveless childhood, then in the murky world of 1940s Madrid, where betrayal is the order of the day, or in the public school environment where Harry and the opportunistic Sandy first meet. Similarly, the reader is catapulted from Barbara's relationships with her very different lovers Sandy and Bernie to the humiliations of her childhood, where her unhappiness over her unprepossessing appearance is to mark her for life. But as *Winter in Madrid* progresses, Sansom adroitly draws the disparate strands of his ambitious saga together, and his recreations of time and place anchor his characters with satisfying precision.

Does it matter that various literary ghosts haunt the shadows of this novel? If an Englishman adrift in a foreign city were not sufficient homage, there are many other touches reminiscent of Graham Greene, such as the threatening eruptions of the brutal, anti-English Falangists, after the fashion of the Tontons Macoutes in Greene's *The Comedians*. Hemingway is in here too, in the terse, economical prose. But Sansom transfigures his sources into a moral universe that is very much his own, and the orchestration of sexual and moral equivocation between his characters is handled with cool assurance.

PHILIP GOODEN (Elizabethan England, Fourteenth-century Britain)

Philip Gooden's Shakespearean mysteries are set in the Elizabethan era and feature the canny Nick Revill, and he has also penned a fourteenth-century sequence (as Philippa Morgan) featuring Geoffrey Chaucer as the central character. Revill is an inhabitant of Shakespeare's world and appears as an inexperienced actor from the West Country who also does service as a tyro detective figure. The writer's decision to set the series in the early 1590s demands a level of historical verisimilitude that Gooden delivers with a sure touch. *Sleep of Death* is the first and one of the most distinguished of the series, with Revill recruited to the Chamberlain's Men and looking into a death that closely reflects Shakespeare's *Hamlet*, with the Bard, no less, in the frame for the murder. Gooden's Chaucer series is equally impressive, with *Chaucer and the House of Fame* a notably strong entry – during the Hundred Years War between England and France, Chaucer becomes involved in the solving of a murder. Gooden has also tackled the Victorian era with *The Salisbury Manuscript*, which is set amidst the cathedrals of England.

Other key books: *The Pale Companion* (Nick Revill), *Chaucer and the Legend of Good Women*, *Chaucer and the Doctor of Physic*.

🎙 Interview: Philip Gooden

I've written historical mysteries set in Geoffrey Chaucer's time, featuring the poet himself tumbling into murderous trouble in medieval England, France and Italy – not totally implausible since Chaucer most likely undertook secret diplomatic work on behalf of the court of Edward III. And I've jumped half a millennium to the Victorian era with three murder stories set in different cathedral cities. But the period and setting I feel most at home in is the decade or so that bridges the sixteenth and seventeenth centuries, and the London of Shakespeare's Globe. It was a turbulent time and place, full of conspiracies and anxiety because Elizabeth I's reign was coming to an end, and no one was certain who was going to succeed the Virgin Queen. But at home it was also a time of artistic exuberance and swagger, while out at sea glamorous figures such as Francis Drake and Walter Raleigh were flexing their imperial, piratical muscles. I contemplated having William Shakespeare himself as a detective but preferred to keep him in the wings, contributing occasionally, a shadowy presence, gliding off and on. There's a theatrical legend that Shakespeare played the ghost in *Hamlet*, and I used this in the first book in the series, *Sleep of Death*. Instead of Shakespeare as a detective, I created a youngish man, Nick Revill, up from the West Country, left bereft by the death of his parents in the plague, and desperate to become an actor. Taken on temporarily by Shakespeare's acting company, the Chamberlain's Men, he soon becomes a permanent fixture at the Globe. Each book in the series uses a Shakespeare play as a kind of backdrop. In *Sleep of Death* it's *Hamlet*, chosen because it's a play everyone sort of knows even if they've never seen it and because it is a murder mystery. It even contains a play within the play called *The Mousetrap*. I was surprised when I started writing the Nick Revill series to discover that, although the Shakespearean era had been covered by other mystery writers, it hadn't been – as it were – done to death. There was still some space.

There are six books in the series and Nick Revill also features in several of the short stories I contributed to the sequence of anthology novels written by the mystery collective the Medieval Murderers (ten books to date). Of the novels, I particularly enjoyed writing *Mask of Night*, set in Oxford and containing a version of a locked-room murder, and *An Honourable Murderer* because it does something rarely – never? – done in a murder mystery. But my probable favourite out of the Shakespearean mysteries is *The Pale Companion*, not just because it was short-listed for the Ellis Peters Historical Award but because it was my stab at a country house mystery and set in a glorious summer at the end of Elizabeth's reign. I discovered later that I got the weather wrong. The summer of 1601 was cool and wet. But then that's the difference between history, where the writer is accountable to fact, and fiction, where the writer can get away with murder... and unclouded skies.

SJ PARRIS (Sixteenth-century England)

Sacrilege is SJ Parris's third book to feature the real-life sixteenth-century monk Giordano Bruno as sleuth, and the character is becoming even more complex and interesting – as is the work of Bruno's chronicler. England's future is at stake as Bruno investigates the disappearance of the corpse of St Thomas Becket in a well-written adventure. Historical crime fiction is a burgeoning field, and something special is required to rise above the thronging competition. *Heresy* showed that SJ Parris (a nom de plume for Stephanie Merritt) possesses that something special; this was a strikingly accomplished first outing for Giordano Bruno, who is simultaneously a monk, a poet and a highly accomplished sleuth. His investigation here takes place in Elizabethan Oxford, and Parris has the measure of all the necessary period scene setting. Giordano Bruno is a truly memorable figure, with his keen mind and anachronistically modern sensibility; *Heresy* also paints a sharp picture of a society riven by religious intolerance. It is in the texture of Parris's books that she excels at every point, with elements of research always worn lightly.

Interview: SJ Parris

I've always been fascinated by the Tudors, and the world of political intrigue in the late sixteenth century, but it was the story of Giordano Bruno that was the starting point for the series. When I came across the theory that he had worked as a spy for Elizabeth I while he was living in England in the 1580s, I realised I could bring together two of my greatest passions – history and detective stories. My inspiration in the genre has always been Umberto Eco, since I read *The Name of the Rose* as a teenager. I can only dream of creating a novel as complex and intricate as that, but I feel that *Conspiracy* is the best of the series so far; there was more of a challenge because it was set in the Valois court in Paris, which is less familiar to British readers, but allowed for a multi-layered plot and the chance to introduce readers to some fascinating historical characters, such as the formidable Catherine de Medici. Among my contemporaries, I always read CJ Sansom's Shardlake series, since he's just before the period I'm writing about, but I deliberately don't look at any other Elizabethan crime as I want to avoid unconscious influence. I'm also a big fan of MJ Carter's Victorian series, and Arturo Pérez-Reverte's historical mysteries.

Although I enjoy straightforward historical fiction, the added pleasure of historical crime for me is that it offers an exploration of a society – and that society's idea of justice – from a different angle, with the bonus of a page-turning plot. As a writer, it allows for the return of the amateur sleuth in a way that is difficult to achieve in contemporary crime fiction, when so much detection relies on technological access.

JAMES FORRESTER (Sixteenth-century England)

James Forrester is the fiction-writing alter ego (utilising his middle names) of the historian Dr Ian JF Mortimer. As Ian Mortimer he has written guidebooks for those 'visiting' the past (such as *The Time Traveller's Guide to Medieval England*) as well as a day-by-day account of a king over a particular year (*1415: Henry V's Year of Glory*). As James Forrester he traverses the gap between historical fact and fiction, creating rich tapestries. *Sacred Treason* is set in 1563 with England a troubled nation as Catholic plots against the young Queen Elizabeth leave the country in a state of fear and suspicion. The respected herald William Harley, known to all as Clarenceux King of Arms, receives an unexpected visitor: his fellow Catholic, Henry Machyn. Machyn is desperate for Clarenceux to hide a manuscript he possesses, but it soon becomes apparent that it contains a secret so dangerous that their lives are at stake.

SIMON LEVACK (Sixteenth-century Mexico)

Simon Levack's initial endeavours were in the legal profession before he took up writing full-time. His long-standing interest in Mesoamerican history, especially the Aztecs, was set in motion by reading Inga Clendinnen's book *Aztecs: An Interpretation*. His atmospheric series, with its unusual Mexican historical settings, includes an impressive debut in *Demon of the Air* and the equally vivid *Shadow of the Lords*.

🎤 Interview: Simon Levack

Let me set the scene for what was my first novel, *Demon of the Air*. It is Mexico in 1517: the eve of the Spanish Conquest.

Aztec Emperor Montezuma rules the known world. Daily canoes and trains of sweating bearers carry tribute to his island capital, Mexico-Tenochtitlan, while squadrons of ruthless warriors enforce his will. Gold, silver, cotton, jewels and precious feathers change hands in his markets. The temples run with the blood of human sacrifices. All seems well, but Montezuma is troubled. Mysterious strangers have appeared in the east. Are they men or gods? Visions and rumours disturb his dreams. The soothsayers he turns to for guidance give him only enigmatic answers and he knows he cannot trust his advisers – especially his chief minister, the unscrupulous Lord Feathered-in-Black. Yaotl, the chief minister's slave, is troubled too. He was ordered to escort a sacrificial victim up the steps of the Great Pyramid, but the victim ran amok, uttering a bizarre and sinister prophecy and leaping to his death before the War God's priests could cut out his heart. Then he learns that the Emperor's soothsayers have vanished. The Emperor scents a connection between these two events and orders Yaotl to find it – on pain of death if he fails. But it soon becomes clear that whatever the connection is, Yaotl's own master will stop at nothing, including murder, to keep it secret. To get to the truth will take all Yaotl's wits and will to survive. It will lead him into confrontations with the peril destined to overwhelm his whole world and with a monster from his own past – and into the hands of a sadistic killer. *Demon of the Air* is the first in a series of crime novels depicting the colourful and bloodthirsty Aztec civilisation at the height of its glory, and featuring as its hero a wily slave, Yaotl (pronounced Yah-ot). Yaotl is something of a dropout in a community that has no time for social misfits, and as a result lives constantly on his wits. The crimes that he is forced to solve – usually against his will – reflect features of the strange society in which he lives: mysteriously botched human sacrifices, vanished soothsayers, a massacre carried out by fanatical warriors.

5: The Seventeenth and Eighteenth Centuries

EDWARD MARSTON (Sixteenth, Seventeenth and Nineteenth Centuries)

The prolific Edward Marston (the pseudonym of Keith Miles) has made his mark as a playwright and has run his own professional theatre company, but this Renaissance man among crime writers has one real métier: his impeccable series of atmospheric crime novels, such as the Domesday series exploring crime in Norman England. *The Frost Fair* (subtitled *A Restoration Mystery*) is perhaps his most accomplished and richly detailed piece: historical crime of the first order. The novel is set in the terrible winter of 1669; London ignores such hardships as a frozen Thames by celebrating Christmas with a traditional 'frost fair' on the banks of the river. Amidst the carousing throng is a talented young architect who is escorting the daughter of one of his clients. The architect, Christopher Redmayne (a recurring character), has romantic designs on the delightful Susan, and he is further pleased to encounter his friend Constable Jonathan Bale, who is also there with his family. Christopher and Jonathan, while saving a boy from a freezing death in the river, discover a frozen cadaver underneath the ice. The corpse is that of an Italian fencing master, and despite Christopher's best efforts, he finds himself further embroiled in the mystery when his brother Henry is accused of the murder. As in all Edward Marston's previous books, there is an assiduously maintained balance between authentic period touches and lively, intelligent characterisation. When so much historical crime seems to be dispatched by rote these days, it is refreshing to encounter a writer like Marston, who never gives less than his best.

Other key books: The Nicholas Bracewell sequence (set in the late sixteenth-century Elizabethan theatre), the Railway Detective series (Victorian England).

Interview: Edward Marston

It was Robert Louis Stevenson who first gave me the urge to write; novels such as *Treasure Island* and *Kidnapped* are exciting adventure stories and colourful evocations of the past. Since I worked in the theatre for many years, it's not surprising that my first historical crime series featured an Elizabethan theatre company, living precariously and assailed on all sides. Its hero is Nicholas Bracewell, the 'book holder' (or stage manager), a pivotal figure in the boisterous troupe. The novel that gave me most satisfaction was *The Roaring Boy*, centred on an anonymous play that lands the company in grave danger because it offends the wrong people. My six Restoration novels explore the rebuilding of London after the Great Fire of 1666. My protagonist is Christopher Redmayne, a talented architect in the unfortunate position of having to get commissions via his brother, Henry, an outrageous rake. The series is set in one of the most vibrant, dissipated and politically fascinating periods in English history. Where else could you invent a Society for the Capture of Araminta's Maidenhead then depict the horror of its four members (Henry Redmayne included) at the appalling news that the woman had married? Inspector Robert Colbeck investigates crime on Victorian railways and will travel anywhere, even America, to catch a villain. The books show how completely railways transformed society. I come from a railway family and, as a boy, was often smuggled on to the footplate when my father was shunting. The novels celebrate the age of steam and are a joy to research. Historical noir is a flowering genre, taking the reader back into lost worlds full of danger, excitement and ferment. The past is another country. It's more fun there.

MICHAEL GREGORIO (Enlightenment Prussia)

References to the philosopher Kant in a thriller? The heavyweight intellectual baggage of Gregorio's ambitious historical novel is there in the title of *Critique of Criminal Reason*, which might suggest we're in *Name of the Rose* territory. If the achievement of Michael Gregorio (aka British-born Michael Jacob and Italian Daniela De Gregorio) is not as prodigious as Eco's, this is still a sweeping and brilliantly detailed read. It is the Age of Enlightenment and Immanuel Kant's writings are realigning approaches to reason and science. Prussian magistrate Hanno Stiffeniis will find Kant is to aid him in investigating a series of violent deaths that have terrified the town of Königsberg. But does the hunt for a murderer matter when Napoleon's troops threaten the borders? The premise may owe something to *The Night of the Generals* (criminal investigation in a time of war), but Gregorio threads philosophical underpinnings through the dark narrative with genuine assurance. In *A Visible Darkness*, Stiffeniis is called to the Baltic Coast, where the mutilated and naked body of a woman has been found. More recent work includes the impressive *Lone Wolf*, a contemporary thriller set in Umbria.

🎙 **Interview: Michael Gregorio (Michael Jacob and Daniela De Gregorio)**

We got caught up in the Napoleonic era by chance. Daniela had an idea for a short story based on the odd relationship between the philosopher Immanuel Kant and Martin Lampe, his eccentric valet. This was the seed for *Critique of Criminal Reason*, our first novel featuring the young Prussian magistrate Hanno Stiffeniis. The book was published worldwide, and we were suddenly the experts on everything Prussian. We weren't, of course, but that didn't seem to bother anyone. Very few people seemed to know that the Kingdom of Prussia had even existed. As an American lady asked us at a literary festival: 'Don't you mean Russia?' Faber and Faber commissioned three more Stiffeniis novels, so we had a lot of research ahead of us, learning about Prussia as we went along, reading everything we could find about the period – the standard histories, soldiers' letters, memoirs of generals who had fought against Napoleon, and, of course, the French *Encyclopédie*, of which we found a copy in the town library. It's an amazing compendium of society in the eighteenth century. Which instruments did doctors use? How did engineers build bridges? How did towns deal with sewage? This was essential background material for us, although we needed to spread the net even wider as the series progressed. We could never have written *Days of Atonement* without knowing how Prussian soldiers lived and died. *A Visible Darkness* owes much to *Succini Prussici*, a remarkable history of Baltic amber written in 1677 by a scholar, Philipp Jacob Hartmann, while *Unholy Awakening* was inspired by a treatise on vampirism that was published in southern Italy in 1739. Any serious attempt at convincing historical fiction involves serious study, as writers such as Andrew Taylor, CJ Sansom and Hilary Mantel will tell you. We're up to our eyes in Fascism at the moment as a new publishing project takes shape. One hundred and eighty thousand people were murdered in Italy immediately after World War Two as old scores were settled and a republic replaced the monarchy, which means that we have a wealth of material to work on!

ANTONIA HODGSON (Eighteenth-century England)

Antonia Hodgson proved with her first novel, *The Devil in the Marshalsea*, that she was, at a stroke, one of the most impressive practitioners of historical crime fiction, fully deserving the breathless encomium from Jeffery Deaver on the jacket. Her territory is London in 1727, and her protagonist, Tom Hawkins, has been enjoying the fleshpots of the capital, luxuriating in the brothels, coffee houses and gambling dens. But he is about to enter a world grimly familiar to anyone who reads Charles Dickens: the debtors' prison, Marshalsea. As sweepingly evoked by Hodgson, this is virtually an entire city within stone walls, with its own ruthless rules and hierarchies. There is one certainty here: those who have connections (either family or friends) who provide some remuneration enjoy a degree of comfort denied their fellow debtors. If you are unlucky enough to have no access to such largesse, your future probably consists of disease and death. And escape from the iron fist of the governor and his henchmen is only the remotest of possibilities. Tom Hawkins finds it very difficult to adapt to this brutal universe, not least because of his inability to follow rules. And when the gruesome murder of a fellow debtor, Captain Roberts, spreads fear among the inmates, the captain's widow is out for retribution for the killing. The man immediately in the frame is the mysterious Samuel Fleet, who is much feared – and he happens to be the man with whom Tom Hawkins is sharing a cell. It's up to Tom to discover who is the real murderer, a quest that may cost him his own life. Hawkins is a winning protagonist, and *The Devil in the Marshalsea* really was something new in the world of historical crime fiction. Such is the detail and atmosphere of Hodgson's writing that at times she even rivals the Master, Dickens (but with added crime). Any lovers of the historical crime genre need to keep a weather eye on Antonia Hodgson, whose subsequent book, *The Last Confession of Thomas Hawkins*, is equally accomplished.

DERYN LAKE (Georgian England)

The time that Deryn Lake spends on research certainly pays off in the admirable John Rawlings series. *Death in the Setting Sun* has all the key elements of her books, with a notably ingenious narrative. This tenth book in the series has Rawlings involved in a prestigious theatre party at Gunnersbury House. The hostess, Princess Amelia, is distressed by the sudden death of one of the party – and Rawlings, to his dismay, is suspected of the murder. All of this is handled with the usual aplomb, but there's something else here – notably the death of a major series character. But the only way you'll find out the identity of the victim is by reading the book – and you should. If the characters in Lake's books don't always behave in a strictly plausible fashion (given the eighteenth-century setting), the assiduously researched detail allows us to accept all the murderous shenanigans, however outrageous.

The earlier *Death in the West Wind* is also vintage stuff, with Lake on her most assured form. Her customary protagonist, the resourceful apothecary John Rawlings, is enjoying his honeymoon in Devon, but, needless to say, marital bliss is interrupted when the mutilated body of a young girl, Juliana van Guylder, is found on a schooner. Then the young girl's brother Richard vanishes, and Rawlings traces a sinister trail to the Society of Angels, a clandestine group that appears to have something to do with the mystery. But thrown into the mix is a highwayman and even a phantom coach, so Rawlings calls for help from the canny Joe Jago and the Flying Runners, his London cohorts. As in her other books, Lake is adroit at creating a satisfyingly knotty plot for Rawlings to solve, and the Georgian period has rarely been evoked with such colour, whether in the fields of the historical thriller, romantic fiction or even the literary novel.

Other key books: *Death in the Dark Walk, Death on the Romney Marsh, Death and the Black Pyramid.*

🎤 Interview: Deryn Lake

I think all my work, the John Rawlings series and my other crime novels, reflects my early reading influences. I have always been attracted to the slightly bizarre, the gothic, and all my childhood tastes reflect this. When I was just seven, reading voraciously, I adored the scene in which the god Pan came down to earth and rescued a baby badger – or was it an otter? – in *The Wind in the Willows*. In fact, I would read that particular scene over and over again. I also adored Edgar Rice Burroughs' Tarzan books, together with his lesser known Barsoom series, which I thought were terrific. At the age of about 13 I graduated to crime novels. I remember being awake till dawn came up I was so engrossed with Agatha Christie's *And Then There Were None*. I know it is fashionable for snotty-nosed modern-day crime writers to sneer at her, and though her writing style is somewhat dated, I consider her plots second to none.

Nowadays, of course, I tend to read the work of people I like and avoid completely those I don't. Steven Saylor is one of the few American writers I feel totally at home with, and I consider *Rubicon* to be quite masterly. But the hard-bitten hard-boiled stuff that comes from across the Atlantic is generally not for me. I think one of the most stunning books I have ever read was Ruth Rendell's *A Sight for Sore Eyes*. The feeling it left me with was quite extraordinary. It is a book that I reread every so often and I shiver deeply every time. I also enjoy the work of Hilary Bonner and Ruth Dudley Edwards. Ruth's books make me laugh a lot, which is good. I do spend quite a bit of time researching, which I am sure is part of the appeal of the John Rawlings series. But mainly it is the family saga that my readers love. For example, they adore John's adoptive father, Sir Gabriel Kent, who always dresses in black and white. And John's love life is of consuming interest.

SHONA MACLEAN (1620s Scotland and Ireland)

The astonishing success of Hilary Mantel's prize-winning *Wolf Hall* has rekindled readers' taste for period-set novels, but such writers as CJ Sansom (as mentioned elsewhere) had already been paving the way. And if your taste is for such fare, you would be wise to pick up Shona MacLean's *A Game of Sorrows*, a diverting historical mystery that combines the ironclad plotting of Sansom with the artful historical recreation of Mantel. MacLean's protagonist is once again the eponymous hero of *The Redemption of Alexander Seaton*, a book much praised for its atmospheric evocation of Scotland in the 1620s. Seaton is a disgraced cleric whose love affairs have cost him his job. In the first book, he undergoes a double journey, which involves uncovering a murderer and regaining his own faith. But does this second outing for MacLean's sleuth match the panache of its predecessor? It is 1628, and Seaton has a new life as a university teacher in Aberdeen. A stranger arrives – an emissary from his family in Ireland. Seaton listens in amazement as he is told that his clan has been placed under a poet's curse. His relatives are to die, one by one – and this may not be superstitious nonsense, as the curse is (apparently) already claiming victims. Against his will, Seaton returns to Ulster and finds himself embroiled in bitter internecine family squabbles. As he attempts to track down the individual who placed the curse, he quickly finds that his own life is in just as much danger as those of his benighted relatives. Although the brio of the earlier book is more fitfully evident here, MacLean once again demonstrates that she is a distinctive talent. The seventeenth-century Celtic atmosphere has pungency, and Seaton is a nicely idiosyncratic protagonist. It is a commendable touch that his sometimes anachronistic modern mindset is balanced against the received prejudices of his time. If your taste is for a trip to seventeenth-century Carrickfergus in stimulating company, you could do worse than investigate *A Game of Sorrows*.

HANNAH MARCH (Eighteenth-century England)

In *The Devil's Highway*, the year is 1761 and Robert Fairfax is on his way to the country house of his new employer when he finds himself on a desolate stretch of road that is known as the haunt of a dangerous highwayman. Fairfax discovers the London stagecoach in a ditch with the driver shot through the head and two passengers dead. His new employer, the local Justice of the Peace, asks him to investigate, and Fairfax discovers that there is far more to this affair than mere highway robbery. One of the corpses appears to be that of a wealthy banker, Nicholas Twelvetree. But who is the Nicholas Twelvetree living in the neighbouring village, alive and well but in mortal fear for his life? And is the other corpse that of a lunatic escaped from the local asylum, as the much-disliked Methodist preacher claims it is? March is particularly skilled at this kind of period mystery, and all the sharp observation and carefully textured historical detail that distinguished the first Robert Fairfax outing, *The Complaint of the Dove*, are in evidence. Fairfax is an intriguingly drawn hero, and March never allows the period trappings to slow down the necessary tension. As Fairfax comes nearer to finding out who the third passenger on the coach was, readers are likely to find themselves turning the pages ever faster.

JEAN-FRANÇOIS PAROT (Pre-revolutionary France)

Perhaps the centuries-old enmity between Britain and France is over; certainly, a literary *entente cordiale* is in place in Jean-François Parot's novel. Early in *The Phantom of Rue Royale* (set in eighteenth-century Paris), it is clear that the writer exerting a not-so-subtle influence on the text is English rather than French; there are references to the 'best' and 'worst' (of Parisians, not times), and someone is knocked down by a dangerously driven carriage and left to bleed on the ground ('from inside the carriage, an arrogant voice gave the order to push the rabble aside and carry on'). But these signs that we might be in for a reworking of Dickens' *A Tale of Two Cities* from a Gallic perspective are misleading, although Parot certainly shares Dickens' taste for an operatically staged set piece. And the set piece that opens this latest outing for Parot's highly intelligent Commissioner Nicolas Le Floch is a doozy, setting a kinetic pace for the narrative that is rigorously maintained. It is May 1770, and the whole of Paris is in a frenzy of anticipation: the Dauphin has married Marie Antoinette, and the city authorities have laid on a spectacular firework display. But as the youthful Commissioner observes the excitement, he realises that the preparations for the event are wholly inadequate. The fireworks display is mismanaged, and wreaths of black smoke and flame engulf the pyrotechnicians' platform; the crowd panics and the Rue Royale and the Tuileries are plunged into chaos, with people crushed by the carriages and the crowds. But there is one body among the dead that appears to be a victim not of the disaster, but of a cold-blooded murderer. Le Floch is determined to track down her killer – even though his boss has handed him a more dangerous assignment: find out who is behind the debacle of the wedding celebrations that ended in death.

As in such earlier books as *The Châtelet Apprentice*, Parot demonstrates that he has few peers in marrying a colourful historical narrative with the exigencies of the crime novel. The translation by Howard Curtis does full justice to the assiduously detailed prose, and, at the centre of things, Nicolas Le Floch is an engaging conduit for the reader through the teeming and phantasmagoric capital city that is Paris in the eighteenth century. Perhaps a little pruning might have been applied to that besetting sin of historical fiction – characters needlessly telling each other things they already know ('Pont du Corps-de-Garde, which leads to the Tuileries Gardens, is closed') – and a supernatural element may be a genre-shift too far for some, but such is the momentum of the storytelling here that few readers are likely to be worried by this.

IMOGEN ROBERTSON (Eighteenth-century England, Belle Époque Paris)

When she is not penning her insidiously diverting historical crime novels, Imogen Robertson spends her time playing the cello music of Bach and Shostakovich – proof (if proof were needed) of her civilised nature. But what makes her books so unusual is their audacious mix of a cultural gloss (as in Robertson's leisure activities) and uncomplicated, straight-ahead storytelling. Both the multi-layered nuance of a Peter Ackroyd and the buttonholing narrative grasp of a Stephen King may be found stirred into the mix here – and although such a combination shouldn't really work, Robertson makes the various elements of her literary personality coalesce to good effect. *Island of Bones*, the third novel in her Crowther and Westerman series, has all the panache of its predecessors, *Instruments of Darkness* and *Anatomy of Murder*, with a particularly strong picture of the Lake District (the book was inspired by her childhood trips to the area). Of course, the Lakes in the eighteenth century, with its rich and fey mix of legend and magic, was markedly different from the region we know today. Robertson's ill-matched protagonists are Harriet Westerman and Gabriel Crowther; the former is a strong-willed Sussex landowner, while the latter is a severe anatomist who prefers his own company – but is prepared to help Harriet in her sometimes dangerous mystery-solving activities. The tomb of a nobleman, the first Earl of Greta, appears to have lain untouched (on the eponymous 'island of bones') for hundreds of years, but when the ancient stone lid is pried loose, there is one body too many in the tomb. Gabriel Crowther's family now owns the land that belonged to the Earl (he of the overcrowded tomb), and Crowther sports a family history quite as chequered (and sanguinary) as the late Earl's: Gabriel's brother, in fact, was executed for the murder of their father, the Baron of Keswick. Gabriel has been enjoying his self-imposed seclusion, but both he and Harriet Westerman are soon in dark and threatening territory. The duo's journey into a mysterious ancient town – in search of the identity of the second skeleton – has its share of unsettling encounters, not so much with the supernatural 'boggles' said to walk the streets as with more corporeal menace. And there is a personal significance for Gabriel in their discoveries. A particular inspiration for Robertson has been the poet Thomas Gray, who, for her, evokes the sinister beauty of the landscape in the eighteenth century – as well as virtually single-handedly creating the tourist industry; both of these notions are creatively utilised in this splendid mystery. What's more, Robertson is to be commended for not having her Lake District-travelling characters encountering William Wordsworth, wandering lonely as a cloud. The most recent novel in this sparkling series, *Theft of Life*, displays an extra depth, as Robertson tackles the subject of the slave trade and how much Georgian high society depended on its profits. Shocking but not didactic, the novel reminds us of a bleak part of our heritage while also providing two first-class and cleverly intertwined mystery plots.

Imogen Robertson may not thank me for doing so, but I think I've rumbled the secret of her success. As a writer of historical thrillers, her reputation is beginning to outpace those of most of her rivals, and *The Paris Winter* is quite as accomplished as her earlier books. But there is a canny Robertson strategy, also evident in the earlier *Anatomy of Murder*, which, despite its historical crime trappings, employed a radical shift of gears. The opening section of that book started as a rumbustious naval adventure in the tradition of such writers as Patrick O'Brian, before settling into its comfort zone of malign deeds in the malodorous streets of London. Similarly, *The Paris Winter* begins as an elegant Henry James-style novel of class and manners, with an innocent abroad finding herself up against more worldly (and corrupt) foreigners; the naïf here is an impoverished young English girl. But suddenly the narrative (with its adroit evocation of early twentieth-century Paris) has a bone-shaking twist that no one with a trace of humanity would reveal – and we move from a novel of art and character into a Stygian, edgy thriller with the reading pace moving from *andante* to *allegro*. But if this makes the novel sound broken-backed, that is certainly not the case – as in her earlier work, Robertson absolutely justifies her tactics. Maud Heighton escapes from a stifling Darlington and joins the celebrated Lafond *Academie* in Paris to join an unorthodox group of young women art students learning their craft in a cloistered, all-female environment. But while Maud finesses her artistic skills, she lives in the most desperate poverty, almost always on the point of fainting through lack of food. But then a glamorous and exotic fellow student, the wealthy Russian Tanya, opens the door for her to become the companion to Sylvie Morel. Maud begins to believe that her luck has turned. It has – but not in the way she expected. Sylvie is an opium addict, and the dark, secret world in which she moves begins to pull the luckless Maud into its embrace. And the young Englishwoman is singularly ill-equipped to deal with the dangers she encounters. Anyone familiar with Imogen Robertson's work will not be surprised to hear that the period aspects here are impeccable, with the reader transported into the exhilarating Paris of Manet and the Belle Époque. But what is perhaps more developed here is Robertson's subtle and nuanced grasp of character, notably of the vulnerable Maud (a heroine almost worthy of Thomas Hardy). It is this characterisation – as much as the labyrinthine narrative – that lifts *The Paris Winter* into a category of its own.

🎤 **Interview: Imogen Robertson**

Long before I thought of writing a novel I read *The Wickedest Age* by Alan Lloyd and was seduced by the contrasts of the eighteenth century. It became a mild obsession while I was still working in TV – a time of civility, growing artistic confidence, scientific discovery and a developing consumer culture, but it was also brutal, messy, violent and cruel. I thought it would be both accessible to a modern audience and endlessly strange. I also enjoyed how often my assumptions and preconceptions were overturned by what I read. What better place to set a murder and have amateurs investigate? I feel Westerman and Crowther give me a licence to explore the period – all of its horrors and charms. I find it impossible to choose between my books but I felt I had a very powerful story to tell in *Theft of Life*, and I'm quietly proud of how it came out. *Island of Bones* is another favourite because I love the Lake District and fell in love with the folklore of the area. Writing about the landscape was such a pleasure as well as a challenge. That book also gave me a chance to get to know Crowther better and understand something more about how he became the man he is. I think we are very lucky as readers of historical noir at the moment. I'm a great fan of Andrew Taylor, Antonia Hodgson, SJ Parris and MJ Carter in particular. There are always passages in their novels of which I am deeply jealous as a writer, but as a reader I find they just sweep me away. I like the way my contemporaries are using the genre to investigate the lives of the unrecorded, the material culture of their chosen periods and the social shifts or absolutes which throw such interesting lights on our own age.

MOLLY BROWN (Seventeenth-century England)

Molly Brown is perhaps most celebrated as a writer of science fiction and fantasy, genres in which she has won several awards, including the BSFA Award for her short story 'Bad Timing'. But among her novels, many would argue that her *chef-d'oeuvre* is the highly impressive murder mystery *Invitation to a Funeral*, with its pungently evoked period setting of Restoration London. The American-born writer, long resident in the UK, demonstrates her love and knowledge of the capital and its past, with the tongue-in-cheek attitude often present in her fantasy fiction kept firmly in check.

IAIN PEARS (Seventeenth-century England)

The literary writer Iain Pears made a considerable mark with his historical mystery *An Instance of the Fingerpost*, an epic novel set in Oxford after the end of the English Civil War and Cromwell's republic. An Oxford don dies and a woman is tried for witchcraft, while several different unreliable narrators paint a picture of a world of superstition and nascent science. The novel was rapturously received, and rightly so – less so its successor, *The Dream of Scipio*, which is an ambitious misfire. Pears' other work features art crime with art historian Jonathan Argyll.

ROBERT LEE HALL (Eighteenth-century England)

The list of unlikely figures in history who have been dragooned into service for detective work in the historical crime genre grows ever more lengthy – and in the case of Robert Lee Hall ever more outrageous. The conceit of his books featuring the American statesman and scientist Benjamin Franklin is that Hall discovered a secret compartment containing decaying manuscripts that describe crime cases solved by Franklin – much in the way that many Conan Doyle pastiches take as their starting point the finding of a lost manuscript by Dr John Watson. In the first book in the series, *Benjamin Franklin Takes the Case*, Hall has Franklin investigating a murder in the Stygian alleys of old London, with slave trafficking and prostitution stirred into the mix. Hall makes Franklin a lively sleuth.

Other key books: *Benjamin Franklin and a Case of Christmas Murder*, *Murder by the Waters*.

JANET LAURENCE (Eighteenth-century London)

Her love of fine cuisine may be discerned in her Darina Lisle sequence with their toothsome gastronomic underpinnings, but for Janet Laurence (who began her career as a cookery writer), her real *chef-d'oeuvre* as a writer consists of her highly enjoyable series of novels featuring the Venetian painter Canaletto as protagonist. The latter series began in 1997 with *Canaletto and the Case of Westminster Bridge*, in which Laurence imagines the larger-than-life figure of the artist travelling to Georgian London in an attempt to sell his paintings – but he quickly finds his life under threat. Subsequent visits imagined by Laurence have the painter encountering no less than Bonnie Prince Charlie. All of the books are characterised by both their intelligence and their utter accessibility.

Other key books: *Canaletto and the Case of the Privy Garden*, *Canaletto and the Case of Bonnie Prince Charlie*.

JAKE ARNOTT (Eighteenth-century London)

Do you feel the need to access London's hidden historic past? There's an easy way: stroll from Farringdon Road to nearby Crawford Passage, and if you kneel down by a grid in the road, you can hear the long unseen Fleet River still flowing underneath. And there's another method of time travel: pick up Jake Arnott's novel *The Fatal Tree*, through which the Fleet River runs (then still above ground). Set in the Stygian underworld of Georgian London, *The Fatal Tree* is a distinct change of pace from Arnott's visceral modern crime fiction – bawdy and as rich with authoritative images of the past as the work of such writers as Andrew Taylor. Arnott's signature novel *The Long Firm* was a complex picture of 1960s London criminality – social history with impeccable thick-ear credentials – and the surprising analyses of cultural behaviour (not least from the mouth of the brutal protagonist Harry) showed that Arnott was an ambitious writer. Here, the template is not Ronnie Kray, but the go-getting prostitute/thief created by Daniel Defoe, Moll Flanders (duly namechecked). Arnott's heroine, however, was a real-life character.

The notorious eighteenth-century robber and folk hero Jack Sheppard claims that one woman led him into crime: Elizabeth Lyons, better known as 'Edgworth Bess', who was both his lover and his associate in his lawbreaking activities. But Bess herself is having none of this, and relates her own version of the couple's colourful life from a condemned cell at Newgate. (Billy, the man setting down Bess's story – and that of the thief-taker who was her nemesis, Jonathan Wild – is himself a sexual outlaw, a gay writer.) We are told how Elizabeth was disgraced after being made love to by the son of the country house in which she lived. She flees to London, where her friendship with the prostitute Punk Alice soon has her leaving her respectable ways far behind. Bess's erotic life is notably busy, and among the many men (corrupt and otherwise) she encounters is the Machiavellian Jonathan Wild, another of the novel's real-life figures, whose power and reach extend from the corridors of the law to the city's criminal underbelly. Bess also tangles with charismatic Jack Sheppard, and after a tumultuous physical attraction leads to marriage, the couple conspire on robberies of great audacity. When he is captured, Sheppard breaks out of his cell time and again, but shades of the prison house are finally closing in on both of them, and the eponymous fatal tree – Tyburn gallows – is in view. As we are taken on a helter-skelter ride through the lowlife pubs, brothels and malodorous streets of 1720s London, Arnott allows us to realise how much this distant era has in common with our own, including a parlous economy leading to a financial crash and an ever-widening divide between the privileged few and the underclasses. All of this – notably the sexual episodes, both straight and gay – is delivered with precisely the kind of brio that we would expect from Arnott, who also successfully tackled turn-of-the-century Paris in *The Devil's Paintbrush*. A caveat, though, has to be registered: the bizarre and pungent language in which the book is delivered. The eighteenth-century slang is partially explained in a useful glossary ('Ride dragon on St George', for instance, means sexual intercourse with the woman on top), but some will find its extensive use wearying. This reservation aside, *The Fatal Tree* is Jake Arnott on beguiling form, with the libidinous Bess a wonderfully multifaceted character. Who would have thought that a cult crime writer would become the Daniel Defoe of our day?

PATRICK EASTER (Eighteenth-century London)
At a Dickensian riverside pub in Wapping, a charismatic ex-policeman gazes out at the swinging hangman's rope which is kept for the tourist trade. Patrick Easter, who spent 30 years in the Met, is intelligent and bookish, and might well have been the model for PD James' copper-cum-writer Adam Dalgliesh (but wasn't). The occasion is the launch party for his series featuring former naval officer Tom Pascoe. But while in the present Easter is looking at the misty glimmer of Canary Wharf in the distance, his hero would have seen a very different view

of the Thames. *The Watermen* is set in 1798, and it's a historical thriller brimming with atmosphere and colour – an exhilarating debut. In the Port of London in the eighteenth-century, a ruthless figure is the linchpin of many illegal activities in the bustling, dirty capital. Boylin's face is mutilated by lime and his back bears the scars from the lashes he received at a naval court martial. He is a man burning with hatred, all directed against the person he considers responsible for his blighted existence: river surveyor Tom Pascoe, who works for the newly inaugurated marine police. Pascoe has been charged with finding out the reasons for the fall in government revenue that is crippling Britain's capacity to wage war against France (as well as the country's dealings with a mutinous Ireland). It's soon apparent that Pascoe's old adversary is somehow at the heart of this problem, and the bitter antipathy between the two men spills over into a conflict that will affect the military and naval fate of a nation. Rarely has a modern novelist evoked the fascinating London of this era (with its murderous docklands, crowded river and sinister narrow streets) with such vividness as Easter does in *The Watermen*, though perhaps the nautical glossary included here won't be used by many readers. We've got a plethora of historical crime writers producing strong work at present, but what distinguishes Easter is the skill with which he delineates the clash between his two strong-willed protagonists, who fairly leap off the page – and that's not to forget the Thames itself, almost a major character in the novel. It is an attractive proposition to travel back to the eighteenth century to take another dangerous river trip in the company of Patrick Easter's doughty nautical hero.

LC TYLER (Seventeenth-century England)

LC Tyler is a former Chair of the Crime Writers' Association, a member of the prestigious Detection Club and the award-winning author of contemporary crime novels (the Herring mysteries), historical crime fiction and short stories. His accomplished historical books are set in the seventeenth century at the time of the Commonwealth and the Restoration. Tyler develops the character of main protagonist and narrator, John Grey, as the series progresses. In the first book, *A Cruel Necessity*, Grey has just graduated from Cambridge and is (as one of his enemies kindly points out) merely a lawyer with no clients. He becomes involved in espionage when, after a drunken evening, he stumbles across the body of a murdered spy and is drawn into a web of intrigue spun by Cromwell's spymaster, John Thurloe. Grey survives despite his touching naïvety and with a lot of help from his sidekick and childhood friend, Aminta Clifford. In the later books he becomes older and wiser, a sort of seventeenth-century Philip Marlowe, literally bearing the scars that he has acquired in the service of Thurloe and his Royalist successor, Lord Arlington. By the third book in the series, *The Plague Road*, Grey has a large and successful legal practice and is wealthy enough that, in the best Golden Age tradition, he can afford to carry out his detective work more or less as a hobby. Over the course of the series, Aminta becomes a talented but perpetually impoverished playwright (a brief and unfortunate marriage leaves her with a title but no money). Her contacts, both with the aristocracy and with London low-life, prove invaluable to Grey, and their professional partnership and on–off romance are recurring themes of the books. Real people featuring in the novels include a pompous and self-serving Samuel Pepys and the self-obsessed Lady Castlemaine.

Though set in the past, Tyler draws frequent parallels with contemporary society. In *The Plague Road*, the hardships suffered by those fleeing the Great Plague bear comparison to those of modern refugees. In *Fire*, the account of the incompetence of relevant authorities during the Great Fire of London and the recriminations after the event also mirror more modern disasters. This is history that has relevance today.

Tyler combines the humour that typifies his contemporary series with meticulous period accuracy. Although he spares us few of the horrors of the plague pit and the pest house, the tone is light and there are plenty of laughs to be had as the dead cart tours the streets and as London burns to the ground.

🎙 Interview: LC Tyler

When I was studying history at school, the Stuarts had seemed a bit dull. The Tudors were ruthless and erudite (Queen Elizabeth spoke ten languages, including Welsh and Cornish). The Georgians gave us the agricultural revolution and the industrial revolution and always beat the French at everything. The Stuarts were a sort of interlude in the middle – neither one thing nor the other. Only gradually did I begin to appreciate the exuberance of the late seventeenth century, its ready acceptance of licentiousness and corruption of all sorts. When I started writing historical fiction, there could have been no other era that I could have opted for. I set the first book, *A Cruel Necessity*, in 1657, on the cusp between the efficient and puritanical English Republic and the restoration of the more laid-back Charles II. I wanted to convey the tensions in society at that time – religious, political and cultural. Oliver Cromwell was alive and Parliament was firmly in control, but how long would that last? People were busy hedging their bets, ostensibly supporting the Lord Protector, while secretly corresponding with the exiled royal court in Brussels. Being an informer was a full-time job. If a dead body showed up, there'd be no shortage of reasons for a murder.

Of course, I've never restricted my reading to that period. My introduction to historical crime fiction was Ellis Peters and her twelfth-century monk. Since then I've gone backwards and forwards in time, from Ruth Downie's excellent Ruso series, set in Roman Britain, through Antonia Hodgson's bravura account of life in a Georgian debtor's prison, to Roger Morris's haunting, beautiful evocations of nineteenth-century St Petersburg.

There is no doubt that historical crime is a growth area, and we've moved away from a narrow focus on the Tudors and the Victorians. There's probably not a single year that hasn't had a fictional crime visited upon it – tricky for anyone looking for a new furrow to plough, but great for fans of the genre.

ROBIN BLAKE (Eighteenth-century Britain)

Robin Blake read English at Jesus College, Cambridge, where his director of studies was the Marxist critic Professor Raymond Williams, whose work (Blake has admitted) 'left some sort of mark on my general outlook. I was a typical long-haired leftie student at the time.' Blake's highly accomplished historical novels feature the lawyer Titus Cragg, who first appears in *A Dark Anatomy*. Apart from running his own legal practice, Cragg is coroner for Preston, with the job of holding inquests into unexpected deaths. His friend and colleague Luke Fidelis is a young doctor who acts as a kind of pathologist. As Blake admitted, 'This is long before any such medical specialism existed, yet it was a golden age of enquiry into what was then called Natural Philosophy – that is, science – so Fidelis is a less unlikely figure than he might seem. Rational, experimental and quick-witted, he is a man of the Enlightenment, and of the future – a modern who acts as a foil to the more classical temperament of Cragg.'

🎙 **Interview: Robin Blake**

My chosen historical period? All my Cragg and Fidelis books are set in Lancashire in the 1740s. It's sometimes seen as a time of war between new reason and old superstition. I prefer to think of it as an older kind of reason beginning to lose out to a newer one. Dr Fidelis is the eager representative of that new 'enlightenment' thinking. The narrator Cragg is more balanced, seeing ancient and modern ideas as equally worth attending to. Books of mine that most achieve what I'm aiming at? I think my novels are like brothers and sisters to each other. They have family traits in common, but different personal characteristics. As with my real family, I try hard not to indulge in favouritism. In fiction I read rather unsystematically except when doing historical research. The most inspiring historical novelists for me have been Robert Graves and Mary Renault, both of whom I read as a teenager. I like writing about the past because, whenever I run out of ideas, I can go back to the library, as you go to a well for water. It is refreshing. Why I write about crime and the investigation of crime in the past is more complicated. There is the fun of setting puzzles in an unfamiliar context. There is also a pleasure to be had from plotting the effects of emotions we can all recognise – passion, greed, anger, justice – in legal territory that is rather strange.

ROBERT BARNARD (Eighteenth-/Nineteenth-century London, 1930s England)

Wit and intelligence are the primary characteristics that distinguish the novels of the late Robert Barnard, who in 2003 received the CWA Cartier Diamond Dagger. The urbane writer was a great admirer of Agatha Christie and, unsurprisingly, demonstrated a preference for the English country house murder in his own work. Of his novels set in earlier periods, *Skeleton in the Grass* had at its centre a murder in the 1930s, with a resolution that finally takes place during the Blitz. Under the name Bernard Bastable, Barnard created two quirky and unusual (if slightly absurd) books with the composer Wolfgang Amadeus Mozart as the detective figure, who, despite his astonishing musical fecundity, still apparently found time (in Barnard's alternative history) to solve murder cases in *Dead, Mr Mozart* and *Too Many Notes, Mr Mozart*. Mozart also manages to live rather longer in Barnard's universe – the second book is set in 1830.

AJ MACKENZIE (Late Eighteenth-century England)

A J MacKenzie is the pseudonym of Marilyn Livingstone and Morgen Witzel, an Anglo-Canadian husband-and-wife team of writers and historians. As a medievalist, Marilyn often asks how she ended up writing novels set in the late eighteenth century. Morgen Witzel grew up in the wilds of northern British Columbia and has written or co-written 22 books as well as articles for many journals and newspapers. He began reading historical novels at a young age, and blames Sir Arthur Conan Doyle for turning him into a historical novelist. Rafael Sabatini and John Buchan were and remain strong influences. The duo's Romney Marsh books, notably *The Body on the Doorstep*, bristle with energy and imagination.

🎙 **Interview: AJ MacKenzie (Marilyn Livingstone and Morgen Witzel)**

Our chosen historical time and place is Britain at the very end of the eighteenth century, with war and the French Revolution raging across the English Channel. We set the novels in Romney Marsh, where on a clear day you can see the French coast. We wanted that sense of vulnerability and ever-present fear of invasion. Romney Marsh was also a hotbed of smuggling, and the worlds of smuggling and espionage often overlapped. Lots of things could happen there. Lots did.

The book that most achieved what we were aiming at is probably *The Body in the Ice*, the second in the Hardcastle and Chaytor series. It had to be better than the first book and not disappoint readers, and the feedback coming our way suggests we hit the target. But some of the themes, of loss and longing for what might have been, of racial prejudice and the bitterness stirred up by war, are quite powerful (again, so people tell us).

We both read quite different things, but we do come together at some points. In terms of crime fiction, Donna Leon, Andrea Camilleri, Lawrence Block and older writers such as Dorothy Sayers, Ngaio Marsh and Agatha Christie influenced both of us. For historical fiction, George MacDonald Fraser and Georgette Heyer – and you don't often see those names in the same sentence – are big influences for both of us, but the master is still the late Dorothy Dunnett.

Historical crime fiction can be absolutely fascinating, so long as it remembers that it is crime fiction. The temptation to stop and give history lessons is often very strong. It must be repelled at all costs. History is the set dressing. The story is everything.

REGINALD HILL (Seventeenth-century England, World War One)

Apart from his Dalziel and Pascoe novels, Reg Hill penned historical pieces such as *No Man's Land*, and, under the name of Charles Underhill, he wrote two exuberant books featuring Captain Fantom, an adventurer from the pages of John Aubrey's *Brief Lives*.

TV: ANNO 1790 (Rickard Petrelius et al., directors)

The Scandinavian crime invasion produced some anodyne offerings along with more quality fare, but *Anno 1790* is a persuasive example of why the genre has such staying power: this compelling drama rings several very satisfying changes on established formulae. The Swedish historical crime piece (which stars Peter Eggers, Joel Spira and Linda Zilliacus) boasts an acute sense of period. Johan has served as a doctor in the Russo-Swedish war of the eighteenth century, but is now a police inspector in Stockholm. He is a modern man of the day: he rejects religion and is inspired by the French revolution and Voltaire. An ill-advised love affair (with the wife of his commanding officer) complicates his life, as do his attempts to ensure that the revolution he desires is a bloodless one. But violent death is to remain an immovable presence in his life. The real achievement of *Anno 1790* is its canny combination of historical detail and the suggestion of a twenty-first-century consciousness in its hero. Peter Eggers is a charismatic actor who commands our attention throughout this powerful drama.

6: Victorian Britain

ANNA MAZZOLA (Nineteenth-century Britain)

Anna Mazzola's impressive first two novels (*The Unseeing* and *The Story Keeper*) are set in a strongly evoked nineteenth-century Britain. Her debut, *The Unseeing*, is based on the life of a real woman called Sarah Gale who in 1837 was convicted of aiding and abetting the murder of another woman in Camberwell, London. *The Story Keeper* is set on Skye in 1857, in the aftermath of the Highland Clearances, and follows a young woman who is tasked with collecting stories for a folklorist. She finds that young girls are going missing, supposedly taken by spirits. Mazzola's future in the genre – on the strength of these books – is assured.

> 🎤 **Interview: Anna Mazzola**
>
> My key influences are Margaret Atwood, Daphne du Maurier, Shirley Jackson and Sarah Waters, together with a few from rather further back: Charles Dickens, Edgar Allan Poe, Wilkie Collins and Emily Brontë, among others. I have something of a taste for nineteenth-century gothic. I also read a lot of historical crime and am a particular fan of the work of contemporary writers such as Robert Harris, Andrew Taylor, Antonia Hodgson, Andrew Hughes, Jane Harris, SD Sykes, Katherine Clements, Hannah Kent and Abir Mukherjee. Recent favourites include Laura Purcell's *The Silent Companions*, *Little Deaths* by Emma Flint, *His Bloody Project* by Graeme Macrae Burnet and *The Lie Tree* by Frances Hardinge. The latter, though classed as YA, deserves to be read by all ages. Historical crime opens a window onto the past: how did people in that era perceive crime and justice? What drove them to commit terrible acts? How were they investigated and punished and how were their crimes

reported? How were the victims treated? The best historical crime authors show us how the causes and impact of the crime reflect the wider world that the characters inhabit. They also give us insight into the lives of people entirely different from ourselves. We're lucky to have a wide range of gifted writers in this genre who wear their learning lightly and keep us turning the pages for the compelling plots, not even noticing how much we're learning about the past and its people. There's also fantastic range across the genre, from the medieval murders of SD Sykes' Somershill Manor mysteries to the 1950s setting of Denise Mina's brilliant *The Long Drop*, and from the historical thrillers of Robert Harris and CJ Sansom to the darker and quieter-flowing waters of writers such as Sarah Waters and Jane Harris. If the past is another country, it's certainly not one in which we'd take a nice family holiday.

KIM NEWMAN (Victorian London)

When then Culture Secretary Tessa Jowell responded to an attempt to save Arthur Conan Doyle's house Undershaw by insouciantly underplaying the importance of the novelist and his creation Sherlock Holmes to British culture, her remarks seemed particularly philistine. And wrongheaded, given that Sherlock Holmes is one of the most instantly recognisable characters in fiction (a recent worldwide poll placed him alongside Tarzan and Superman). And there is his famous nemesis, Professor James Moriarty, the ultimate criminal genius. The line of Moriarty's evil descendants stretches down to Hannibal Lecter and beyond, and just as all fictional detectives live in Holmes's shadow, so criminal masterminds are similarly judged against the yardstick of the Napoleon of Crime. What is surprising for many readers is how little time his creator spent on Moriarty, and how few appearances he makes in the Holmes canon. The reason for his imperishable reputation may be due to the number of people who have taken up the character both in films and on the printed page after the death of his creator. The novelist John Gardner wrote a series of enjoyable Moriarty pastiches, but it has taken Kim Newman to do something really audacious with the master criminal – and his conduit for a new approach is the rambunctious, sexually decadent, self-regarding journal of his lieutenant Colonel Sebastian Moran (a figure who appears even fewer times in Conan Doyle stories). The notion of reinventing Moriarty and Moran as malign doppelgängers of Holmes and Watson may have been touched upon before, but not with the firecracker exuberance that Newman brings to *Moriarty: The Hound of the D'Urbervilles*.

The masterstroke here is making the narrator a libidinous scoundrel à la George MacDonald Fraser's Flashman, and allowing us to see the bloodless, asexual Moriarty through the eyes of his boastful, utterly amoral lieutenant. Moran, who both loathes and respects his employer, sees him as a solitary masturbator, which for Moran (always on the lookout for female conquests to whom he can administer a 'Moran special') is a contemptible activity.

The other entertaining conceit Newman comes up with here is the series of spins on other writers, not just Conan Doyle but HG Wells and (notably) Thomas Hardy, whose Wessex Moran dismisses as 'one of the shit-holes of the world', where a corrupt, phoney scion of the D'Urberville family is pestered by a throat-ripping hound. And is the ghostly female figure with a neck broken by hanging the late Teresa Clare, née Tess Durbeyfield?

Moriarty: The Hound of the D'Urbervilles is essentially a collection of lively linked tales rather than an organically conceived novel, but it should be remembered that Conan Doyle did his best work in the short stories rather than the novels.

🎤 Interview: Kim Newman

Though I've written about other periods – including the 1970s – the time I tend to be drawn back to the most is the late nineteenth century, which features (in variously fantastical forms) in *Professor Moriarty: The Hound of the D'Urbervilles*, *Anno Dracula* and *Angels of Music*. The late Victorian era is interesting in terms of what was going on in politics, arts, sciences and society – but my point of entry in all these books is the popular fiction of the era. These novels are, among other things, 'answer songs' for Bram Stoker's *Dracula*, Gaston Leroux's *The Phantom of the Opera* and Arthur Conan Doyle's Sherlock Holmes stories. The quarter-century or so leading up to World War One produced an extraordinary number of lasting pop culture literary figures – most of which I've repurposed in my books – and arguably the foundation of whole genres of fiction like crime, detective, horror, science fiction, fantasy and mystery. I've always thought of the 1890s as the beginning of the modern age rather than a remote, sealed-off era – so many things that we now cope with (celebrity culture, sensationalist press, fad diets and medicines, serial murder, mass media) began with the late Victorians. I tend to look back at that time to find resonant parallels with the present – though I have also occasionally dealt with specific historical events (the climax of *Angels of Music* is set during the Paris flood of 1910). I grew up reading Doyle, Wells, MR James, Stevenson and the like – and was led by Hugh Greene's *Rivals of Sherlock Holmes* anthologies (and the cool ITV series adaptation) to look at Arthur Morrison, Grant Allen, Guy Boothby, Fergus Hume, Richard Marsh, etc. A feature of crime fiction in general that's especially apt for historical crime is that a criminal investigation allows for a tour of a whole society, from palaces to gutters – I certainly built *Anno Dracula* around the Jack the Ripper murders because it let me do that.

CHARLES PALLISER (Victorian Britain)

The very British Charles Palliser was born in New England and is an American citizen, but he has lived in the United Kingdom since the age of ten. He has published five novels, which have been translated into a dozen languages, and has also written for the theatre, radio and television. However, it has to be admitted that if one talks of Palliser, one book looms above all others. As a very clever synthesis of Dickens and Wilkie Collins, Charles Palliser's labyrinthine magnum opus *The Quincunx* is carried off with supreme élan. But although all the tropes of historical mystery developed by the masters of an earlier century are reactivated with great skill, it's the infusion of a modern sensibility into these dark deeds of the past that makes this arm-straining volume so distinctive. John Huffam and his mother have been leading clandestine lives for as long as he can remember. John's potential inheritance is formidable, but there are many people laying claim to this wealth. The proof of John's right to his estate lies in a missing will – and the search for this proof in the dark corners of a cathedral town is the engine for the vast, baffling narrative that is often as redolent of Mervyn Peake as it is of Dickens (though neither author created so many carefully orchestrated suspense sequences – John Huffam's life is often under serious threat here). While characterisation is writ large, the naïve hero is particularly well-honed – though it's the fustian period atmosphere that claims the attention. In 1991 *The Quincunx* was awarded the Sue Kaufman Prize for First Fiction by the American Academy of Arts and Letters. Subsequent novels have been less ambitious in scope, but have gleaned a host of new admirers, notably the disturbing *The Unburied* in 1999. Aficionados of *The Quincunx*, however, live in hope that Palliser will again tackle something on the same massive scale as his breakthrough novel.

🎙 Interview: Charles Palliser

I've set three of my five novels in the period 1820 to 1890 for several reasons. One is that I am completely smitten by novelists of that era (especially Austen, Dickens, Wilkie Collins, Eliot, the Brontës, James and Hardy, as well, of course, as the French and the Russians) and my own books are in part a blend of homage and critique of their work. Secondly, those 70 years arguably saw the most dramatic changes of any comparable span. So in *The Quincunx* I can play with elements in 1820 that are almost medieval: the legal system, the treatment of the poor and the insane, the oppression of women and children, and the class system. But all of those were being challenged by technological innovation and economic turmoil so that by 1890 we virtually had the modern world. We're now going through another period of rapid change and I believe that what happened in the Victorian age offers insights into our current situation.

I read a wide variety of novels. In my teens I devoured Waugh and Greene and then Murdoch, Golding, Spark, Fowles and the Americans: Bellow, Updike, Roth and Malamud. When I started to write I was fascinated by the technical innovations of Conrad, Joyce, Woolf, Kafka and Faulkner. Among the novelists I most admire who are writing now are Franzen, Smiley, Morrison, Ishiguro and Joyce Carol Oates. In the crime genre – if that's the right term – I'm a fan of Patricia Highsmith above all others because of her unnerving entry into the mind of a sociopath but also of Raymond Chandler for his stunning prose and dialogue. More recent writers I admire include Rendell/Vine, James Ellroy, Michael Connelly and Scott Turow. I write fiction with an unsolved crime at the centre because a mystery opens up a space that the reader's imagination is invited to fill. A mystery requires a revelation and that should always come as a surprise. I find all of that a fascinating challenge. Wilkie Collins invented that structure and I'm not sure anyone has done it better.

MJ CARTER (Victorian Britain and India)

MJ (Miranda) Carter's writing career has taken off on surprising tangents: biography (a book on the duplicitous Anthony Blunt), history (*The Three Emperors*), then a header into ripping yarn territory with the deliriously enjoyable *The Strangler Vine*, which fused Wilkie Collins with Sax Rohmer via Conan Doyle. That book introduced her ill-matched sleuths Jeremiah Blake and William Avery in a colourful Victorian India. *The Printer's Coffin*, the second outing for the duo, is even more fun, with the same audacious blend of derring-do and elegant writing (the latter not necessarily a sine qua non of this genre). Back from India, Blake and Avery find Britain in 1841 a changed place and struggle to readjust, not least to the English cold. But a series of brutal killings in the world of London's yellow press re-energises their faltering association as they track down a killer enjoying the protection of people in high places. Delicious stuff, to be consumed at just a few sittings.

🎤 Interview: MJ Carter

My thrillers are set in the 1840s, the first decade of Queen Victoria's reign. It's a fantastic but little-known period of tumultuous transition and conflict: the decade of railways and telegraph, Dickens and the Brontës, and terrible hunger. London became the biggest, richest, most thrilling city the world had ever seen, but inequality between rich and poor had never been more gaping and the urban poor lived and worked in conditions as bad as anything ever. There were the first race riots, foreign émigrés preaching revolution, bank crashes, failed harvests. Sounds familiar? I love the constant surprising parallels with now that keep emerging.

I'm still learning with each book so it's hard to choose one that succeeds best. I find plot the hardest. It's like a puzzle you have to solve anew each time. It's what keeps me awake at night. I felt with *The Strangler Vine* I made lots of mistakes with pacing, but I was proud of the world and the setup – I spent years thinking about it. With *The Printer's Coffin*, I'd learned a lot and I thought I'd written a better book, but not everyone agreed. I like the claustrophobia of *The Devil's Feast*, the character of Alexis Soyer, the sense of the comfort and danger of food, but I still worry about the all-important balance between background and plot...

Favourite writers in the genre? Wilkie Collins – *The Moonstone* particularly. It was reading CJ Sansom's Shardlake books that made me feel I might be able to do this too. The historical novel/thriller I love and press on everyone is Iain Pears' 1997 *An Instance of the Fingerpost*: a clever, moving, multifaceted, enormously satisfying book. Antonia Hodgson's Thomas Hawkins is a great, vivid creation, and I like Imogen Robertson's Crowther and Westerman books, and Ray Celestin's *The Axeman's Jazz* – wonderfully put together, jazz and violence rippling through its pages.

KATE GRIFFIN (Victorian London)

Boasting one of the most unusual detectives ever to appear in historical fiction – a plucky 17-year-old trapeze artist – Kate Griffin's exuberant debut novel, *Kitty Peck and the Music Hall Murders,* is a glorious romp through the seedy yet irresistible world of the East End music halls of 1880s London. Griffin has got Kitty's voice spot on, the period is pungently evoked and the eventful plot doesn't let up for a moment. Griffin is a former journalist who works part-time for Britain's oldest heritage charity, the Society for the Protection of Ancient Buildings, a job that aligns with her own personal interests. At the time of writing, she has written three historical crime novels, maintaining the promise of that impressive first book: the follow-up is *Kitty Peck and the Child of Ill Fortune*, with the third book being *Kitty Peck and the Daughter of Sorrow.* Griffin's future in the genre is assured.

🎙 Interview: Kate Griffin

I am almost ashamed to admit this, but I suspect the main reason I was drawn to the 1880s as the setting for my books was based largely on the childhood hours I devoted to watching TV in the 1970s when Victoriana was having a moment. (Think Biba, Liberty prints, and all that mauve!) It's a period with a strong and exciting visual identity. In my imagination (and probably everyone else's), the Victorian era is characterised by swirling fogs, steam trains, galloping hackney carriages, cane-twirling toffs, veiled mediums and cloaked villains. Yes, all the tropes! It is cosily familiar, but actually it is utterly alien too. Beneath that completely artificial surface lurks an age of extreme warring contrasts – old and new, tradition and discovery, truth and hypocrisy, wealth and poverty. This is a world of ripe opportunity for a crime writer. You only have to read Dickens and Mayhew to understand how the majority really lived and the heavy price paid for progress and Empire. The Victorian era is beautiful and beguiling, but also deeply troubling. And that makes it a fascinating and richly rewarding setting.

In the Kitty Peck books I'm consciously throwing all the tropes of Victorian melodrama and the penny dreadful together and turning them on their heads. It's knowing and playful, but that doesn't mean I shy away from darkness. It's hard to single out the book where I feel I've most achieved what I was aiming at – does a writer ever pull this off? But I think the juxtaposition of shade and light is especially successful in book three, *Kitty Peck and the Daughter of Sorrow*, where Kitty's bold, cockney narration belies real tragedy. I am a voracious reader of historical fiction with or without a crime element.

I am in awe of CJ Sansom's Shardlake series in which the dangerous world of Henry VIII's schismatic England is as much a character as the hunchbacked lawyer/detective. I greatly admire MJ Carter's ingenious Blake and Avery series, a riff on the partnership of Holmes and Watson. And I always recommend Phil Rickman's Merrily Watkins series set on the borders between England and Wales – a perfectly realised landscape where the darkness of the distant past continually shadows the future. Christopher Fowler does something similar in his deceptively entertaining Bryant and May series. It's perhaps stating the bleedin' obvious, as Kitty would say, but everyone who writes about the past is influenced by their present. If a dozen crime writers were asked to describe a Georgian street, I suspect that the differences in the scenes would be more notable than the similarities. Writing about the past is an act of imagination. It doesn't matter how many hours of research we put in, it will never be real because we simply weren't there. We all

> bring our own interests, influences, prejudices and beliefs into play when we write – it's unavoidable and part of the fun. The one thing that will always be 'real' is our delight in human foibles – and they never change.

JOHN HARWOOD (Victorian England)

'I am Miss Georgina Ferrars of Gresham's Yard, London. I am. I swear that I am. And I shall prove it.' With John Harwood's beguiling pastiche *The Asylum*, we're once again in a contemporary version of the Victorian gothic mystery, with a lineage that stretches back to Wilkie Collins' *The Woman in White* and beyond. And although it's not a comfortable place for the beleaguered heroine, readers are guaranteed a thoroughly diverting time in Harwood's not-to-be-trusted hands. A young woman wakes up to find herself in an unfamiliar bed with coarse sheets, in a room with sickly green walls and with light feebly filtering through a metal grille. A middle-aged man with an air of authority appears and announces himself as Dr Maynard Straker, saying, 'Have no fear, Miss Ashton, I am entirely at your service.' But despite the young woman's distress and confusion, she is sure of two things: Ashton is not her name, and she does not belong in the asylum in which she has awoken. But when she asks the doctor to send a telegram to her uncle in London, to verify her identity as Georgina Ferrars, the reply that comes back is devastating – the real Georgina Ferrars is safe at home, and so the woman claiming to be her must be an impostor. What follows is a richly textured, sometimes overcooked, but always masterfully constructed narrative in which the reader is placed at the heart of Georgina Ferrars' nightmare, with her own memory being the clue to unravelling a skein of deceit and venality. As in John Harwood's earlier *The Seance*, the creaking apparatus of the Victorian novel of suspense (with all its fog-shrouded obfuscation) is given an energetic shaking up here, demonstrating that there is plenty of life in the old genre yet, provided a contemporary author is in charge who can utilise all the requisite elements (such as the convoluted mystification provided by the ruthless villains) without self-consciously guying such things (always the kiss of death in this kind of enterprise).

In fact, though, the modern dabbler in the waters of the Victorian mystery has a problem to overcome that was less onerous for the likes of Wilkie Collins and co. The latter's readers would have been quickly onto the fact that Count Fosco with his unpleasant pet mice was up to no good, although the basic deceptions would have been airtight. But the modern reader will have mental feelers extended for such things from the first line – we are perhaps not quite as ready to be led up the garden path as the Victorians. But the fact that John Harwood trots us up and down that path in a dizzying dance – and that we love every minute of it – is proof of his casual command of this shamelessly enjoyable idiom.

LM JACKSON (Victorian London)

There are readers who buy their crime fiction on the strength of a reliable author's name, banking on a known commodity. And there are those who pick up novels after encountering pieces such as the one you're reading now. But writers really value the third method by which their work slowly and surely achieves popularity: good old word of mouth. Let's face it, we're all persuaded by the enthusiasm of a trusted friend – and LM (Lee) Jackson must have relished the fact that many of us responded to the vox pop buzz about his Victorian-set mysteries. Not enough, mind you, to propel him into the upper echelons – but quite enough, thank you, to build up a real head of steam after only a slim body of work. His first novel, *London Dust* – with his heroine Natalie Meadows tracking down the killer of her best friend and musical star Nelly Warwick – signalled that we had another writer who could evoke the colour and danger of Victorian London with a master's touch – there were those who even breathed the sacred name of Conan Doyle in comparison. In the following three books, featuring the unorthodox Inspector Decimus Webb, the reader is taken into such unfamiliar areas as the recently built underground (in *A Metropolitan Murder*), Victorian pleasure gardens (*The Last Pleasure Garden*) and even department stores (*The Welfare of the Dead*).

Moving with Jackson's mystified characters through the swirling fogs of a pre-electric capital city is an exhilarating experience – and it's a trick he also brings off in *A Most Dangerous Woman*, this time with total assurance (some of the earlier books gave the sense that the Dickensian atmosphere was laid over the narrative rather than growing organically out of it). Leather Lane is the location of Sarah Tanner's Dining and Coffee Rooms – and her clients and fellow traders are intrigued by this enigmatic woman who clearly harbours some secrets in her past. Those who have read Jackson before will know that security for his protagonists is an illusion – like William Faulkner, Jackson believes that the past is not only still with us, the past is not even the past. A friend of Sarah's is savagely killed, and she is the only one to witness the murder, but she cannot inform the police. She enlists a motley group to aid her in cracking a sinister mystery – all the time stalked by a master criminal with a finger in many pies. If this brilliant miscreant owes a little to Holmes's nemesis Moriarty, who cares? Jackson is very much his own man in this phantasmagoric tour through the squalor and splendour of the greatest city in the Empire – and the resourceful Sarah is a wonderfully multifaceted heroine, risking all in a highly dangerous gamble.

JANE JAKEMAN (Victorian London)

It's a real pleasure to come across something as inventive as Jane Jakeman's *In the Kingdom of Mists*; not only is this a carefully detailed piece of work, there is no sense of reaching for novelty – Jakeman's narrative strategies are not unfamiliar, but they remain fresh. *In the Kingdom of Mists* is set in London in 1900, and the painter Monet is central to the macabre mysteries here. As the great Impressionist paints his celebrated visions of the Thames, that same river is a repository for hideously mutilated bodies. There are fears of a return of Jack the Ripper. Tyro diplomat Oliver Craston just happens to be present when the bodies are pulled from the Thames, and finds himself drawn into the investigation against his better judgement and his wishes. The Foreign Office has jitters over French sympathies with the Boers, and Craston is instructed to follow the doings of the Monet family, who are staying at the Savoy Hotel. But there is a terrifying secret in the rooms above their suite, and grim events in the slums of Lambeth across the river draw Craston into a nightmare from which he will be lucky to emerge alive. *In the Kingdom of Mists* functions as a compelling thriller with the requisite set pieces, and even as an intelligent discourse on art itself. Readers should try to seek out the edition with a dozen colour Monet reproductions, which add an extra dimension.

ALIS HAWKINS (Nineteenth-century Wales)

Alis Hawkins was born in the Forest of Dean and grew up on a dairy farm in Cardiganshire. Her first novel, *Testament*, is set in both the Middle Ages and the modern era. For her more recent historical crime series, Hawkins has moved 500 years forward from the medieval era and 300 miles west to Cardiganshire's Teifi Valley in the 1850s. The series features blind ex-barrister Harry Probert-Lloyd and his assistant, solicitor's clerk John Davies. Critic Mike Ripley compared the first in the series to Graeme Macrae Burnet's Booker-shortlisted *His Bloody Project*, while Phil Rickman, on BBC Radio Wales's 'Phil the Shelf', described it as 'the most interesting historical crime creation of the year'.

In 2016, Hawkins founded Crime Cymru, a collective of Welsh crime writers whose aim is to promote and support the reading, writing and publication of crime fiction in Wales. With pleasing circularity, she now lives once more in the Forest of Dean and nips over the border to Monmouthshire for the day job, where she has occasional opportunities to speak Welsh.

Interview: Alis Hawkins

Having done huge amounts of research for *Testament* (and a subsequent novel) I assumed that I would quite happily become a medieval mystery-cum-crime writer. But, to follow a compelling storyline, I leaped forwards and sideways into nineteenth-century West Wales. And there, for the moment, I shall stay. I've always been fascinated by the present's relationship with history. I wanted to use *Testament*'s dual narrative to highlight the fact that, however much we think we've understood the past, we've only ever seen a partial and fragmentary slice of it. *None So Blind* was written for a similar reason: I wanted to know why nobody in contemporary West Wales talks about the Rebecca Riots; why the whole area isn't lit up with stories of Victorian farmers going out at night, disguised as women, faces blacked, to destroy tollgates and bloody the noses of the moneyed class. And, by living through the aftermath of the central murder with my characters, I answered my own question: fear.

In terms of influences, the Teifi Valley Coroner series is influenced less by individual writers and more by a genre: Nordic noir. According to Paul Hirons, there are two fundamental elements that characterise that sub-genre: a clear sense that place is fundamental to the action, and what Hirons calls the 'second story' – a social issue that underlies the crime narrative. Of course, there are authorly influences too. Joanna Trollope's use of telling details and dialogue. Geraldine Brooks' masterclass in writing historical novels as if they were contemporary fiction. JK Rowling's brilliant exemplification of the importance of throughline in a series. Contemporary crime writers are also important but as inspiration rather than direct influence. The two giants, for me, are Phil Rickman and Harry Bingham. Is it a surprise that most of my influences write contemporary fiction? Good. I want my nineteenth century to feel contemporary. Unlike my own work, much current, Victorian-era crime fiction is set in a recognisably Holmesian environment and, like Conan Doyle's stories, tends to the gothic. It is also largely dominated by women writers. Understandably, therefore, the issue of gender is a major one with gender-bending a staple and characters expressing proto-feminist views. Of course, to give these fictions historical credibility, those protagonists have to exist on the very margins of society, different in some fundamental way from the conservative majority or, at the very least, prepared to be at the sharp and sometimes personally cutting end of social change.

ANDREW PEPPER (Nineteenth-century London)

Andrew Pepper is adroit at conjuring up a rich period atmosphere in *The Last Days of Newgate*, his first mystery featuring sometime Bow Street Runner Pyke. The reader is taken from the squalor of Seven Dials (Pepper reminds us that this now chic district of London was not ever thus) to the sectarian tensions of Belfast – here Pepper points out the still existing parallels with neighbours who find it difficult to live together. People have been savagely killed, amidst religious and political turmoil. When the resourceful Pyke, who also has criminality in his past, becomes involved, he treads on the toes of several powerful individuals, and ends up being unjustly accused of murder.

GYLES BRANDRETH (Victorian London)

So many real-life figures have been dragooned as detective heroes that readers are likely to be blasé unless a writer can come up with something special. And that's what Gyles Brandreth did in his highly unlikely utilisation of writer/raconteur Oscar Wilde as sleuth in such diverting mysteries as *Oscar Wilde and the Candlelight Murders*. It's a brave man who attempts to match Wilde in wit, but Brandreth's skills in this area are well known. The playwright discovers the naked body of youthful Billy Wood in an attic room, and enlisting fellow writer Sir Arthur Conan Doyle (no less), he searches through every stratum of Victorian society to track down a brutal murderer.

PETER LOVESEY (Victorian England)

Peter Lovesey's much-admired series of novels began after he won a publisher's contest in 1970 that bagged him a prize of £1,000 and the guaranteed publication of his first book. That novel, *Wobble to Death*, introduced his Victorian copper Sergeant Cribb; the setting is Islington's Agricultural Hall, and it features a Victorian version of an endurance contest rather like that in Horace McCoy's *They Shoot Horses, Don't They?* The other Cribb novels touch upon a variety of aspects of Victorian society, from bare-knuckle boxing in *The Detective Wore Silk Drawers* to the spiritualist movement, which takes centre stage in *A Case of Spirits*, and several were filmed by Granada TV (see box). Lovesey's subsequent historical crime moved to other time periods: an Atlantic liner in the 1920s is the setting for *The False Inspector Dew*, a book that bagged Lovesey the CWA Gold Dagger, while *Keystone* has an early film industry milieu. Next for the writer was a series of novels and stories with Bertie, the Prince of Wales (destined to become Edward VII) as an unlikely crime solver. Real-life figures of the day have walk-on parts, including Sarah Bernhardt and Toulouse-Lautrec. But the protean Lovesey has several other series and eras under his belt, all delivered with his customary expertise.

🎙 Interview: Peter Lovesey

Mystery readers watch out. Your favourite bookshops are under siege by Ancient Egyptians, conquering Romans, medieval monks, cloaked Elizabethans and crinolined Victorians. The rise and rise of the historical mystery has been the dominant trend of the last 30 years. Authors such as Ellis Peters, Anne Perry and Lindsey Davis have achieved bestselling status. Other high-profile writers better known for their modern settings – I'm thinking of Ed McBain, Michael Crichton, John Gardner, Colin Dexter and Ken Follett – could not ignore the trend and produced their own history mysteries. In the days when there were fewer of them, I wrote eight Victorian mysteries between 1970 and 1978 and I am often asked what inspired them. The answer is simple: the lure of money. In 1969 I saw an advert for a crime novel competition with a first prize of £1,000, which was about as much as I was earning as a teacher. The script had to be delivered in a little over four months. Not much time for research and plotting. I'd already published a non-fiction book on the history of athletics, so it seemed sensible to write about something I'd already mugged up – a long-distance running race in 1878. Tossing in a couple of murders, some steamy sex and Scotland Yard's finest, I concocted a whodunit that was different, if nothing else. The title, *Wobble to Death*, was catchy, and it won the prize. In the next seven years I wrote a series using Victorian enthusiasms as backgrounds: prize-fighting, the music hall, the seaside, inventions, spiritualism, boating and the waxworks. They were dramatised for the TV series *Cribb* in 1980 and, together with my wife Jax, I wrote six additional TV scripts using the same characters, Sergeant Cribb and Constable Thackeray. I was in serious danger of being pigeon-holed as a history mystery man and nothing else. I started plotting my escape, writing books set rather later in the twentieth century. I suppose they qualified as period pieces, if not what most of us think of as history. One called *On the Edge* was set in 1946, well within my memory. It took me 21 years to break out completely and write my first contemporary crime novel, *The Last Detective* (1991).

So what is the appeal of the historical mystery? I doubt if I'm qualified to judge. I enjoy writing them, but I don't read many. I've heard it suggested that readers like to escape into the past when so much about the present is depressing. That may be so, but it isn't obvious to me when I write them. I find I'm more intrigued by things that haven't changed. It's amusing to discover that human nature hasn't altered in thousands of years. The little vanities and the bigger enmities are much the same whether the characters are living in caves or travelling through space. Take many of today's hot political topics and you find that people in the past were having to deal with similar problems in their own way. As I write this, the headlines are dominated by drug use in sport. In *Wobble to Death*, the athletes were taking drugs to improve their performance. The motives were the same, even if the chemistry was different. They pepped up their performance with strychnine; the modern athlete takes something called THG. The wider use of drugs in society is not a modern phenomenon. Victorians had their opium dens, which were thought iniquitous by respectable people – who took chloral and laudanum as sedatives. Queen Victoria herself was said to have been a cocaine freak, addicted to Marioli's Cocoa Wine, in which pure coca was the main ingredient. What else are our newspapers preoccupied with? Terrorism? The Fenian campaign of the 1880s (the basis of *Invitation to a Dynamite Party*) was quite as serious and scary as the IRA attacks more than a century later. The Fenians succeeded in bombing Scotland Yard, the House of Commons, the Tower of London, Westminster Hall, the Admiralty and Victoria Station.

One of the delights of weaving history into the mystery is that trivia found in memoirs and biographies can be used to bring colour to the characters and their motives. I like the story of Bertie's brother, Prince Leopold, having such a crush on Lillie Langtry – the Jerry Hall of her day – that he bought a portrait of her by Frank Miles and hung it over his bed. Queen Victoria spied the drawing and was so scandalised that she climbed on a chair and removed it. I read somewhere else that Victoria in old age achieved the perfect symmetry of 58 inches both in height and waistline. Climbing that chair couldn't have been easy.

TV: CRIBB (various directors)

Set in an economically realised (but persuasive) Victorian era, the TV cases for Peter Lovesey's Detective Sergeant Cribb of Scotland Yard's newly formed Criminal Investigation Department were professionally dispatched with the actors Alan Dobie, William Simons and David Waller acquitting themselves well. In one of the

> best episodes, *Wobble to Death*, the pedestrian Championship of the World is taking place in London's Agricultural Hall, an indoor marathon lasting six days with the winner being the individual who can be proved to have walked the greatest distance. But murder – rather than what first appears to be cramp – brings about the involvement of Cribb, very ably played by Dobie.

GRAEME MACRAE BURNET (Nineteenth-century Scotland)

There is always a level of excitement around the announcement of the Man Booker Prize shortlist – but in 2016, there was an added layer. The buzz was not over 'readable versus inaccessible' books, but over the fact that the shortlist included a crime novel. However, in *His Bloody Project*, Burnet proves that the undeniable pleasures of the crime novel need not represent a sloughing off of literary value. The book appears to channel a bookish version of the currently fashionable 'found footage' film genre, in which verisimilitude is granted by randomly cobbled together material that forms a fragmentary narrative. This includes witness statements, post-mortem documents on murder victims, a documentary account of a trial and the lengthy memoir of an incarcerated man accused of triple murder. The subtitle reads 'Documents relating to the case of Roderick Macrae', and these ersatz papers build a picture of an insular crofting community in the nineteenth century while also presenting a fascinating picture of attitudes to criminology at the time. The premise, wholly fictitious, is that the author, Burnet himself, while looking into his own Scottish roots, discovered a fragment of a memoir that apparently had set Edinburgh society alight. A young crofter, Roderick Macrae, has written up the catastrophes of his life while sitting in a cell in Inverness in 1869, accused of three savage killings. Macrae appears to have entered – with the intention of murder – the house of his deeply unpleasant neighbour Lachlan Mackenzie, a local constable. But the truth of the events that led to these three deaths is pieced together through contemporary statements and reports, from witnesses, experts, dodgy phrenologists and journalists. The most telling evidence is provided by the prison doctor, James Bruce Thomson, who holds ironclad views on the behaviour of the criminal class. Roderick, surely, is guilty, not least because of his open admission that he had no love for the dead man, who both ruled the community and made Macrae's life a particular hell. His soul-baring at the trial brings forth condemnation from the pulpit as well as from the new discipline of psychological observation, which analyses character in more scientific – but no more helpful – terms. What, Burnet teasingly asks us, is truth? Ironically, although Burnet would appear to see himself as part of a Scottish literary tradition, there are other Celtic influences at work: Joyce's fragmentary assembly of narrative and that blackly comic strain that is characteristic of so many Irish writers. And don't for a second imagine that this is just a tricksy literary experiment (although, admittedly, it is that) – Burnet is a writer of great skill and authority, and the central notion is sure-fire in dramatic terms: a thuggish bully (who had even impregnated Macrae's sister and dispossessed his father) receiving some bloody justice. And it is all freighted with acute historical detail: the poor crofting community, the dead hand of the Scottish church crushing free spirits. What's more, the hapless Roderick Macrae, writing from his jail cell, begins to grow in authority as a human being, realising that an accusation of murder is the existential fact that has made him a person of note – even if he may have to die for it. But – finally – is *His Bloody Project* a crime novel? The author has said that it might better be described as 'a novel about a crime', but readers won't care about the definitions. Whatever the genre, Burnet's book is energetically written – and the provocative absence of a linear narrative is actually a sleight of hand: few readers will be able to put down the novel as it speeds towards a surprising (and ultimately puzzling) conclusion.

This is the second of Burnet's books to be published by the small Scottish publisher Saraband/Contraband – his first, *The Disappearance of Adèle Bedeau*, was a low-key, French-set detective story, rather in the manner of Simenon, which enjoyed respectable reviews but no conspicuous success, although a second book in the series, *The Accident on the A35*, appeared in 2017.

SARAH PINBOROUGH (Victorian London)

The writer Sarah Pinborough has long been interested in testing the parameters of fiction, a concern that she attacks with relish in such books as *Mayhem*. Is it a piece of historical crime fiction? Or is it located within the supernatural genre that the author has also profitably explored? Whatever the answer to this question, the result in *Mayhem* is spellbinding and original – and, what's more, it is a book that manages to find something new in the well-trodden Jack the Ripper territory, although the book is not about Saucy Jack, but another murderous figure. A decomposing torso is found within the vaults of New Scotland Yard, and police surgeon Dr Thomas Bond becomes aware that there is another killer plying his bloody trade in London apart from the Ripper. Bond, unhappy in his own skin, becomes dangerously involved when, escaping from his problems in an opium den, he sees another figure who doesn't belong there – a man in a black coat. Who is this sinister figure? This is deliciously inventive stuff, delivered with the narrative nous and sense of atmosphere that lifts *Mayhem* above the raft of many similar novels.

RICHARD MARGGRAF TURLEY (Nineteenth-century London)

The lists of historical crime fiction grow ever longer, and something special is required to raise a book above the throng. *The Cunning House*, by academic and poet Richard Marggraf Turley, is precisely that kind of novel; it is both a mesmeric thriller and a fascinating insight into a clandestine world that few of us know about. In London in 1810, male brothels offer for their clientele rent boys known as 'Mollies', but the city has a visceral hatred of these young men, allied to a suspicion about their political sympathies, and there is a raid on one of the houses in Vere Street. At St James's Palace, the Duke of Cumberland's valet is killed, and Turley's protagonist, the canny and unconventional lawyer Wyre, finds a link between these two events and the war against France. This is a dark side of London that Charles Dickens could never have dared show us, evoked here with tremendous panache.

🎙 **Interview: Richard Marggraf Turley**
By setting *The Cunning House* in 1810, I was able to murder two birds with one stone. With my professorial cap on, I teach Romantic poetry and culture at Aberystwyth University, so any archival

excavation I did for the novel was pressed into double service. For instance, the book's protagonist, homophobic lawyer Christopher Wyre, gets around Regency London's mean streets on a velocipede, a pedal-less precursor to the bicycle. My interest in these quirky contraptions quickly became serious, and led to an academic article on the poet John Keats' own adventures on two wheels. *The Cunning House* delves into a real-life scandal: murder at St James's Palace, and a royal conspiracy centred on the city's most notorious gay brothel, the White Swan. Over 20 men sporting monikers such as Blackeyed Leonora and Miss Sweet Lips were arrested in July 1810 for sodomy and attempted sodomy, and two – who weren't actually present in the pub on the night of the raid – were publicly hanged. Insofar as I was able to throw a spotlight on the brutality of attitudes towards homosexuality in the supposedly polite age of Jane Austen, while taking a pop at entrenched power, I felt *The Cunning House* had achieved its goal. I'm a fan of Christie, Rankin and Chandler, and I greatly admire David Mitchell's *The Thousand Autumns of Jacob de Zoet* and Michel Faber's *The Book of Strange New Things*, both of which I read, and reread, while writing *The Cunning House*. I think that novel is a strange mash-up of all the above. If science fiction offers cautionary futures, historical crime fiction allows us to explore the twisting, torturous, labyrinthine ways that brought us to the all-too-often violent present.

ANTHONY HOROWITZ (Victorian London, Twentieth-century Britain)

Anthony Horowitz's career includes TV scriptwriting for the BAFTA-winning *Foyle's War* and bestselling young adult novels, but a new level of fame and achievement arrived with his move into Conan Doyle territory. When it was announced (with much fanfare) that Horowitz would be dusting off a hansom cab for Conan Doyle's Great Detective, few were surprised that the facsimile of Conan Doyle's style in *The House of Silk* was unerring. Next up in terms of reinvention of an existing character was Ian Fleming's durable 007, and it was quickly apparent that the writer was doing something both clever and risky, playing several games with readers – not least with his mischievous attitude to political correctness in his Bond book *Trigger Mortis*, set in the same period as Fleming's originals. Having these successful tilts at Ian Fleming and Conan Doyle pastiches under his belt, with *Magpie Murders* he attempted something different: a take on a typical Christie-style whodunit.

ALANNA KNIGHT (Victorian Scotland)

Alanna Knight is one of the most popular authors in UK libraries. Named as one of *The Times'* '100 Masters of Crime', she is a leading crime writer with three historical crime series, featuring the Victorian detective Inspector Jeremy Faro, lady investigator Rose McQuinn, and time-traveller Tam Eildor. Her more than 60 published works include romance, thrillers, historical novels and non-fiction. She is an authority on Robert Louis Stevenson and has written true crime, 'how to write' guides and biographies.

Key book: *The Inspector's Daughter.*

🎙 Interview: Alanna Knight

Writing Victorian crime with both Inspector Faro and his daughter, Rose McQuinn, evolved quite naturally in Edinburgh where I had walked the streets and touched the stones for 15 years writing about Robert Louis Stevenson. Research at the National Library while living in Aberdeen before the computer age resulted in an invitation to a friend's Georgian house. One afternoon, a man in a deerstalker hat and Inverness cape walked by. My immediate thought: Sherlock Holmes! He could be a Victorian detective. I never saw him again but Inspector Jeremy Faro was born that day, and having just completed a trilogy of historicals for Macmillan, I had a new series to offer. Living in the heart of Edinburgh is a gift to writing historical crime, with no lack of plots or inspiration from the windows of my home on the slopes of Arthur's Seat, within crow-flying distance of Holyroodhouse and Craigmillar Castle, and citywards close to the dark shades of Burke and Hare, Flodden Wall, our tragic Mary Queen of Scots, and the Scotland that never was, with Prince Charles Edward Stuart. The past is everywhere. I want readers to share its atmosphere through my two series and hope I have achieved this from the first Faro, *Enter Second Murderer*, and the first Rose, *The Inspector's Daughter.* I have enjoyed moving them around Scotland and to my second best love, Orkney. My life of literary crime developed seamlessly from historicals (with their share of murders and mayhem), and from an addiction to crosswords, jigsaws, sudoku – in fact, any kind of puzzle or brainteaser. Long before I became a published novelist in 1968, I had read every Agatha Christie, Sherlock Holmes and most of the Golden Age classics. With one book a year, my leisure reading tends to useful non-fiction such as historical biography rather than contemporary crime, apart from a select few authors such as PD James, who became a personal and much-missed friend.

LINDA STRATMANN (Nineteenth-century London)

A characteristic entry in Linda Stratmann's impressive series of London-set mysteries is *A True and Faithful Brother*. The year is 1882, and a wealthy philanthropist disappears from a locked and guarded room. Stratmann's protagonist Frances Doughty is reluctantly drawn into a case that tears the veil of mystery from her own past. The author's skill in crime fiction narratives and in writing about Victorian England is based on solid research undertaken before the launch of her Frances Doughty series, which is set in Bayswater in the 1880s. She has also written true crime and historical biography.

Interview: Linda Stratmann

I love the carefully crafted old-fashioned 'locked-room' mysteries, and for book seven in the Frances Doughty mysteries, I set myself the challenge of writing one – but with a difference. Instead of finding the body of a murder victim in a room locked from the inside, I wanted to make a man disappear. A wealthy philanthropist is last seen in a locked and guarded room together with a number of his friends. The lights go out, and when they are relit, he has vanished. The guards have seen no one leave and the doors remain securely locked, the only keys undisturbed. How and why did the man leave? Was it voluntary or was he abducted? And where is he now? I decided to avoid the tricks used by many of the classic authors of the Golden Age – wires, invisible threads, trapdoors, false ceilings, mirrors, etc. – and make it a more plausible, less mechanical mystery. It was a mystery I had to solve myself before I could even begin to write it. The nature of that locked room is also crucial to the plot. It is no ordinary room, but the lodge room of the Literati, a fictitious lodge of Bayswater Freemasons. The vanished man is a distinguished guest, and his disappearance takes place during the performance of a ceremony, one during which the lights are lowered for several minutes. The subject naturally required considerable research – and what a fascinating one it is! Not all writers like research but I love to immerse myself in the past, and discover new things in our wonderful rich history. There was considerable reading to be done on Freemasonry, its origins, structure and practice, and I also had taken into account how a lodge might have been organised in the 1880s. Despite its reputation as a secret society, Freemasonry really has very few secrets. Most of the ceremonies can be found on the internet with very little effort, and I came to enjoy the archaic expressions and rhythm of Masonic ritual. That gave me the basic information I needed, but I also took care to seek expert advice, from which I gained additional knowledge and was also able to hone my work to give as accurate a picture as possible. At the heart of the story, however, is Frances Doughty, lady detective, who has suffered many sorrows. At the end of book six she is in an unhappy place, but this is the adventure in which she will find herself again. Solving a crime in an all-male organisation is the least of her worries; after all, she lives in a society dominated and controlled by men, but has been able to remain her own woman despite everything fate can throw at her. Not only will she unravel the mystery of the disappearing Freemason, she will also uncover secrets in her own family that have dogged her since her very first adventure, and emerge stronger and more confident than ever.

JAMES MCCREET (Victorian London)

McCreet's colourful and involving *The Incendiary's Trail* is a Victorian detective thriller based in London and is typical of his work. His subject is the very beginnings of detection – pre-Sherlock Holmes – and pits the minds of policemen against criminals who lurk in a city caught between modernity and darkness. Later books by McCreet include *The Vice Society*, *The Thieves' Labyrinth* and *The Masked Adversary*, all featuring the Detective Force's Inspector Albert Newsome.

DAVID MORRELL (Nineteenth-century England)

Famous for such novels as *First Blood* (though Morrell's Rambo is a very different figure from the one represented in the Stallone film adaptation), the Canadian author has created a strong period series featuring the writer Thomas De Quincey and his daughter, Emily. *Murder as a Fine Art* was followed by *Inspector of the Dead*, set in 1855, as the British are coping with the fallout of the Crimean War and London is at the mercy of a ruthless killer.

JOAN LOCK (Nineteenth-century England)

A former policewoman, Joan Lock is the author of 11 non-fiction police/crime books, including three on Scotland Yard's first detectives; she is also an authority on female police history. Her crime fiction includes short stories and eight crime novels, one modern and seven in the popular Victorian series that features the charismatic Inspector Ernest Best. *Dead Letters* is a characteristic title.

JULIAN SYMONS (Victorian England)

Julian Symons was perhaps the most celebrated critic of crime fiction in the history of the genre. His study *Bloody Murder* is sui generis, and the urbane Symons was also an accomplished practitioner of the genre himself, noting that he was interested in the 'violence behind respectable faces, the civil servant planning how to kill Jews most efficiently, the judge speaking with passion about the need for capital punishment, the quiet obedient boy who kills for fun'. His novels *The Blackheath Poisonings* and *Death's Darkest Face* both examined dark familial undercurrents. In the former novel (which is set in the Victorian era), a generational clash prompts a series of deaths by poison and a surprising postscript in which the identity of a murderer is revealed. Symons practised what he preached, writing well-turned, elegant crime fiction.

🎞 TV: THE BLACKHEATH POISONINGS (Stuart Orme, director)

Much applauded on its first showing, the Victorian murder mystery series *The Blackheath Poisonings* is based on the celebrated

---

novel by Julian Symons and was the brainchild of producer Kenny McBain (who also had under his belt the TV *Inspector Morse*). The tone of this atmospheric period drama is nicely judged: there's a subtly sardonic air, but no parody – and there are lashings of nicely calculated suspense. It is essentially a family drama: the Collards and the Vandervents are the two distinguished families in the moneyed, comfortable setting of Albert Villa, near the London suburb of Blackheath. But the bourgeois respectability conceals a disturbing turbulence beneath the surface, with internecine squabbles over control of the family toy business. A Machiavellian stranger arrives, and Albert Villa is thrown into barely disguised chaos, with – inevitably – murder on the menu. The production looks splendid, but the top-notch cast is the thing here: Zoë Wanamaker, Judy Parfitt and (most divertingly) the saturnine Patrick Malahide using all their considerable skills to stir the ingredients of the brew.

MARK GATISS (Nineteenth-century England)

Mark Gatiss is something of a renaissance man with a wide range of skills, from cultural commentator and writer (including considerable expertise regarding his beloved Hammer films) to showrunner and actor – the latter accomplishments were all combined in the modern-day reimagining of Conan Doyle's character in the television series *Sherlock*, in which Gatiss made a memorable Mycroft Holmes. A lesser-known element of his CV is a series of period-set crime novels beginning with *The Vesuvius Club*, which received a nomination for best newcomer at the 2006 British Book Awards. This features quirky sleuth Lucifer Box, who moves from era to era in a series of satisfyingly eccentric adventures (the 1890s here, the 1920s in *The Devil in Amber*, and the 1950s in *Black Butterfly*).

KATE SUMMERSCALE (Victorian England)

So festooned with awards and acclaim is Kate Summerscale's remarkable book *The Suspicions of Mr Whicher* that a further rehearsing of its many virtues is probably redundant – except perhaps to say that anyone interested in utterly compelling crime narratives, brilliantly realised historical milieus or simply elegant writing should have acquired it by now. Summerscale's first book, *The Queen of*

Whale Cay, was inspired by an obituary she had written for the *Daily Telegraph*; that book won the Somerset Maugham Award. *The Suspicions of Mr Whicher* won the Samuel Johnson Prize as well as the British Book Awards for both popular non-fiction and book of the year.

TV: THE SUSPICIONS OF MR WHICHER (various directors)

Based on the highly original book by Kate Summerscale and written by Neil McKay and Helen Edmundson, *The Suspicions of Mr Whicher* is a British series of television films produced by Hat Trick Productions for ITV. Crucial in the success of the series was the casting of the diffident, superficially unconfrontational copper whose name the series carries, and with Paddy Considine skilfully underplaying as Detective Inspector Jack Whicher of the Metropolitan Police, success was assured. Broadcast in 2011, the first film in the sequence, *The Murder at Road Hill House*, was Summerscale's 2008 take on the real-life Constance Kent murder investigation of the year 1860. This highly successful first outing for Whicher was followed by less impressive fictitious extensions of his career as a private enquiry agent, starting with *The Murder in Angel Lane*, filmed in 2013 and broadcast that year. Two more episodes followed, *Beyond the Pale* (broadcast in September 2014) and *The Ties that Bind* (also 2014). While the continuing episodes are ably written and directed, the first remains the series' high point, with the most personal involvement of the Whicher character.

SK RIZZOLO (Regency England)

The American author SK Rizzolo developed an interest in history from seeing a BBC series about Henry VIII's 'headless wives' (as she calls them), after which she became obsessed with all things British. Her series featuring the unlikely alliance between John Chase (a Bow Street Runner) and Penelope Wolfe (wife of the chief suspect in the first book) includes *The Rose in the Wheel* and *Blood for Blood*. The setting in Regency England is strongly evoked with period accoutrements nicely judged (such as the penchant of the upper classes for the waltz, the notion of King George III being regarded as mad, and the ever-present bogeyman Napoleon).

JUDITH CUTLER (Nineteenth-century Warwickshire)

Judith Cutler has written several different series of crime novels, all accomplished, but for the purposes of this study, the books featuring the Reverend Tobias Campion, a nineteenth-century parson, are the most relevant. The first in the series, *The Keeper of Secrets*, marked her out as a talented practitioner in the historical crime genre, and the subsequent Campion novels – *Shadow of the Past* and *Cheating the Hangman* – continue her exploration of early nineteenth-century life. This was marked by the excesses of many of the Upper Ten Thousand, who made and enforced the law, often with quite disproportionate punishments, and the extreme poverty pervading both town and countryside. As the son of an aristocrat and a cleric, Tobias has access to all strata of society, dealing with crime – and indeed sin – wherever he finds it. Jem, his former groom, and Dr Hansard, the local doctor, help him in his search for justice, but no more than two redoubtable women – Campion's housekeeper, Mrs Trent, and Mrs Hansard. The series is darker than many of her others, although – as you would expect with Cutler – there is some social comedy. Without attempting to write a pastiche of Jane Austen, Cutler writes in a much more formal style than usual, just as her characters are expected to follow the very strong contemporary codes of behaviour. But expect blood and gore rather than heaving bosoms.

OSCAR DE MURIEL (Victorian Edinburgh)

Oscar de Muriel was born in Mexico City in the building that now houses Ripley's Believe it or Not museum and currently lives in North Cheshire, but his series featuring Inspector Ian Frey and Detective McGray is based in Edinburgh – after several visits, it seemed that the city was the perfect setting for a crime mystery. For years de Muriel had been meaning to write a story about the Devil's Sonata (de Muriel plays the violin), and it was appropriate as a subject for the first case for his protagonists, *The Strings of Murder*. This intriguing series combines history, horror, and the occasional supernatural element.

🎤 Interview: Oscar de Muriel

Historical research is a tricky thing. It's pretty much impossible to tell when you've done enough, and there's always the temptation to google for another reference or to open another book. In my case, this comes from the ever-present fear that one day I'll be 90,000 words into a first draft, merely weeks from my deadline, only to find a tiny historical detail that will render my plot completely absurd – luckily, that hasn't quite happened yet! This was a particular concern while writing *A Mask of Shadows*. The entire plot revolves around Victorian theatre and the real lives of some of the most famous personalities of the 1880s: Bram Stoker, Ellen Terry, Henry Irving – even Oscar Wilde has a delightful cameo. It was a heavenly coincidence that the most celebrated theatre company of the time was presenting Macbeth in 1889, when my detectives Frey and McGray were solving their first spooky cases, but it was also a curse: with the plethora of online resources available nowadays, and the fact that you can carry thousands of files in a tablet, very soon I found myself drowning in books, history journals, biographies and photographs. And what I kept finding was so rich I simply didn't know when to stop. Theatre back then was a dangerous affair. Special effects involved naked wiring, red-hot embers to create steam, explosives, live animals on stage, limelight that heats up to thousands of degrees... I wonder what they'd think of today's safety assessment forms! I also found all these wonderfully rich and twisted details about the famous Stoker, Irving and Terry – so juicy Jeremy Kyle would blush. Ellen Terry married three times, had children out of wedlock (in Victorian times), had ongoing affairs with married men... and yet was so charismatic she managed to remain the darling of British audiences, even performing privately for Queen Victoria. And Bram Stoker turned out to be entirely different to what I'd expected: I was surprised to find out he was rather shy, a workaholic, incredibly tall and broad-shouldered, and ginger (and then his private life...). The more I delved the more possibilities came to mind. The plot thickened and I ended up with a fiendishly complicated Excel spreadsheet, colour-coded, so that I could follow every strand and loose end. I remember printing it out (A3 sheets were required), looking at the tiny font and thinking, 'It's time you stopped researching.' I knew there were still tomes upon tomes to look at, but I had a story to tell (and a deadline). In the end, my fear of missing out an exciting detail did come about, although thankfully not in a way that would thwart my plot. In fact, it was something that planted the seed for a follow-up case featuring the celebrated trio. And that's how addictive research can be: I finished the book a while ago, yet I can't wait to delve into the lives of these fascinating people one more time.

DAN SIMMONS (Victorian London, Late Nineteenth-century America)

Lengthy, futuristic epics such as *Hyperion* were in the purview of American writer Dan Simmons, who bagged the prestigious Hugo Award for his efforts in creating alternate worlds and societies. *Drood*, however, is Simmons's venture into nineteenth-century Britain and the work of two of its greatest writers: Charles Dickens and Wilkie Collins (the title, of course, is a reference to Dickens' final, unfinished novel, *The Mystery of Edwin Drood*). Simmons' book, however, is a very different literary creation, with the two novelists and friends venturing through a darkly atmospheric Victorian world where supernatural creatures haunt the shadows and an alternative cityscape exists beneath the streets. The narrative is dispatched with the energy we have come to expect from Dan Simmons, and along with his eventful plotting, he is able to take on notions of creativity and the gulf between genius and talent (Dickens and Collins are pungently characterised). An interest in the two writers and in the nineteenth-century classics is definitely an advantage here, but for those persuaded to join Simmons and his two protagonists on their sinister and terrifying odyssey (a rather long one, it should be noted – the book is nearly 800 pages), this is a journey they will not regret undertaking. Simmons' early work utilised elements from the horror genre (a constant here) and horror reappears frequently in Dickens' world, making this a strong literary marriage.

Simmons ventures into the past in another novel, *The Fifth Heart*, in which he channels two characters – one real and one fictitious. *The Fifth Heart* is almost as massive (over 600 pages) but is continuously entertaining. Sherlock Holmes and the writer Henry James in 1893 America join together to investigate the suicide of Clover Adams, wife of the esteemed historian Henry Adams – a man whose family hobnobs with US presidents. The upper reaches of American society are to be shaken by their findings…

ALEX SCARROW (Victorian London)

Earlier books by Alex Scarrow (such as *Last Light* and *Afterlight*) gleaned much critical praise, but his Victorian thriller *The Candle Man* was his breakthrough novel. In 1912, a man relates a story in a ship's cabin to a young girl – a cabin, in fact, on the *Titanic* – which is just about to sink. The story relates to events in Whitechapel in the nineteenth century. A young woman, Mary Kelly, comes across a man lying in the gutter suffering from head injuries and loss of memory. He is American, but has no idea how he will find his way home. This provocative opening premise is explored with great imagination and flair by Scarrow, proving that there is still more to explore in the saga of Jack the Ripper. The felicitous descriptions here match those in previous entries by the author.

LYNN SHEPHERD (Victorian London)

You may feel that after all the film and television adaptations, you've had a surfeit of Charles Dickens, but we can hardly blame the writer for what other people choose to do with his work. Similarly, does the fact that her publishers evoke *Bleak House* persuade you to read Lynn Shepherd's *Tom-All-Alone's*? Or does it make you feel that this is one contribution too many to the world of Dickensian London? It should be the former – for in the army of novels written under the spell of Dickens, this is both an intelligent simulacrum of the great man's style and something subtly individual and inventive. Dickens it isn't – although the journey into the darker alleyways of Victorian London is a memorable one. *Tom-All-Alone's* is a title that Dickens considered for *Bleak House*; the area was one of the most squalid and filthy slums in Victorian London, emblematic of the need for social reform that so energised the writer. But what Shepherd has done here is to forge an intriguing spin on something that has become rather a truism: *Bleak House* as the first detective novel. Shepherd has taken that conceit (rather than the myriad other aspects of the original) and developed it in idiosyncratic fashion. Charles Maddox, nephew of the identically named protagonist of the author's tribute to another great British writer, *Murder at Mansfield Park*, has been dismissed from the Metropolitan Police for an offence he did not commit. The younger Maddox is hired by Mr Tulkinghorn (the imposing lawyer from *Bleak House*) after a series of anonymous letters has been delivered to the home of wealthy banker Sir Julius Cremorne, as well as to other prestigious figures in London. As Maddox tries to track down a shadowy blackmailer, he (and we) embark upon a sometimes nightmarish odyssey through a sprawling, crowded London that contains wealth and privilege alongside thieves' drinking dens, prostitutes and murderers. As with Michel Faber's *The Crimson Petal and the White*, Shepherd is at liberty to deal more frankly with some of the social ills that novelists such as Dickens and Hardy were obliged to be circumspect about, and it is an opportunity she grabs with both hands. The prose here is vibrant, and a tightrope is skilfully walked: finding something else for Dickens' Inspector Bucket, Lady Dedlock and Mr Jarndyce to do without ever making the reader frown at such hubris on Shepherd's part. As the author would no doubt admit, she does not have Dickens' genius, but *Tom-All-Alone's* is such an enjoyable novel that one hesitates to use the word 'pastiche'. More recently, Shepherd has published another excellent historical novel, *The Pierced Heart*, before moving into contemporary fare.

🎤 **Interview: Lynn Shepherd**

In a sense, my period chose me – at least to start with. The first book, *Murder at Mansfield Park*, turned Jane Austen's 'problem child' into a murder mystery, so that anchored me firmly to the Regency. I never thought it would evolve into a series, but as it turned out, no one else was writing precisely that combination of literary/historical noir. But when I started thinking about a follow-up I made the very conscious decision to move forward, away from Austen's refined universe to the much coarser and (for my purposes) richer territory of the mid-nineteenth century. Choosing Dickens' *Bleak House* as my inspiration was a big part of that, of course, but I've always felt very much 'at home' in the Victorian period. It's at a fascinating intersection – far enough back to be strange, but close enough to feel 'like us'. The fact that we have photographs of Victorians, for example, makes them seem so much easier to 'recall to life' (in Dickens' fabulous phrase). When I started writing *Tom-All-Alone's*, I deliberately chose a narrative style that would allow me to exploit both the strangeness and the familiarity. My great model there was John Fowles' *French Lieutenant's Woman* – a neo-Victorian novel endowed with all the awful clarity of twentieth-century hindsight. In the same way, *Tom-All-Alone's* shows us Victorian London with a very modern knowingness, which makes the story bleaker, darker and more brutal than anything Dickens could ever have written, even if he did indeed see his contemporaries 'dying thus around him every day'. *Tom-All-Alone's* is my most unflinching historical noir, taking my readers down and dirty (literally and metaphorically) into the terrifying underside of what was then the world's greatest city – a London that, 'night and day, moves and sweats and bawls, as riddled with life as a corpse with maggots'.

LLOYD SHEPHERD (Nineteenth-century London)

There are several elements that mark out *The English Monster* as a striking novel, not least its remarkable depiction of the labyrinthine streets around Wapping in 1811. But this compelling piece is based on the real-life story of the Ratcliffe Highway murders, and the canvas utilised is impressive, with its evocation of a Regency London. Two families are suffering from the effects of murder, and Magistrate John Harriott has his hands full. But he has an ace in the hole – Senior Officer Charles Horton, who is proving himself adept at something which has only recently acquired a name: detection. This is splendid stuff.

PETER ACKROYD (Victorian London)

Stroll down London's Stoke Newington Church Street, and at one of the chic wine bars you'll see a plaque informing you that Edgar Allan Poe was once a pupil at a school that stood on the site. The author of 'The Pit and the Pendulum' and 'The Raven' – a London schoolboy? This is precisely the sort of curious historical fact that fascinates Peter Ackroyd (who has written about Poe) and versions of such things find their way into his highly accomplished historical crime novels – such as the groundbreaking *Hawksmoor* (which set a modern-day policing narrative against a more interesting historical one) and *Dan Leno and the Limehouse Golem*. In fact, the polymath Ackroyd has been charting a course through history in both his fiction and non-fiction – his baggy Dickens biography, with its controversial 'fictionalised' sections, reads rather like one of Ackroyd's novels. In so much of his work, Ackroyd vibrantly conjures the reality of Victorian life, and the issues that concerned the Victorians energise his characters, both real and fictitious.

Film: THE LIMEHOUSE GOLEM (Juan Carlos Medina, director)

Peter Ackroyd's *chef-d'oeuvre Hawksmoor* was inexplicably passed over by filmmakers, so I suppose we should be grateful that the writer's *Dan Leno and the Limehouse Golem* enjoyed a creditable film adaptation, although it is one that did not quite do justice to the source material. The vengeful monster of Jewish mythology is – apparently – incarnated in nineteenth-century London as refugees arrive in Britain from Europe. Detective Inspector John Kildare (nicely underplayed by Bill Nighy – the only underplaying in a film full of larger-than-life characterisations) is tasked with tracking down the serial killer of the title. Visually stylish and full of the kind of Victorian music hall exuberance found in the novels of Kate Griffin rather than Ackroyd's original.

SARAH WATERS (Victorian London)

Sarah Waters has produced a variety of acclaimed novels, including *Tipping the Velvet*, which won the Betty Trask Award; *Affinity*, winner of the Somerset Maugham Award; and the novel most appropriate for this book, the much-acclaimed *Fingersmith*, which was short-listed for the Booker Prize and the Orange Prize and won the CWA Historical Dagger. Almost equal acclaim was to follow for the subsequent *The Night Watch* and *The Little Stranger*. However, in the view of many readers, *Fingersmith* remains Waters' *chef-d'oeuvre*.

In nineteenth-century London, the Borough – a slum area near Southwark Bridge – is a hotbed of crime, all of which is described unsparingly by Waters. The youthful Sue's mother was hanged for murder, and she is in the care of Mrs Sucksby and Mr Ibbs – both petty criminals but they provide a sympathetic environment. But into Sue's world comes the attractive forger Richard Rivers, and her life is to change irrevocably. It's splendid stuff: vital, atmospheric and teeming with a keen literary energy.

TV: RIPPER STREET (various directors)

There were those who were resistant to the glossy period production design of *Ripper Street* – a little too visually pleasing, they muttered – but the BAFTA-nominated crime series inaugurated a notable first: a resurrection from the dead after it had been cancelled, despite its clear popular success. Series 3 begins four years after the culmination of the previous series (the action jumps from 1890 to 1894) and represents another heady descent into the lives of the denizens of the dangerous streets of Whitechapel in late Victorian London. The rich scene setting and atmosphere of the earlier series are satisfyingly in place, and the slightly anachronistic acting styles well integrated.

7: The Rest of the World in the Nineteenth Century

KATE GRENVILLE (Nineteenth-century Australia)

What is the appeal of Kate Grenville's writing? Is it her evocative use of language, with every word burnished until it shines like a jewel? Actually, no: what makes such books as *The Secret River* so impressive is her ability to marry character with plot, setting with period. *The Secret River* starts in nineteenth-century London. William Thornhill is content with his marriage to the woman he has loved since he was a boy, and he has a job working on the Thames. But he finds himself in trouble with the law and is transported for life (along with his family) to New South Wales. The family finds their life among the convicts a trial. So when William hears that an escape may be bought, and that uncharted territory far away from Sydney holds the promise of a new life, he grabs the chance. But the family's happiness is to be short-lived: terrifying times are ahead. In their new home, they find themselves having to coexist with aborigines living on the river as well as other non-natives who are struggling to cope, including Thomas Blackwood and the forceful Smasher Sullivan. If you're under the illusion that historical fiction by women writers may be less tough than that by men, *The Secret River* will quickly disabuse you of that idea. The life that William Thornhill and his family live is harsh indeed. As her protagonists struggle to survive in the face of danger from people far more attuned to the land than they are, they find it equally difficult to relate to the other white settlers they are obliged to live with. And although the struggle with a menacing environment is conveyed with tremendous skill, this is also a book about the search for identity. William Thornhill and his wife Sal must decide what is the real essence of their nature – and the clash between staying civilised and simply surviving will change them both irrevocably. Kate Grenville won the Orange Prize for her book *The Idea of Perfection*, and she shares with other Australian writers (such as Peter Carey) a luminous skill for evoking her native land in all its beauty and threat. A few sentences of Grenville make one realise that much of the writing one encounters in a novel these days is thin and perfunctory. Reading *The Secret River* may put you off anything less accomplished for a while.

MATTHEW PEARL (Nineteenth-century America, Victorian Britain)

In Matthew Pearl's *The Last Dickens*, it is 1870, and Charles Dickens is dead. The last instalment of his final manuscript has disappeared, last seen addressed to the publisher whose livelihood depended on it. But the clue to its disappearance lies in a series of savage killings, and it is up to Dickens' publisher – with his own life on the line – to crack the mystery. In Pearl's intense thriller, we are taken through lively West End locales and the more threatening back alleys of the East End of London. It is a stunningly realised piece of historical crime writing – and readers who know Pearl's name will know that he is top-notch at this sort of stuff.

Interview: Matthew Pearl

My first novel was called *The Dante Club*, a historical thriller set at a crossroads in literary history. The title refers to a small group of poets and professors based around Boston who were the first to translate Dante into English in America during the 1860s. Most people think of literature's classic pantheon – Shakespeare, Dante, etc. – as having always been part of our cultural canons. In fact, Dante was an extremely controversial poet in Britain and even more so in America, because of the violence of his work and the Catholic doctrines it highlighted. It took some temerity to overcome that in puritanical, Protestant and xenophobic nineteenth-century America. *The Dante Club* dramatises the courage and dedication of those first Dante scholars by converting the controversy into *actual* violence: a series of murders inspired by Dante that only the Dante Club could put to an end. I am sometimes asked how it occurred to me to combine poets with a story about gruesome deaths and the criminal mind, but it is hardly a new idea. In fact, Dante made his two protagonists who must descend into the deepest regions of hell and face its horrors not soldiers or warriors like Ulysses or Aeneas, but Dante himself and Virgil, two rather unheroic poets. There is a philosophy inherent in that which I share: literature does not arise from a landscape, but rather a battlefield.

Two writers who influenced my approach to this project were Umberto Eco and Iain Pears, both of whom did much to define our modern historical fiction, in very different ways. Both proved that historical fiction is at its best when the fiction pressures the history but does not puncture it altogether. When thinking of writing and politics, I think it's very important to recognise that it's a choice a writer makes to inject political viewpoints or not. I find fiction a strange place to encounter politics, and as for myself I have no ambitions to make political points in my fiction.

ARMAND CABASSON (Napoleonic France)

Armand Cabasson has written several highly accomplished detective novels set during the Napoleonic Wars which have been bestsellers in France. A typically engaging entry is *The Officer's Prey*. Set in Poland and Russia at the time of Napoleon's ill-fated Russian campaign, Cabasson's protagonist here, Captain Quentin Margont, is a principled French army officer, charged by Napoleon's son-in-law Prince Eugène to look into the killing of a Polish woman, a servant. As in Hans Hellmut Kirst's *The Night of the Generals*, the murder seems to have been committed by a high-ranking army officer, and Margont is counselled to be discreet. And also as in Kirst's novel, several officers are the main suspects. With a background of war and non-cooperation, Margont's task looks insoluble.

CALEB CARR (Nineteenth-century New York)

Some authors may toil ceaselessly for years before achieving a modicum of success. Others may be catapulted into the limelight after only a couple of books. Caleb Carr is of the latter breed: the remarkable acclaim that greeted *The Alienist*, however, was not so enthusiastically echoed by similar attention for the subsequent *The Angel of Darkness*. Carr's speciality is a canny synthesis of the Holmesian novel of deduction, a Thomas Harris-style pursuit of a serial killer, and the detailed topography and historical verisimilitude of Doctorow's *Ragtime*. While Carr's preternaturally brilliant detective/alienist Laszlo Kreizler is at the centre of the books, there is a shrewd strategy at work in allocating the peripheral characters their share of attention in successive outings.

🎙 Interview: Caleb Carr

I feel a writer has two jobs: to educate and to entertain. I'm not interested in being treated as a serious novelist, but I am interested in what I think writing should be doing now. Too much of the autobiographical, introspective style of novel being written today is really a dead horse that's being mercilessly flogged. It's a cliché, I know, but people are still desperately thirsty for stories. And in America, where educational standards are falling, I think there's a real importance in the concept of accessible books that teach something. You have to do it in a way that is entertaining to readers. I'm not claiming that I do this quite as well as I'd wish; there are some historical details in my books that seem to me, in retrospect, a little stuck on. It's essential that this sort of thing is organic to the narrative. Maybe I haven't mastered that technique yet. I see my descriptive passages as purely functional. I don't tend to wax very rhapsodic in my use of language. I go for language that is strictly utilitarian. I think that certainly since Hemingway (and certainly since my father's old friend Jack Kerouac), everything that can be done with language *has* been done. All the experiments you can perform with language have been tried. I do try to keep the description as straightforward as possible – it should serve a function. I began with the concept of a psychiatrist and a killer who had certain things in common. But I appreciated that this sounded like a hundred other books, and I thought to myself, 'What am I going to do to make this distinctive?' So I went for something which wasn't quite a thriller and wasn't quite a historical novel – hopefully it was a new departure. My publishers, of course, said, 'What are we going to do with this?' So it was decided to present this as part of a new genre: the psychological/historical thriller. To my editor's credit, she was right behind this idea, but the marketing people were deeply unhappy. They said, 'We can't do this – this is too new!'

As for my New York setting, part of the reason I wrote the books was because I was getting so tired with hearing people say, 'New York's gotten so rough – it was so charming in the old days, the gay 90s, the golden age.' And I'd look at them and think, 'Come on, the

> city's always been a sinkhole of corruption and crime and absolute degeneracy.' That's what I try to address in the books.

STEF PENNEY (Nineteenth-century Canada)

Stef Penney (who was born in Edinburgh) was nonplussed by the remarkable acclaim garnered by her novel *The Tenderness of Wolves* and fought shy of the attendant publicity, although she has since allowed herself to become a more public figure. The novel, which is set in Canada in 1860s, won the 2006 Costa Prize and is a triumph of research over experience: despite its strongly realised Canadian setting, the author never travelled to the country but did all her research in London libraries. The story begins with the murder of Laurent Jammet, a trapper scraping a living in a secluded settlement. He has been scalped, and his throat has been slit. Penney's protagonist, Mrs Ross, is distressed by the fact that her son has gone missing on the day she finds Jammet, and she hires an Indian tracker (a suspect in the murder) to trace him. Subsequent books by Penney have not achieved the same level of success, but she is nevertheless a formidable writer.

MICHAEL DIBDIN (Nineteenth-century Florence)

Dibdin inaugurated his serious writing career with an unorthodox (but very clever) reworking of the familiar Sherlock Holmes versus Jack the Ripper plot in *The Last Sherlock Holmes Story* – a book that upset Conan Doyle purists (for reasons not to be enumerated here for spoiler reasons). He followed this with a beguiling adventure for the poet Robert Browning as detective in *A Rich Full Death*, set in Florence in 1855 – at which point it became clear that each new book would be radically different from its predecessors, except in terms of adroit plotting. His series detective, Italian Police Commissioner Aurelio Zen, is contemporary and not relevant to this volume, but his period-set mysteries are worth the attention of any fan of historical crime fiction.

ANDREW WILLIAMS (Nineteenth-century St Petersburg)

Andrew Williams' background is in television journalism, and while making a BBC series on the IRA, he met one of their most successful bombers, who had destroyed the centre of Derry. Williams asked why he had laid waste to his own city, and the cool reply was 'because the IRA instructed me to do so'. In *To Kill a Tsar*, Williams has translated this chilling encounter into a seething revolutionary Russia, and has suggested telling parallels between the different cultures, despite the separation of nearly a century between the Russian terrorists and the members of the IRA he interviewed. The business of compromised characters with difficult moral choices to make in fraught situations clearly fascinates this writer. It was also the fulcrum of his World War Two-set debut novel *The Interrogator*, which synthesised historical writing with the excitement of the thriller (à la Robert Harris's *Enigma*). And Williams has come to grips even more authoritatively with the notion in *To Kill a Tsar*. Essentially a morality play set in a deftly realised nineteenth-century St Petersburg, the protagonists are Dr Frederick Hadfield, making a great deal of money from the privileged Anglo-Russian gentry, and a seductive femme fatale, Anna, working for pitiless revolutionary groups to overthrow the corrupt ruling elite. In the summer of 1879, Russia threw up the first significant terrorist cell of the modern era, the People's Will. An energetic war of bombings and assassinations was waged on Tsar Alexander II and his government (the parallels here, of course, are not just with the IRA but with Al Qaeda). Williams presents Frederick as off-balance in his professional life and ripe for suborning by Anna, who seduces him into a desperate game in which he becomes the target of both the revolutionaries and the Tsar's equally implacable police. As well as Dostoyevsky's *The Devils*, there are echoes here of Conrad in the unsparing picture of terrorist cells, but Williams, despite his well-turned prose, is essentially a popular writer, plying these themes in relatively straightforward fashion. The book is none the worse for that, and the bravura of the storytelling registers strongly, even if some may feel that the moral dilemmas of hero and heroine might have been more thoroughly excavated. Nevertheless, *To Kill a Tsar* is proof that Williams is the real thing: a writer who can marry a popular genre to a sophisticated treatment of political arguments.

ANTONIN VARENNE (Nineteenth-century Burma and Britain)

Varenne is not lacking in audacity. *Bed of Nails* undertook a radical shaking-up of the detective story, while in *Loser's Corner* he utilised the experiences of his own father for an excavation of France's murky colonial past. In *Retribution Road* (translated by Sam Taylor), however, Varenne strikes out in a new direction. He has created a sprawling but rigorous epic evoking such great adventure novelists of the past as Conrad and Buchan. In nineteenth-century Burma, Bowman, a soldier, is dispatched on a clandestine mission that ends with the capture and torture of his men. Bowman survives and ends up in London, drink- and drug-addled. But a mutilated corpse is found that has undergone the same tortures that Bowman did in Burma. His tracking down of a vicious killer takes the reader on a picaresque – and always dangerous – odyssey. What is most bold here is the genre splicing, with elements from the Western, detection and even war novel kept in exhilarating balance.

CAROL MCCLEARY (Nineteenth-century Paris)

Carol McCleary's heroine Nellie Bly is an amateur detective, feminist and investigative reporter – America's first woman to hold that job, in fact. In *The Alchemy of Murder*, she is in Paris on the track of a mysterious murderer. Paris is not a safe place to be; the Black Fever holds the city in thrall – but at least Nellie can call on some very famous artists and writers for help. Some missteps, but, in general, *The Alchemy of Murder* is wonderfully inventive stuff from an intriguing writer.

LYNDSAY FAYE (Nineteenth-century New York)

'Seven for a secret, never to be told' runs the nursery rhyme, but we can be grateful that the talented Lyndsay Faye *does* tell us the grim secrets here. The heady narrative of *Seven for a Secret* involves kidnapping on the streets of nineteenth-century New York and centres on the 'blackbirders', slave catchers whose violent trade is in fact state-sanctioned. The star policeman of New York's recently formed police force, Timothy Wilde (a character we first encountered in the author's baggy and impressive *The Gods of Gotham*), takes on the sinister traders and is shocked to find out that he is not quite as inured to the malignity of human behaviour as he believed. Lyndsay Faye is a member of the 'Baker Street Irregulars' and a worshipper at the shrine of Conan Doyle – but it is her own skill at evoking the dark world of the nineteenth century, crammed with plausible detail, that distinguishes this slice of historical crime writing.

PABLO DE SANTIS (Nineteenth-century Paris)

The Paris Enigma is both a prize-winning mystery and a highly diverting riff on the classic detective themes of Conan Doyle and co., but it is ingenious and solid fare that is no mere pastiche. The legendary group of sleuths the Twelve Detectives arranges a meeting at the World's Fair in Paris in 1889. But one of the group, Louis Dabon, is discovered murdered at the foot of the newly built Eiffel Tower. The Twelve know it is necessary to pool their considerable talents to track down the killer, as the next victim is likely to be another member of the group.

RN MORRIS (Tsarist Russia)

A mother and son have died a hideous death, poisoned by a box of chocolates given to them by the dead woman's husband. The detective on the case shuffles papers in his stuffy office, and has his patience tested by a new recruit before setting out for the crime scene. But the reason that the detective's office is stuffy is because the windows are closed to keep out the stench of raw sewage coming from a ditch outside. For this isn't a modern police procedural; in *A Vengeful Longing* we are in nineteenth-century Russia, and the police magistrate suffering from the heat is Porfiry Petrovich – the dogged copper, in fact, who solved the double axe murder in Dostoyevsky's *Crime and Punishment*. The British crime novelist RN Morris has made the Russian writer's sleuth his own, both here and in the earlier *A Gentle Axe*. While the details of the murder investigation are familiar, Morris's skill is to take us into a totally different world and century; right from the start, we are hooked by his storytelling panache as the once beautiful Raisa Ivanovna Meyer sits on the veranda of her dacha, watching her obsessive young son Grisha copy out meaningless passages from a newspaper. Neither is particularly pleased by the appearance of the boy's father, a doctor with little time for his family, who presses on them a box of chocolates. Raisa struggles with thoughts of what the chocolates will do to her spreading figure, but indulges. She is soon paying a heavy price, as the pair die in unspeakable agony (Morris spares us nothing here – or in the grisly autopsy scene that follows). It's time for the plump, deceptively ordinary (but brilliant) investigator Porfiry Petrovich to find out the identity (and motives) of the murderer. Is it the doctor, who seems anxious to convey his guilt to Porfiry? The latter is alternately helped and hindered by his gauche new assistant Virginsky (the too obvious metaphor of the inexperienced assistant's name is one of the few missteps by the surefooted Morris). The creators of Peter Falk's rumpled TV detective Colombo admitted to borrowing from Dostoyevsky – the irritating, 'just one more thing' detective wears down a murderer until the final confession is a mere formality. But Morris has burnished the technique to a fine art. And the recreation of pre-Soviet Russia is painted with a master's touch.

🎤 Interview: RN Morris

I've written books set in two historical periods and settings, nineteenth-century St Petersburg and London just before the outbreak of World War One. The reason I chose the first period was because I had an idea for a detective novel featuring Porfiry Petrovich, the investigating magistrate from Dostoyevsky's masterpiece, *Crime and Punishment*. I had the idea because I loved the book. Something about the febrile atmosphere of it, as well as the mixture of philosophy, metaphysics, theology and axe murdering, just captured my imagination. I remember seeing Dostoyevsky's name on his books in my school library and being intimidated by it, and by the titles of his books – as well as the thickness of them. It was quite a long time before I plucked up courage to take one out – and that was *Crime and Punishment*. The blurb, I seem to remember, described it as one of the earliest detective novels, which it isn't really. I was expecting a Russian Sherlock Holmes and got something very different! (At the time I was very into Sherlock Holmes, and had grown up watching Sexton Blake and Lord Peter Wimsey on TV.)

After I wrote four of those books, I needed a break from all things Russian, so I turned to a setting nearer to home: London. I was fascinated by the period at the beginning of the twentieth century, before all the horrors of that century had been unleashed. Two World Wars, trench warfare, gas attacks, aerial bombing, the Holocaust – those things were still in the future and unimaginable.

I see it as a time of great innocence. I wanted to write a series of books in which terrible crimes would be committed, which would disrupt that innocence, but would be nothing compared to what was to come. These are my Silas Quinn novels, which I don't think have got as much attention as the Porfiry books, but I think I've been able to do things in them which I'm very proud of. I set out to explore the idea of crime fiction as a sub-genre of surrealism, in which the psychological atmosphere is as important as the physical setting. The Fantômas novels first planted that seed in my mind. Then there were GK Chesterton's Father Brown stories, which are also quite bizarre, as is his novel *The Man Who Was Thursday*. Surrealism is a way of unlocking the subconscious, and subconscious desires resulting in violence seem to be quite a good engine for a crime story. I really push my detective to the limit psychologically. Like all fictional detectives he has his demons to contend with. But I really wanted to take him far beyond the cliché into a very dark place.

CLAUDE IZNER (Nineteenth-century France)

Claude Izner is a bifurcated writer. The author of the bestselling *Murder on the Eiffel Tower* is actually the pseudonym of two sisters, Laurence Lefèvre and Liliane Korb. Their detective is Victor Legris, a bookseller – they have both been booksellers themselves on the banks of the Seine, one on the right bank, one on the left. In *Murder on the Eiffel Tower*, perhaps their signature book, the spanking new structure is the glory of the 1889 Universal Exposition. But one day a woman collapses and dies on this great Paris landmark; she appears to be the victim of a bee-sting, but youthful bookseller Victor Legris was on the Tower at the time of the incident and is keen to learn the real truth behind the death. With a stunning conjuring of late nineteenth-century Paris as backdrop, the investigation takes Victor all over the city.

Other key book: *The Père Lachaise Mystery*.

BORIS AKUNIN (Imperial Russia)

Among modern Russian crime writers, Boris Akunin's is a name with distinct lustre. Akunin's quirky Erast Fandorin and Sister Pelagia series both transport the reader to the Imperial Russia of the late nineteenth and early twentieth centuries, while channelling the personalities of two notably distinctive sleuths. In the benighted Soviet era, the detective genre was dismissed as bourgeois and reactionary, but in present-day Russia (for all its problematic elements), such books as Akunin's *The Death of Achilles* are – thankfully – not on the radar of a newly interventionist regime. The novel is set in Tsarist Russia, and after a sojourn elsewhere, Erast Fandorin returns to Moscow only to become involved in court intrigue, with his associate, national hero General Sobolev, discovered dead in a hotel room. Fandorin is convinced that his friend was murdered. *The Death of Achilles* is typically astringent and atmospheric Akunin fare.

JASON GOODWIN (1830s Istanbul)

You might feel that we don't need another exotic foreign detective, but you'll change your mind after encountering Goodwin's Yashim in *The Janissary Tree*, an Ottoman detective in a highly unusual novel. Certainly, a eunuch detective is a first in the field, but that's only one element of the novelty that Goodwin brings to this strongly written thriller, set in Istanbul in the 1830s and crammed with fascinating detail. The author studied Byzantine history at Cambridge and knows his subject – hence the exemplary detail.

TV: THE LEGEND OF LIZZIE BORDEN (Paul Wendkos, director)

Director Paul Wendkos enjoyed a reputation in his day as a minor auteur, and this 1975 film has something of a following – not least because it stars the actress Elizabeth Montgomery (best known for TV's *Bewitched*) as the legendary New England woman who (as the children's rhyme says) 'took an axe and gave her mother forty whacks'. This made-for-TV piece takes a clear position on the much-disputed guilt of Lizzie Borden, and the sequences shot in the courtroom utilise actual court records. The night in which Lizzie's parents were chopped to pieces with an axe remains, however, shrouded in mystery.

TV: COPPER (various directors)

Set in 1860s New York during the American Civil War, this unusual series stars Tom Weston-Jones as an Irish immigrant policeman – the eponymous 'copper'. The show, fitfully successful, ran for two seasons and had a distinct, quirky identity quite unlike that of most American television crime shows.

Film: GANGS OF NEW YORK (Martin Scorsese, director)

From a screenplay by Jay Cocks, Steven Zaillian and Kenneth Lonergan, Scorsese's 2002 epic *Gangs of New York* is a period drama set in the Five Points district of New York City in the mid-nineteenth century. Based on Herbert Asbury's 1927 non-fiction book of the same name, the movie was not filmed in the titular city but in Rome's Cinecittà studios. However, despite its nominations for numerous awards (including the Academy Award for Best Picture, among nine other Oscar nominations), it is not – for all its virtues – vintage Scorsese. With a characteristically barnstorming performance by a bizarrely garbed Daniel Day-Lewis, the film centres on fictional gang leader Bill 'The Butcher' Cutting (Day-Lewis), who is both crime boss and political kingmaker under the patronage of 'Boss' Tweed (Jim Broadbent). The climax features a violent clash between Cutting and his mob with Amsterdam Vallon (Leonardo DiCaprio) and his allies, which preceded the real-life New York draft riots of 1863.

TV: MURDOCH MYSTERIES (various directors)

Distinctly traditional in approach, this Canadian mystery series (promoted as a 'Canuck Sherlock Holmes') can always be guaranteed to ruffle no feathers, but proves to be undemanding entertainment. The show (also known as *The Artful Detective*) features Yannick Bisson as William Murdoch, a police detective working in Toronto, Ontario, at the end of the nineteenth century. *Murdoch Mysteries* riffs on characters from the books by Maureen Jennings, who declared herself to this writer as relatively happy with the series.

8: The Early Twentieth Century and World War One

DAVID DICKINSON (Edwardian England)

Not to be confused with the orange-hued TV antiques expert of the same name, the crime writer David Dickinson has made a speciality of ingeniously turned narratives largely set in Victorian and Edwardian England (with occasional forays abroad). His protagonist is Lord Francis Powerscourt, a detective figure whose stamping ground is Edwardian-era Britain and who appears in 15 novels, beginning with *Goodnight Sweet Prince*, a particular favourite with readers. Powerscourt is a scion of the Irish aristocracy with an ancestral home in County Wicklow, and Dickinson pays considerable attention to the family tree of his aristocratic sleuth. As well as the obligatory Eton education, Powerscourt is furnished with an early career in army intelligence in India and Afghanistan. For his subsequent role as detective, he relies on such associates as Lord Johnny Fitzgerald and the Prime Minister of the day, Lord Rosebery. Throughout a lengthy series, Dickinson's skills as a writer have been unfaltering.

Other key books: *Death and the Jubilee*, *Death of a Chancellor*.

GIL ADAMSON (1900s Canada)

Shortlisted for the Commonwealth Writers' Prize, Gil Adamson's *The Outlander* is a remarkable novel: plotted with complexity but always utterly sure in its narrative grip. In some ways, the book is a reinvention of the classic Western manhunt. It's 1903, and a young woman is on the run across the Canadian forests, her pursuers close behind. She has killed her husband – and her implacable trackers include two terrifying red-headed brothers. It's their brother she has killed, and their thirst for revenge is keen. But for the woman, the real enemy is within – her own mind. And there is the strange group of misfits and cast-offs of society she meets; some help her, some have their own personal terrors to deal with. This sprawling but tense odyssey is a remarkable synthesis of chase narrative and literary novel, with powerfully etched characters and locales. Adamson is a writer of real distinction.

MARTIN EDWARDS (Early Twentieth-century England)

As an expert on the history of crime fiction – and a specialist in the British Golden Age, as his award-winning *The Golden Age of Murder* attests – it's no surprise that one of Martin Edwards' most distinctive books takes readers back to a vividly realised past. *Dancing for the Hangman* is a departure from Edwards' contemporary novels featuring Liverpool lawyer Harry Devlin and his Lake District mysteries, even though the author had previously written pithy short historical stories set in previous eras. The book is Edwards' reinvention of the notorious Hawley Crippen case, with the narration in the voice of the murderer himself. Edwards finds black humour in the gruesome tale of Crippen's murder and mutilation of his wife, Cora, who sang in music halls as Belle Elmore. Edwards ingeniously draws parallels between Crippen's character and the modern celebrity murderer, particularly in terms of the bizarre scenarios built around Cora's death, and his filling in the blank spots in the historical case is very satisfying. It's a book to make readers wish that the versatile Edwards might tackle the historical crime genre more often.

🎙 **Interview: Martin Edwards**

Dancing for the Hangman covers the lifetime of Dr Hawley Harvey Crippen (1862–1910). For me, Crippen is not only one of the most famous of murderers, he is also among the most fascinating. Executed for an apparently horrific crime, in person he was meek and genial. Hardly anyone had a bad word to say about him. To this day some people believe that he wasn't a murderer at all. The Crippen case is full of contradictions that have baffled experts ranging from Raymond Chandler to Francis Iles. When writing *Dancing for the Hangman*, I wanted to stay true to the established facts of the case. What makes it a work of fiction is that I've used a novelist's imagination to solve the mysteries surrounding Crippen's life – and his death on the gallows. It is, despite gratifying reviews here and in the US, the least well-known of my books, but a personal favourite. Among contemporary writers of historical mysteries, I greatly admire Peter Lovesey and Andrew Taylor, while Sarah Waters' *The Paying Guests* is a spellbinding fictional version of a famous case of the past, as F Tennyson Jesse's *A Pin to See the Peepshow* was in the 1930s. I've written plenty of short historical crime stories – set in periods as diverse as the pre-Conquest era, the eighteenth century, Sherlock Holmes's England and World War Two – since the short story form is, for writers and readers alike, an ideal way of dipping into days gone by. My love of history is reflected in the fact that Daniel Kind, protagonist of my Lake District mysteries set in the present, is a historian. One day I'd love to publish another historical mystery. Perhaps set in the era of the Golden Age of murder between the wars...

PETER MATTHIESSEN (Turn of the Century Florida)

After the success of such books as *The Snow Leopard*, Matthiessen established a reputation as one of the most gifted of writers, whose occasional missteps were subsumed in an impressive oeuvre of consistent achievement. *Shadow Country* (weighing in at 900 pages) is one of his most ambitious books. The inspiration behind the novel lies in an event from the untamed Florida frontier at the turn of the twentieth century, in which an Everglades sugar planter and outlaw finds his violent career brought to an end at the hands of his neighbours. His son Lucius becomes obsessed with the killing, and his investigation is to prove a life-changing experience. Matthiessen's trilogy enjoyed great acclaim when it originally appeared in the 1990s, and its incarnation as a single volume will please a new generation of readers – at least those readers prepared to settle in for a long (but rewarding) haul.

FRANK TALLIS (Early Twentieth-century Vienna)

A middle-aged man begins a punishing climb. On reaching the summit, he is startled by an unexpected voice: 'Are you a doctor?'

He is not alone – it is a serving girl from his hotel. 'How did you know I'm a doctor?' he asks; she replies that it is in the visitors' book. She tells him that sometimes she can't breathe, and there's a hammering in her head. And something very disturbing happens. She sees things – a face that fills her with horror... The historical crime writer and clinical psychologist Frank Tallis is fond of relating this fragment of story: an isolated locale, an unexpected encounter, an unnerving confession. So what is it exactly? A little-known work by a celebrated crime writer? An early film by Alfred Hitchcock? Actually, it's neither. This is a précis of the first pages of 'Katharina' by Sigmund Freud, case number 4 in *Studies on Hysteria*, published in 1895. While the classic detective story may have sprung from the literary loins of Poe and co., there is an argument for the indirect cross-fertilisation of the genre via the influence of psychoanalysis. Freud has long been an *éminence grise* behind crime fiction, even appearing in person in such novels as Nicholas Meyer's *The Seven-Per-Cent Solution*, and Frank Tallis's fiction is transmuted through his own experiences as a clinician. His Liebermann Papers series, murder mysteries set in Freud's Vienna, makes assiduous use of psychology; Dr Max Liebermann is an early acolyte of Freud and utilises the new science of psychoanalysis as a forensic tool – a distinctive feature is his use of authentic techniques, such as the close observation of small errors and dream interpretation. Typically, plots revolve around an impossible crime in the context of some form of closed community: in *Mortal Mischief*, a spiritualist circle; in *Vienna Blood*, a proto-Nazi secret society; and in *Fatal Lies*, a military school.

Darkness Rising again airs key themes for Tallis: the conflict between reason and emotion, and the origins of National Socialism. The headless corpse of a monk is found in a baroque church, with a municipal councillor another decapitated victim. The murdered men were both passionate anti-Semites, and Vienna's Hassidic Jews appear to be the prime suspects. Psychoanalyst and police aide Max Liebermann may reject the religious certainties of his fellow Jews, but he is drawn into the world of the Kabbalah to discover a dangerous truth. While the mechanics of thriller plotting are handled as adroitly as ever, Tallis has perhaps made a rod for his own back.

The anti-Semitism theme is so trenchantly handled (Liebermann outrages a priest by an act of kindness – preventing the last rites being given to a dying man unaware of his state – and makes himself a target) that the reader may wonder why Tallis doesn't just write about the hothouse mores of turn-of-the-century Vienna, *sans* the mystery elements.

There are three more books in the series. *Deadly Communion*, a work that flirts with gothic tropes, *Death and the Maiden* – the plot of which revolves around several of Tallis's musical obsessions – and *Mephisto Waltz*, in which Liebermann and Detective Inspector Oskar Rheinhardt descend into the underworld of early twentieth-century anarchism.

LISA APPIGNANESI (Belle Époque France)

Polish by birth, Canadian by upbringing and British by adoption, Lisa Appignanesi is a novelist, non-fiction writer and broadcaster with a notable enthusiasm for the defence of literary freedom (she is Chair of the Royal Society of Literature and a former president of English PEN). Her dark psychological thrillers such as *Paris Requiem*, *Sanctuary* and *The Dead of Winter* prod at the parameters of genre fiction. Her most distinguished historical novel is *Sacred Ends*, a follow-up to *Paris Requiem*. Set in the Loire Valley in 1900, the heroine Marguerite is dispatched from Paris to the country at the request of her husband, the Comte de Landois. There, she becomes entangled in a mélange of death and secrets, and, when a girl goes missing, she calls upon Chief Inspector Durand of the Paris Sûreté, a strongly drawn character.

GILLIAN LINSCOTT (Early Twentieth-century England)

The prolific and reliable Linscott also writes as Caro Peacock (her Liberty Lane series is set in Victorian London), but under the Linscott moniker she is the author of the award-winning series about the suffragette detective Nell Bray. The series begins with *Sister Beneath the Sheet*, while impressive later entries include *Dead Man's Music* and *The Perfect Daughter*.

🎤 **Interview: Gillian Linscott**

In *Blood on the Wood*, the eleventh outing for my Suffragette detective Nell Bray, she decides to steal a valuable painting – with the highest motives, of course, and for the sake of the cause. In the course of the theft she stumbles over the body of a fiddle-playing girl, engaged to a socialist folk singer who had acquired two fiancées at the same time – also with the highest motives. One of the recurring themes of the series is that high motives usually lead to bad trouble, especially for Nell. I chose a Suffragette central character because I was interested in women who mostly came from a class on the respectable side of the law finding themselves on the wrong side of it. But I didn't want to make it too dark and serious. There were wild and witty women among the Suffragettes. In real life they carried out stunts such as invading the House of Commons terrace from the Thames with grappling irons, floating over London in a balloon hurling out leaflets, and climbing on roofs to break up meetings addressed by government ministers. In the course of the series I've followed Nell from her decision to throw herself into the struggle for the vote as an Oxford student in 1900 (*Dead Man Riding*) through to the point where the battle is won and she stands for election to parliament in 1918 (*Absent Friends*). The books were not written or published in chronological order and all the early ones are out of print. This makes things more challenging than I'd intended for new readers wanting to follow her career and I'm sorry about that. Nell has served several prison terms, escaped from Holloway, swapped wisecracks with George Bernard Shaw, exchanged lies with Lloyd George, climbed Mont Blanc and mucked out goats in an anarchist commune. While taking some liberties with history, I've kept faithful to the big events of the Suffragette campaign and sometimes used them as the starting point of the books, like the firebomb attack on a house belonging to Lloyd George or the great march through London before George V's coronation. This may be the last Nell Bray, for a while at any rate. I'm not killing her off but have decided to give her a rest.

CHARLES TODD (Post-World War One England)

'Charles Todd' is actually the mother-and-son writing team of Caroline and Charles Todd, residents of the East Coast of the US. Charles in particular was fascinated by the history of Britain and the couple have taken many trips to England, utilising their travels in their subsequent work. A typical novel is *Racing the Devil*, in which Inspector Ian Rutledge (in the nineteenth outing in this series) investigates a case with tentacles reaching back to World War One. The case begins on the eve of the Battle of the Somme with a group of English officers promising that, if they survive the war, they will meet in Paris a year after the fighting ends. Consistency is the watchword of the Todd duo.

DENNIS LEHANE (1910s America)

Celebrated as one of the most accomplished of modern-day American crime writers, Dennis Lehane has also demonstrated a particular interest in America's past. In *The Given Day*, he creates a panoply of Boston during a turbulent period of the city's history – the years 1918 and 1919. Featuring several real-life characters, Lehane's epic incorporates everything from Bolshevist revolutionaries to an unmotivated police force, viewing history through the lives of two families, one black and one white. With matchless storytelling and historical grasp, Lehane demonstrates the sheer reach of his ambition.

ANDREW MARTIN (Edwardian England, 1920s India)

Do you have a keen interest in British history at the start of the last century? Or a taste for finely honed crime novels with plotting as precise as a Swiss watch? Or perhaps a nostalgia for the age of steam? If the answer to all these questions is yes, then Andrew Martin is very much your man. But even if you only checked one of these three, this quirky and highly individual writer will not only get under your skin, he'll convince you that you knew far more about the early twentieth century than you thought you did. In his earlier novels, *The Necropolis Railway* and *The Blackpool Highflyer*, Martin (who is as quiet and unassuming in person as you might expect such an accumulator of facts to be) synthesised something new in the historical crime field: the author's relish for the glorious age of the locomotive was injected into crime narratives dispatched with a real Dickensian relish, and this fog-shrouded world was evoked with a vividness reminiscent of the Victorian Master. Murderous happenings are orchestrated in this Edwardian universe with great panache, and the highly unlikely figure of ex-railway worker Jim Stringer going up against evil criminal masterminds is genuinely piquant. If *The Lost Luggage Porter*, steam detective Jim Stringer's third outing, seems to lack the freshness of its predecessors, that's not really Martin's fault – perhaps the conjuring tricks of the first two books are becoming familiar to us. But admirers of Stringer's earlier cases will still find much to divert them. Jim is depressed by the fact that his days of driving steam engines are over. But his new job as an undercover railway detective gives him little time to lament over things past. With his wife pregnant and a boss who couldn't give a damn about Jim's work, he finds the world of station pickpockets and other minnows of York's criminal classes challenging enough. And then, in a cramped, smoky pub, he finds himself on the trail of a lethal and insane villain who is in a different league altogether. Whether or not you share the writer's love of Yorkshire – and even if you're someone whose hackles rise on encountering professional Yorkshiremen – this is a book to have you looking at timetables for the next train to York. Absolutely delectable stuff, with the historical (and local) detail seamlessly integrated into a mystifying narrative.

After outings for Stringer in World War One France and then Baghdad, the ninth book in the series, *Night Train to Jamalpur*, finds him in India in 1923. Martin's reliable protagonist, now Captain Jim Stringer, has been seconded to the East Indian Railway; his job is to check on security arrangements. And as so often before with Martin's doughty period sleuth, a routine assignment suddenly acquires massive – and dangerous – implications. A brutal murder takes place on the night train from Calcutta to Jamalpur; the victim is a wealthy Anglo-Indian who is shot in the first-class sleeping compartment adjacent to Jim Stringer's own (these things happen frequently in crime fiction). The first traces of evidence point to a straightforward robbery, but then Jim begins to suspect that he himself was the intended target. The first-class compartments of these trains have begun to be very dangerous – lethal king cobras have been placed in them to murderous effect – and it's not clear whether a lone psychopath is to blame or whether the deaths are a manifestation of the political turmoil that is beginning to grip India. As snakes are being used as potential murder weapons, Jim begins to look into the remunerative snake trade of the teeming city of Calcutta – with further complications provided by his daughter's ill-advised relationship with a maharajah's son. For some time, Martin held down a parallel career as a quirky and wry journalist and broadcaster. He made off-beat programmes about, and wrote articles on, such subjects as domestic husbandry of the past and the charisma of Mick Jagger. But those who admire such splendid Martin literary efforts as *The Necropolis Railway* and *Murder at Deviation Junction* will be glad he now seems to be concentrating his efforts on books as sheerly enjoyable as *Night Train to Jamalpur*. Once again Martin sports his customary sparky characterisation and is shored up by the most richly imagined foreign and period detail. If the development of the plot here stretches credulity a little more than usual, few will have cause to complain given the narrative skill that Martin demonstrates. And, as ever, a love of vintage steam railways is not necessary to enjoy the proceedings – although it might help.

In *Soot*, the year is 1799 and we are in Andrew Martin's native town of York, which he writes about with authenticity and historical detail that brings the late eighteenth-century landscape and its brilliant characters to life. Written in epistolary format true to the period, we follow the tale of Fletcher Rigge, a young felon who, to keep himself out of prison, has been given the task of finding the murderer of a silhouette artist, stabbed to death by the tools of his trade, a pair of scissors. The murderer, he concludes, must be one of the artist's recent sitters, but all Fletcher has to identify the suspects are their silhouette portraits, known as 'shades', so he embarks on a journey into the shadows encountering memorable victims and villains along the way.

🎤 **Interview: Andrew Martin**

In early books featuring my Edwardian railwayman, Jim Stringer, I overdid the period detail, like a kid colouring in so fervently that he tears a hole in the page. Later, I relaxed into using small, telling details, for example (in *Death on a Branch Line*) a ladder propped against a hedge in the deep English countryside of 1911... When writing my latest novel, *Soot*, which is set in York in 1799, I had access to mouldering copies of the *York Courant* newspaper. The front pages were given over to horses for sale, upcoming phases of the moon, and pleas for money by debtors. So I was straight into that world. I generally avoid reading historical crime novels, preferring books from the actual past. While I'm happy to make my own distortions of history, I don't want to apprehend somebody else's, and all my favourite crime writers are dead anyway: Doyle, Hammett, Simenon. For a period template, you need a book from the time written in language that is lively and representative *of* the time. For Edwardian language I read Arnold Bennett, for late eighteenth-century English, Fanny Burney.

Concerning authors who've influenced me... one reason I became a historical crime writer was because I so much enjoyed *The Name of the Rose*, which I read on publication, and found totally immersive, but when I picked it up again recently I couldn't get beyond page 30. Perhaps only the young can experience time travel. I have no overview of the genre except to say that it is castigated as a ghetto within a ghetto, and uncool: comfort reading for grannies. But I am stuck with writing historical crime because I love crime fiction and it's easier to evoke the past than the globalised present. I mean, who can be bothered to describe a McDonald's restaurant?

JODY SHIELDS (1910 Vienna)

Hardly surprising that DM Thomas provided an encomium for *The Fig Eater*, as his *The White Hotel* similarly dealt with Freudian sexuality. Shields utilises the same heightened prose in *The Fig Eater*, her tale of murder and eroticism in the hothouse atmosphere of Vienna at the beginning of the twentieth century. The strangulation of a young girl is worrying the Chief Inspector of Police, but his wife Erszébet becomes obsessed with the murder victim and begins a clandestine investigation of her own. Shields adroitly marries the heady psychopathology of her characters with a rigorous narrative.

ROBERT OLEN BUTLER (1914 Mexico)

With echoes of Arturo Pérez-Reverte's colourful, kinetic fare, this is lively historical crime from Pulitzer Prize-winning Robert Olen Butler. *The Hot Country* is the first of an ambitious three-part series featuring determined American war correspondent Christopher

'Kit' Marlowe Cobb. On the surface, it appears to be a cocktail of adventure, romance and espionage, but it's soon apparent that the novel is not only shot through with keen intelligence but couched in elegant prose. The author's own experience as a counter-intelligence agent grants verisimilitude, despite the period setting. It's 1914, and Cobb is covering the Mexican Civil War. As bullets fly, he is in pursuit of a German diplomat en route to a meeting with the larger-than-life revolutionary leader Pancho Villa. But encounters with a strong-willed young Mexican woman, a slippery double agent and an enigmatic sniper make Cobb's trip a lively one, both for him and for the reader.

🎤 Interview: Robert Olen Butler

I am deeply drawn to the 1914–18 era for a number of reasons. War, terrorism, genocide, tsunamis of immigrants, cultural identity, minority and women's rights, brand new technologies that are massively effective at killing, world leaders ranging from ineffectual to evil. In other words, the world of 1914–18 had all the same issues as 2014–18 (and I daresay beyond). So I can write about fascinating history while writing about our alarming present. As for 'noir' itself, I think the classic understanding of a noir central character as a wickedly motivated, blindly driven, morally empty loser who, even if he seems to end up okay, in fact ends up disastrously, is also a fitting description of those two historical periods. The era of my Cobb novels and the present era are *themselves* classic central characters in a vast noir novel entitled *The Human Condition*.

MICHAEL PEARCE (Edwardian Cairo)

One of the most entertaining sequences in crime fiction is Michael Pearce's ingenious Mamur Zapt mysteries. His protagonist, who has been granted the title Mamur Zapt, is a Welsh captain serving as the British Chief of the Secret Police in Edwardian Cairo, ostensibly answering to the Khedive, but ultimately to his British masters. We have observed Gareth Owen's inner struggle over his duties on many occasions, but they are handled in *A Cold Touch of Ice* with a sharply observed and satisfying skill, set against a colourful new cast of characters. As usual, Owen's Welshness grants him an anti-establishment sympathy with the Egyptian natives, and the greatest possible use is made of richly delineated local colour. In fact, the cosmopolitan setting, with its heady mix of religions and social divisions, always affords even more pleasure than the convoluted plots – here initiated by a heated political discussion followed by a brutal murder, with Owen obliged to balance the demands of natural justice and political expediency. In a series as long-running as this, refreshing the customary ingredients must be a Herculean task, but such is Pearce's understated professionalism that we are never conscious of having encountered these particular situations before.

Other key books: *The Mamur Zapt and the Return of the Carpet*, *The Night of the Dog*, *The Mark of the Pasha*.

ELIZABETH PETERS (Turn of the Century Egypt)

At the start of *The Golden One*, Elizabeth Peters' fourteenth adventure for Amelia Peabody (which continues the wartime theme begun in *Lord of the Silent*), it is New Year's Eve 1917. Risking winter storms and German torpedoes, the Emersons are heading for Egypt once again: Amelia, Emerson, their son Ramses and his wife Nefret (the series is also something of a family saga, introducing various friends and relatives). Emerson is counting on a long season of excavation without distractions, but this proves to be a forlorn hope. Yet again they unearth a dead body in a looted tomb – not a mummified one, though; this one is only too fresh – and it leads the clan on a search for the man who has threatened them with death if they pursue the excavations. If that wasn't distraction enough, Nefret reveals a secret she has kept hidden: there is reason to believe that Sethos, master criminal and spy, may be helping the enemy. It's up to the Emersons to find out, and either prove his innocence or prevent him from betraying Britain's plans to take Jerusalem and win the war in the Middle East. Elizabeth Peters (the pen name of Barbara Mertz) was a highly prolific writer with well over 50 novels to her credit, and Amelia Peabody Emerson, her Egyptologist lady sleuth, is a strong creation. At times, Peters' books are workaday, but *The Golden One* is more assured and among her best work.

STEFANIE PINTOFF (1900s New York)

The 2010 winner of the Edgar Award for the best first crime novel, *In the Shadow of Gotham* arrives with something of a reputation to live up to, and it's heartening to report that it does just that. Stefanie Pintoff's artfully constructed serial killer thriller does, admittedly, recycle some familiar elements, but with an imaginative spin that revivifies them. The setting is New York at the beginning of the last century, and a demented killer is wreaking havoc. Detective Simon Ziele has lost his fiancée in a ferry disaster, and is attempting to assuage his grief in a country town near Manhattan. But his involvement in the case begins when a young girl is beaten to death in her bedroom. Criminologist Alistair Sinclair spots a link relating to the remarks of one of his unstable research subjects, and the two men attempt to discover whether the patient (who has a history of violent behaviour) is really a dangerous killer to be reckoned with. There is a pleasing mix here of streamlined plotting and copious, sweeping period atmosphere. It is a debut to take note of.

JED RUBENFELD (Early Twentieth-century New York)

The Interpretation of Murder, the first novel by Princeton philosophy graduate Jed Rubenfeld, represented something of an act of will on the part of the author. Rubenfeld (a professor of constitutional and criminal law at Yale) had written non-fiction and books on his specialist subjects before, which sold (at his own estimate) 'about six copies'. But the author hankered for book sales that at least crept into double figures, and decided to take the route that had brought Umberto Eco such phenomenal success: he would write a 'popular' historical thriller – one with ideas freighted into the context of assiduously researched historical detail. But is *The Interpretation of Murder* as audacious a piece of work as Eco's *The Name of the Rose*? Certainly, Rubenfeld showed real acumen in the choice of the acorn from which his novel grew. In 1909, Sigmund Freud arrived in New York on the steamship *George Washington*. The details of his stay in the city are shrouded in mystery, but it left a psychological scar on the father of psychoanalysis. Freud was haunted by something that happened to him during his brief Manhattan sojourn, and ever after blamed several neuroses on the despised city of New York.

What happened to Freud? Writers in more specialist fields may come up with an answer some day, but Rubenfeld's brilliant conceit is to weave this real-life event into an accomplished fictional thriller, with the glittering, normal-seeming façade of New York concealing dark secrets – a Freudian metaphor, in fact. On the morning that Freud arrives in New York, the body of a beautiful debutante is discovered strangled in her sumptuous penthouse. Then another young member of the social elite, Nora Acton, is found tied to a chandelier, her body mutilated, and her mind damaged by the assault – she has no memory of it and cannot identify her attacker. Dr Stratham Younger, a student of the new science of psychoanalysis, is a dedicated admirer of its Viennese founder, and takes it upon himself to ask the man he so admires to aid him in analysing this beautiful and damaged young victim. All three individuals – Younger, Freud and Nora – are to discover unpalatable truths. With the stolid and difficult Freud as the anchor of his narrative, Rubenfeld takes the reader on a beguiling tour of the opium dens of Chinatown, the haunts of the rich at Gramercy Park and even the subterranean construction site of the new Manhattan Bridge under the East River (Rubenfeld is well aware that tunnels will be open to interpretation here!). If Rubenfeld lacks the rigour of a more experienced novelist in fusing the disparate elements in his narrative, his admiration for the troubled Freud carries all before it.

ROBERT RYAN (World War One Europe)

Does most fiction really take us into a fully imagined world? Many of us would say we are fully conversant with the Victorian universe of Sherlock Holmes: the cobbled streets, the hansom cabs, the all-pervasive fog. But an examination of Doyle's writing shows that he can occasionally be parsimonious with detail, and our mental picture is crammed with imagery supplied by innumerable film and television adaptations – not to mention Sidney Paget's illustrations, which furnished the deerstalker unmentioned by Holmes's creator. Robert Ryan would probably be the first to admit that – whatever his skills – he is not in Doyle's class as a writer, but *Dead Man's Land* reminds us that Ryan is one of the most evocative and assiduous conjurors of the past in historical fiction. This book presents a striking vision of the trenches of World War One, with the scorched countryside, the ever-present 'monstrous anger of the guns' (as Wilfred Owen had it) and the stink of gunpowder and burning flesh stunningly realised. Doyle would simply not have been interested in packing in so much detail and atmosphere. But was Ryan right to take this approach in a new series featuring a volunteer medical man aiding the wounded in France? Particularly as that medical man is none other than Dr John Watson, late of Baker Street, London. Many writers have taken up the Doyle baton – with mostly workaday results, but, with *Dead Man's Land*, Ryan joins the ranks of those who have done something radical with the legacy, and the masterstroke is to put Watson into a setting where death is ever present. The doctor (who has had an acrimonious disagreement with Holmes) is working with the Royal Army Medical Corps in France when a series of deaths takes place, quite unlike the wholesale slaughter of the trenches, involving bodies decorated with Roman numerals. Watson is obliged to investigate and the flare-lit horrors of the Great War become the stage for grisly nocturnal graveyard raids and a mystery quite as baffling as any Watson encountered back in England. Given Ryan's expertise, it's hardly surprising that Watson emerges as a fully rounded, conflicted figure here, although it has to be said that he is quite some distance from the figure created by Doyle. But that's not all this novel has to offer, as Watson realises that his carefully ordered hierarchical society – even when transplanted abroad – is the most fragile of constructs. Less fragile is the relationship between the warring Watson and Holmes, and we read on in hopes of a reconciliation. It's a brave – or foolhardy – writer who takes up the Conan Doyle baton, but with *Dead Man's Land* Robert Ryan places Dr John Watson in the perfect setting. At a time when Sherlockian recreations are ten-a-penny, Ryan's 'Dr Watson at War' series seems likely to be the one that would most have won the approval of Conan Doyle himself.

In the third book in the series, the mesmerising *A Study in Murder*, the year is 1917 and Sherlock Holmes's amanuensis is a prisoner of war in a brutal camp in Germany. The Allied blockade of the country has made food scarce at the camp, and when a new prisoner is killed, the assumption is that he has been murdered for his Red Cross parcel. Watson, however, has been trained by example never to accept the obvious conclusion. However, when it is discovered that there is an escape plan being hatched in his hut, Watson is sentenced to solitary confinement. Grimly he realises that the options open to him are escape or death. But an escape might require some help from a distance, via a brilliant friend and colleague… He is once again required to put into practice the investigative technique he has learned from Holmes, and the audacious setting here – the dangerous world of a POW camp where life is cheap – pays dividends, moving into territory that Conan Doyle's sleuthing duo could not tackle. *A Study in Murder* is proof that this is one of the strongest series in historical crime fiction – and one of the best entries in the post-canon Holmes and Watson library.

Interview: Robert Ryan

I came to World War One by accident (as did many of the warring nations). Sometime in the 1990s, before I was a published author, while on a rainy holiday in Devon, I picked a book off the hotel's bookcase. It was Jack Tracy's *Encyclopaedia Sherlockiana* (I was previously a devotee of both the Arthur Conan Doyle canon and the Jeremy Brett/Granada Holmes). Here, I was reminded that in 'His Last Bow', set in 1914, Conan Doyle claimed that Watson was 'rejoining his old service'. Which was by then called the Royal Army Medical Corps. A doctor in the trenches. Who knows a little bit about detecting. Or knows a man who does, anyway. It crossed my mind that someone really should write the story of Watson in the RAMC during World War One. Little did I know it would be me. After a spell writing about World War Two, my publisher asked me if I fancied producing a novel about a detective in the trenches. Sure, I said. I did some research and came back to report that, logistically, it was hard to make it feel authentic (most policemen were busy tracking down deserters behind the lines). But what about a *doctor*? In fact, what about Dr Watson? It would be written in the third person (unlike the majority of the original stories, but like 'His Last Bow'), not a pastiche, and with Watson acting (mostly) alone in solving murders. Sold. It was only then I realised I not only had to get World War One and the trenches right, I had to keep the Holmes community happy by honouring Arthur Conan Doyle's creation *and* research medical procedures in the war. What was I thinking? So the first book (*Dead Man's Land*) took the best part of 18 months to write, but, with the groundwork done, the next three came easier.

Of my fellow authors in the field, I am always drawn back to Philip Kerr and Bernie Gunther, his 'gumshoe' during the Nazi period. The first trilogy just redefined the idea of the man who must walk mean streets for me. Not every entry in the series is five star, but the character remains so, and Kerr seems to have caught a second wind of late. When I was doing the Dr Watson World War One series, I went back to four little-known Gavin Lyall novels about the early days of the Secret Service – *Spy's Honour, Flight from Honour, All Honourable Men* and *Honourable Intentions*. Excellent period detail plus well-drawn characters, although the plots are not as sharp as his early thrillers (and probably not quite noir enough for Mr Forshaw). For something outside my comfort zone, I turn to Lloyd Shepherd's Charles (and Abigail) Horton's adventures from *The English Monster* onwards, which tick all my boxes. And what are those boxes? I want an unusual setting (think *The Devil in the Marshalsea*, perhaps) or protagonist (William Ryan's conflicted Korolev in Soviet-era Moscow is a favourite), a sense of place (Alan Furst's strong suit is surely atmosphere), and a heinous crime helps, as does some subtle historical education.

ANNE PERRY (World War One Europe)

In Anne Perry's *At Some Disputed Barricade*, Joseph Reavley is a chaplain serving close to the dangerous world of no man's land on the Western Front in 1917. It is his job to keep the morale of his men high, a nigh-impossible task. And there are rumours of mutiny, which makes his job even more difficult. Then an officer dies, and several soldiers are arrested – and it becomes Joseph's task to find out exactly what happened. The World War One books are something of a departure for Anne Perry, whose better known series are set in Victorian London, but then difficult moral choices have always been her speciality – and that consideration is to the fore here.

RAY CELESTIN (Early Twentieth-century New Orleans)

With a variety of unlikely real-life figures being dragooned as sleuths in crime fiction, perhaps jazz trumpeter Louis Armstrong is not such a stretch – Celestin's remarkable debut novel places him as one of a group on the trail of a serial axe murderer in early twentieth-century

New Orleans. *The Axeman's Jazz* gleaned awards and sports an acute sense of period, shored up by an echo of the sound of early jazz – no easy thing on the page. *Dead Man's Blues*, which also features Louis Armstrong, moves forward to Chicago in the 1920s.

TV: PEAKY BLINDERS (various directors)

Steven Knight's larger-than-life family gangster epic set in Birmingham in the years immediately after the First World War has forged something of a cult following over several seasons, not least because of the charismatic turn by Cillian Murphy as ruthless and ambitious gang boss Tommy Shelby. The title refers to the razor blades sewn into the peaks of gang members' caps.

Film: DR CRIPPEN (Robert Lynn, director)

Once a difficult-to-see movie, this sombre 1963 drama features Donald Pleasence, impeccably cast as the henpecked murderer who found his nemesis in (then) modern technology. Robert Lynn's direction is pedestrian, but the subject fascinates. Playing entertainingly over the top is Coral Browne as the strident, blowsy Mrs Crippen, irritating enough to have the most pacifist of viewers nurturing murderous thoughts.

9: The Twenties and Thirties

ABIR MUKHERJEE (Raj India)

The personable Abir Mukherjee grew up in Glasgow – hence the beguiling Scottish accent – before turning to crime (of the fictional variety). His first Captain Sam Wyndham novel, *A Rising Man*, was widely praised as an odyssey into the dark underbelly of the British Raj in 1919. In his second, equally successful novel, *A Necessary Evil*, the heir to the throne of a fabulously wealthy kingdom is both liberal and a moderniser and has (unsurprisingly) upset the hardline religious elements of his country; Mukherjee draws some provocative modern parallels with theocratic intolerance. The heir is assassinated in the presence of Captain Wyndham and the investigation that follows proves to be very dangerous indeed. Defeating the dread 'second novel syndrome', *A Necessary Evil* is every bit as lively and mesmerising an experience as its predecessor.

JACQUELINE WINSPEAR (Post-World War One)

Famous for her popular Maisie Dobbs series, Winspear has bagged a variety of awards and her industrious writing ethos is impressive. The first Maisie Dobbs novel (which simply bears her name) tells readers that, when World War One broke out, she went to the front as a nurse. After the war, she sets up as a private investigator and takes on a case of infidelity with surprising ramifications. The series has built up a considerable following over the years.

ANDREW ROSENHEIM (1930s America)

Frederick Forsyth may have said that he wrote *The Day of the Jackal* purely for the money; however, he not only created what remains his signature book but also forged a genre that is still in rude health: the planned assassination of a real-life public figure which is foiled at the last minute. The latest flowering of the concept is Andrew Rosenheim's accomplished *Fear Itself*, set in the turbulent political world of 1930s America, and the target is President Franklin Roosevelt. But when does a relatively heterogeneous clutch of novels form themselves into a recognisable genre? Perhaps when critical mass is achieved thanks to a series of first-rate entries – such as Rosenheim's book.

In the late 1930s, America is flinching under the Depression. As Europe moves inexorably closer to bloody conflict, America is pulling up the drawbridge, reluctant to identify Germany as a potential nemesis – not least because of its millions of citizens with German ancestry. The FBI is a tyro organisation and not yet the monolith it will become. Jimmy Nessheim, a special agent keen to prove himself, takes on the risky assignment of infiltrating the Bund, a German-American organisation which makes no secret of its passionately held pro-Nazi views. The Bund has one overriding agenda: to bring a halt to President Roosevelt's efforts to sabotage Hitler's ruthless empire building. Jimmy, moving closer to the heart of the powerful association, discovers that there are those prepared to take the fight to the White House in the most direct fashion, with nothing less than the murder of Franklin Delano Roosevelt. There is a host of felicities crammed into this complex and ambitious thriller, not least the sweeping and cogent creation of an America struggling to stay free of the firestorm about to engulf the world. Both the Bund itself and the upper echelons of Washington society are forged with a dynamic that rivals such heavyweights as Gore Vidal, but Rosenheim isn't quite able to pull off the key trick that Forsyth did: orchestrate the suspense around the murder of a world leader that we know did not take place. But in the context of his considerable achievement, this particular caveat doesn't seem too important.

🎙 **Interview: Andrew Rosenheim**

My trilogy of Nessheim novels is set in America in the years just before and during World War Two. All three are what I would call 'realistic counter-factuals' – each is about a conspiracy that doesn't succeed but would have changed history if it had. In *Fear Itself*, for example, Roosevelt decides to run for a third term as President in 1940 because he thought only he could bring America into the war against Germany. His assassination before the election might well have kept America on the sidelines, and from this my plot emerged. Similarly, *The Informant* is based on the fact that, although the Soviet Union learned of Japan's plans to attack America at Pearl Harbor, it didn't tell the United States – with German battalions threatening Moscow itself by December 1941, the Soviets were desperate to have America drawn into a Pacific war, and thus keep Japan from joining the German invasion. In the last of the three, *The Accidental Agent*, Allied efforts to build an atomic bomb were accompanied by Allied fears that the Germans were building one as well. This is my favourite of the three; it has the strongest characterisation, I think, and is set mostly where I grew up in Chicago.

Of contemporary writers in the field, I think no one approaches le Carré at his best (all the Smiley novels) – and few are close to even his less than best. I also read Philip Kerr's books with consistent appreciation and enjoyment, as I do the work of Alan Furst and Joe Kanon. Charles McCarry remains too little known. I admire Raymond Chandler for prose that is very much of its time and place, yet remains uniquely fresh – no mean feat. Historical thrillers, in my view, have to tread a fine line between authenticity and overkill. Too much period detail is the most common mistake – as if the writer can't bear to let any research go unused. I think here less is invariably more. You need a light but confident touch to carry it off, rather than a history degree...

BARBARA CLEVERLY (1920s India and Europe)

The world of historical mysteries had reason to be grateful when Barbara Cleverly gave up her career as a schoolteacher to write bustling, generously populated novels. The first series featured Scotland Yard detective Joe Sandilands and utilised a colonial Indian setting in the 1920s. The inaugural book in the series, *The Last*

Kashmiri Rose, has her expat policeman on the point of returning home when he becomes involved in a possible suicide. The background of India during the Raj is one of the particular pleasures of the series, and in order to freshen the brew, Cleverly took her detective to England at the time of the general strike in *The Bee's Kiss*, and she also moved across the Channel to France, notably in *Folly du Jour*.

Her sequence featuring aspiring archaeologist Laetitia Talbot is her ace in the hole. Typically diverting is her novel *A Darker God*, set in 1928. In the open-air theatre of Dionysus, Laetitia observes a performance of an Ancient Greek tragedy. The synthetic violence onstage is to be matched by the real thing offstage.

GILBERT ADAIR (1930s and 1940s Britain)

In an age in which fiction teems with scalpel-wielding psychopaths and alcoholic coppers, is there still room for crime novels of a more genteel demeanour? Written by novelists who set their faces against cutting-edge grittiness and embrace the gentler, never-never land of an earlier era? The late Gilbert Adair clearly thought so, and *A Mysterious Affair of Style*, the second novel featuring his middle-aged female sleuth Evadne Mount, attempts once again to pull off a double whammy: a reinvention/recreation of the Golden Age crime novel à la Christie, and simultaneously a ruthless parody of the fripperies and absurdities of that era. Does Adair repeat the trick of his earlier *The Act of Roger Murgatroyd*? The answer to that is not as clear-cut as it might initially seem. Adair had an impressive panoply of cultural references, displayed proudly and entertainingly in his books – the first line in *A Mysterious Affair of Style* is the exclamation 'Great Scott Moncrieff!!!' (though the reference to Proust's translator doesn't actually have any relevance beyond showing us we are in for a clever spoof). Adair clearly yearned for a variety of crime fiction in which the spilling of entrails was done tastefully offstage, and pleasure was simply to be found in the solving of an ingenious puzzle – the very artificiality, in fact, that Raymond Chandler so ruthlessly anatomised in an essay, using the darker reality of American crime fiction as a stick with which to beat the thin-blooded British variety of the day. But Adair was having none of Chandler's caveats, and threw himself enthusiastically into the well-heeled 1940s milieu that clearly got his creative juices flowing.

It's a decade since the murder case that Evadne Mount tackled in *The Act of Roger Murgatroyd*, and she accidentally runs into her lugubrious ex-colleague, retired Chief Inspector Trubshawe. The duo are soon on the track of a clever killer who has murdered an actress on the film set of a director (modelled on Hitchcock), even as the cameras rolled. As in classic Christie, we are presented with five suspects who might have slipped the dead woman the poisonous draught. The characterisations here are as outrageously over the top as ever, and the skill with which Adair reinvigorated the tropes of the Golden Age affords some light-hearted fun. But there is a problem with this one that is less evident in its predecessor: Adair so unerringly pointed up the silliness and contrivance of this kind of vintage narrative that the book finally functions only on the level of a rather cold-eyed detonation of the genre. It's almost as if Chandler – with all his loathing of the era – had written a merciless Christie pastiche in order to drive a final nail into the old girl's coffin.

ALISON JOSEPH (1920s Britain)

The British novelist Alison Joseph began her career as a documentary director, making programmes for Channel 4, and has also written for radio, including adaptations of Simenon's *Maigret*. Her signature crime series, which she started in 1993, features the sleuthing nun Sister Agnes, but she has penned a newer series set in the 1920s and featuring Agatha Christie as detective.

Key books: *Murder Will Out*, *Hidden Sins*.

🎙 **Interview: Alison Joseph**

In my historical novels I have found myself firmly in the 1920s, simply because of taking up the offer of writing Agatha Christie as a detective. Of the three novels so far, the first two are set when she's still married to Archie, and the third in 1928 when she is divorced. (I am deliberately ignoring 'The Disappearance', the flight to Harrogate.) For the fourth I am heading into the 1930s when she meets her second husband. Having only written contemporary novels up till now, it has been a revelation to discover the many possibilities of writing within a historical period. The most recent, *Death in Disguise*, is set in the world of theatre – the murder happens backstage at a variety show – and so deliberately plays with ideas of ártifice, disguise and make-believe. Given that I am writing a real person and placing her in a fictional world, the parallels are apposite. It has also given me the opportunity to rediscover the work of Agatha herself. As a teenage reader of the Christie oeuvre, so much went over my head – her wit, her extraordinary elegance and skill with plot.

Of my contemporaries, I really admire Walter Mosley, and I'm also reading a lot of Christopher Priest, who isn't really a crime writer but who has a fantastic page-turning quality in his work. I love being a crime writer. I know this is often said, but as a genre it can do anything. Within my crime novels I can write romance, I can reflect on the philosophical problem of evil, I can comment on historical change and, most importantly, I can tell a story that is un-put-downable.

NICOLA UPSON (1930s Britain)

There are two very different acts of reclamation taking place in Nicola Upson's *Fear in the Sunlight*: we are told that Alfred Hitchcock's seemingly unassuming wife Alma was central to his artistic achievement, and that he relied on her totally in both his personal and professional life; and, secondly, we are shown, sympathetically and unsensationally, the lives of gay women in the 1930s – principally via the crime author Josephine Tey, rejigged by Upson as an amateur detective herself. Actually, the timing of *Fear in the Sunlight* (with its clever use of the Hitchcocks at the centre of the narrative) could not have been more apposite: at the time of its publication, there were two films in production concerning different aspects of the life of England's greatest film director (the actors playing him – under varying degrees of prosthetics – were Anthony Hopkins and Toby Jones, while Helen Mirren and Imelda Staunton tackled Alma). But both of these films focused on the director's American sojourn: Upson's premise has the director making a 1936 visit to Portmeirion to set up a film of a Josephine Tey novel, finessing the reluctant novelist to sign away the rights. Hitchcock was known for his rather juvenile practical jokes, and Upson creates as much intrigue as to what these will be before the book's inevitable murder. The latter, when it happens, is of a Hollywood star, and Tey is obliged to help her policeman friend Archie Penrose, who has appeared in previous books in the series. The mechanics of the murder mystery are worked out with the panache that we have come to expect of this writer, but the real piquancy of the book perhaps lies in its understated feminist/lesbian slant. We are used to Upson presenting Tey as a more glamorous version of the real-life writer than historical facts might suggest, but the picture here of dealings between gay women in a far less liberated era has both truthfulness and sympathy, though – tendentiously – the men (Archie apart) are a sorry bunch. The presentation of Hitchcock's wife Alma Reville, a considerable film talent in her own right, is perhaps the book's most signal achievement; the various appearances of this deceptively self-effacing woman in the narrative provide a genuine frisson, and it might be argued that Upson has performed a re-evaluation of a neglected woman much as Claire Tomalin did for Dickens' lover Nelly Ternan. (Hitchcock himself is equally adroitly characterised, though the couple are prone to tell each other things that they already know, largely for the benefit of the reader.) There is, of course, no earnest proselytising – Upson never forgets that her principal job is to entertain. And – be assured – *Fear in the Sunlight* is highly engaging and intelligent entertainment.

There is a notable strand of Englishness (as opposed to Britishness) in the work of Upson – particularly so in *Nine Lessons*, a later entry in her distinctive historical series, in which Tey is once again dragooned into service as a detective. Apart from the felicitous evocation of a Cambridge setting, Upson references our greatest writer of ghost stories, MR James. Two decades after that writer chilled his colleagues at Kings College with his tales, Tey is spending Christmas in the town, which is gripped by fear because of a serial rapist. Detective Chief Inspector Archie Penrose teams up as before with Tey to solve a series of vicious murders, with the supernatural stories of James proving crucial to the mystery. As well as furnishing a superior piece of crime writing, Upson is perceptive on the place of women in unenlightened 1930s England.

DAN SMITH (1930s Ukraine)

Dry Season marked Dan Smith out as a writer well worth following, with a particularly acute sense of pace and ambience. The setting in *The Child Thief* is the Ukraine in December 1930. Luka, a war veteran, is trying to lead a quiet life with his family. As the brutal Soviet war machine approaches, his village has so far escaped its ravages. But then a stranger appears with a sled bearing a grim cargo. The villagers react violently, and are under the illusion that they have saved themselves from destruction. But in the ensuing violence, a little girl has disappeared, and Luka is the only man who has the ability to find out who could have abducted a child in this chilly landscape. What follows is a pursuit across a war-torn country, with human betrayal always as dangerous as any external threat. *The Child Thief* is delivered with tremendous authority and proves once again that Dan Smith is a writer to whom attention must be paid.

MARK SANDERSON (1930s London)

Over the centuries, much blood has been spilled in the antiseptic corridors of London's Smithfield market. Although the meat market itself is now surrounded by chi-chi bars and restaurants (with nary a bloodstained apron to be seen), there are signs that it is becoming a popular literary destination in the twenty-first century – with the blood flowing in new Smithfield-set novels human rather than animal. Recently, Frances Fyfield's *Cold to the Touch* married Smithfield and murder in sanguinary fashion, but Mark Sanderson's *Snow Hill* makes the earlier book look like *Heidi* in terms of copious bloodletting. And if that isn't enough to ruffle a few feathers, there is some startlingly graphic transgressive sex. The novel, set in an artfully realised London of the 1930s, is not (as they used to say) for one's maiden aunt. Sanderson is a boulevardier of wit and charm, with a gift for the outrageous. Ironically, this novel – despite its unblushing treatment of gay sexual encounters – is in fact more reticent than one might expect; the word 'gay', of course, never appears in the narrative in its modern sense. Struggling journo Johnny Steadman receives a tip-off about the death of a policeman at Snow Hill station, and thinks his luck is in. But Johnny finds himself blundering into a dark mélange of corruption and murder at the heart of the establishment.

To survive, he is even obliged to temporarily join the ranks of the dead and confront a psychotic man of power. The graphically treated male rape in Sanderson's trenchantly written novel is responsibly handled, but the narrative pulls few punches. The characterisation is functional rather than nuanced, but the author sports a narrative grasp that won't let the reader go. However, his ace in the hole is the portrayal of time and place: the London of the 1930s is conjured with immense skill, as are the less than enlightened attitudes of the day (notably towards homosexuality – the casual intolerance on display here is a salutary reminder of a distant time).

ANDREA MARIA SCHENKEL (1930s Munich)

Ice Cold by Andrea Maria Schenkel is set in Munich in the 1930s. This is a dangerous place for young women – particularly for those who cycle along the secluded country lanes on the outskirts of the city. A savage attacker is at work, killing his victims after raping them. The city breathes a sigh of relief when the murderer is caught – a member of the Nazi party, swiftly cut loose by his colleagues (he is an ethnic German – an Aryan – and not from one of the more convenient 'lesser' races, which would have been less embarrassing). The man, Josef Kalteis, is swiftly and expediently executed. But was he, in fact, guilty? Or is the real killer still on the loose? Kathie, young and pretty, takes the train to Munich, hunting for work. But her pipe dreams of success are quickly torpedoed as she sinks into a variety of emotionless sexual encounters and, inevitably, casual prostitution. Kathie struggles to achieve her naïve plans for happiness, but there is another cloud on the horizon apart from her dispiriting lifestyle: darkhaired and attractive, she conforms to the profile of the murderer's prey. And it isn't long before she's in mortal danger.

Schenkel's first book, *The Murder Farm*, marked her out as something very different from most female writers of crime fiction, even those prepared to venture into the more unsettling outer reaches of psychopathology. That first novel drew admiring comparisons to Truman Capote's *In Cold Blood*, as Schenkel tackled in similar fashion the murder of a farmer and his wife in a secluded farm; the use of a dispassionate, documentary-style assemblage of facts had a chilling cumulative effect. *Ice Cold* is more personal, placing the vulnerable Kathie at the centre of the narrative – and Schenkel adroitly involves us with the half-baked romantic dreams of her protagonist, even as we are irritated by her fecklessness. But that's only part of Schenkel's strategy. The pursuit of a serial killer in the Weimar Republic is conveyed through the distancing device of documents, flashbacks and even different fonts – but this hardly prepares us for the graphic horror of much of the narrative here. From the calculating propaganda of the Nazi politicians through the desperate lives of ordinary Munich citizens to the troubles of the sexually abused heroine, Schenkel ruthlessly marshals her material to fashion a novel that, for all its brevity, conveys an ambitious scale.

CATRIONA MCPHERSON (1920s Scotland)

Catriona McPherson's Dandy Gilver series appears to be firmly in the 'cosy' crime camp – but is it? The comparison evoked on the jackets is to Dan Brown and Barbara Pym, but McPherson is more intelligent than the former and more political than the latter. The books (such as *After the Armistice Ball*) demonstrate the author's faultless assimilation of this idiom: a genteel note is sounded throughout, with the middle-class Dandy, an amateur female sleuth in the 1920s, solving knotty mysteries. But McPherson is actually more postmodern than this might suggest; there's a subtle detonation of the cosy genre, soothing the reader while clandestinely taking on more serious concerns. *Dandy Gilver and the Proper Treatment of Bloodstains* is possibly the most radical in that sense, dealing with the politicisation of the serving classes and national strikes under cover of a murder-the-wife plot owing not a little to Patrick Hamilton's *Gaslight*. The nervous Mrs Balfour has a new maid who is not all that she seems. She is, in fact, a disguised Dandy Gilver, hired by the young wife to protect her from the murderous designs of her husband. But can Dandy (in between writing letters back to her husband, complaining about the strikes sweeping the country) foil this bit of domestic malfeasance? The tactics here include an acute sense of period, sharp observation of the mores of the day (both above and below stairs), a nicely judged infusion of humour and a winning (if unlikely) heroine. All this is 'cosy' enough, but Dandy's acid disapproval of the social upheavals of the day is not necessarily shared by her creator, and it is this meshing of gears that adds a piquancy to the untroubled surface of the novel.

MAREK KRAJEWSKI (1920s and 1930s Breslau)

The Polish author Marek Krajewski sets readers a knotty challenge in his rich and idiosyncratic Breslau novels. Atmosphere and piquant visualisation positively saturate the pages and push these books into the upper echelons of literary crime. But Krajewski's cynical, sybaritic Police Inspector Eberhard Mock – with his eternally unslaked appetites and cruel brutality to his beautiful wife Sophie – has the reader wondering: do we really want to spend time in the company of this unattractive protagonist? Krajewski, however, has second-guessed this possible objection: Mock, however unappealing, is not as off-putting as many of the characters he encounters in this privileged, decadent society, so we reluctantly accept him as our guide. *Death in Breslau* had critics scrabbling for superlatives, particularly thanks to Danusia Stok's pellucid translation, with Breslau (now Wrocław) portrayed as a cornucopia of lowlife crime and aristocratic debauchery in the years between the wars. In *The End of the World in Breslau*, Eberhard Mock, locked in a violent relationship with his young wife in a sumptuous mansion, is at home in this society, indulging in its vices with enthusiasm. The body of a man has been discovered bound and walled up alive, another has been dissected, his fingers chopped off. The victims have nothing in common – one is a locksmith, one a musician – but both are found with a calendar page with the date of their death marked in blood. Krajewski's caustic protagonist takes time off from his disintegrating marriage to plunge headlong into the bordellos, gambling joints and bath houses of Breslau to track down a particularly savage murderer. Mock is hardly in a position to make too many moral judgements, but even he is given pause by a series of drug-fuelled aristocratic orgies that have been concealed by an ingenious use of hypnosis. Meanwhile, Sophie, chafing at the abuse meted out by her husband, has initiated her own journey of sexual indulgence with her friend Elizabeth – and she comes into contact with a cryptic figure who is somehow feeding the apocalyptic fever sweeping 1920s Breslau.

Those exhausted by crime fiction set in the violent council estates of modern Britain will pounce on this ferocious odyssey into a lost world of decadence, class and deception. It's not a comfortable journey – particularly in the louche company of its antihero Mock – but Krajewski, as before, performs the key function of the skilful novelist: providing an entrée into a world so far from our own that the Breslau depicted here seems like some bizarre science fiction landscape. If you're looking for a taste of a more comforting age in your historical crime fiction, you'd better steer well clear of the lacerating narratives of Marek Krajewski.

KERRY JAMIESON (1930s New York)

Kerry Jamieson's *The Golden Door* is historical thriller writing of a rare order; characterisation and plotting are commanding, but it's Jamieson's grasp of the historical detail that really sets the seal upon the book – 1930s New York has rarely been evoked with such panache. More than 12 million immigrants entered the United States between 1892 and 1954 in search of a new life. Many were destitute, cast out from their homelands. Their journeys were fuelled by hope and expectation. The main building at Ellis Island was the 'Golden Door' through which all had to pass to gain entry to America. Inspections took place and records were kept. Although relatively few immigrants who landed at Ellis Island were denied entry, anyone who was sick was taken a few hundred feet across the water to Islands Two and Three. Here the diseased, insane, criminal and unwelcome were housed in preparation for deportation. And it was here where, some say, people disappeared. The main building has been restored and now stands as an impressive red brick structure for the tourist trade. But Islands Two and Three are completely untouched. The doors of the buildings are boarded up, the windows remain shattered and the place is dead. Ellis Island has many ghosts but it's the voices of those lost souls from these two islands that clamour loudest to be heard. Jamieson's novel plunges us into a sizzling summer. Irish immigrant Will Carthy works as a riveter on the tallest skyscraper in the world, spending his days high above the ground and fighting loneliness at night. When his half-sister Isobel sails out to join him, Will goes to meet her at Ellis Island but finds that she has vanished before passing through immigration control. Little by little, Will realises that something deeply sinister is behind Isobel's disappearance and that the answer might lie in an altogether wider arena of social and political ambition. *The Golden Door* brilliantly evokes Prohibition-era New York when the glittering towers of modern Manhattan were rising but, for some, the American Dream was collapsing around them. Kerry Jamieson was born in Durban and attended high school in South Africa, but then won a scholarship to study in the US, where she ended up living for six years, eventually making her home in New York. There, she fell in love with the city's history and spent hours in her favourite museums – the Ellis Island Museum and the Immigrant Museum.

TOM BRADBY (1920s China and New York)

Sometimes work appears that synthesises large-scale adventure, sharp historical detail and real storytelling smarts. *The Master of Rain* by Tom Bradby was such an entry, plunging readers headlong into a breathless tale of double-dealing and murder in 1920s Shanghai. A further virtue: Bradby never allows his sprawling canvas to overwhelm his beleaguered characters, who always remain in keen focus. Richard Field, Bradby's resourceful protagonist, has been seconded to the police force in the turbulent city of Shanghai. He finds a jostling throng of British imperial civil servants, American gunrunners and vicious Chinese gangsters. The grisly case he is landed with involves the mutilated body of a young White Russian woman, and Field discovers that her neighbour, Natasha Medvedev, is somehow crucial to the investigation. But Natasha's only agenda is self-preservation, and Field – unwisely – falls in love with her. Can he crack the mystery before the next victim is murdered – particularly as the signs are that it is to be Natasha? This is strong work from the author of the first-rate *Shadow Dancer*, masterly in its depiction of a beautiful, dirty and corrupt city and a population in thrall to the imperatives of the market: human life, like everything else in Shanghai, has its price. Field is the perfect guide to the glittering decay of the city, and his relationships (both with the beguiling Natasha and with the panoply of quirky, dangerous characters he encounters) are adroitly handled by an author who knows exactly what he's doing. Nearly 500 pages – but the reader will find that this one has the pace and compulsiveness of a short story.

Bradby's *Blood Money* displays the same effortless skill at handling both characterisation and tension, dispensed with maximum pace. The plot is very apropos in our modern age of financial meltdown: the setting is New York in 1929, and Joe Quinn of the NYPD has, as his first case, a banker plummeting from a Wall Street building, though all the signs suggest murder rather than despair at financial wipe-out. Other deaths occur, even more gruesome – and the connecting factor is the gangster Lucky Luciano...

MICHAEL RUSSELL (1930s New York)

Having already brought 1930s Dublin and Danzig vividly to life in his outstanding debut *The City of Shadows*, Russell does the same for New York in a sequel, *The City of Strangers*, which is even better. The unique complexity of Ireland's divided loyalties and enmities on the eve of World War Two takes Garda Sergeant Stefan Gillespie to America to apprehend a killer and is explored with unusual clarity and intelligence, while the suspense and tension are keenly maintained.

AC KONING (1920s and 1930s Europe)

AC Koning is the alter ego of award-wining novelist Christina Koning, whose nine published works include several novels with a historical setting. Her protagonist is Frederick Rowlands, a blind veteran of World War One, whose investigations take him from late 1920s London to Berlin in 1933. Over a series of novels – there are currently four – Rowlands is confronted with murder, betrayal, sexual jealousy and kidnapping – all taking place against a meticulously realised period setting. In keeping with the Golden Age tradition of the amateur detective, to which Koning's books pay homage, Rowlands is assisted in this endeavour by the reliably dour Inspector Douglas of the Metropolitan Police Force. The pair appear together in successive books, starting with *Line of Sight*, in which Rowlands, then working as a switchboard operator at a firm of City solicitors, overhears a conversation between his employer and a beautiful society lady, which may or may not point to murder. Because Rowlands is blind – the result of a shrapnel injury – he has to rely on his wits and on his formidable memory, leaving the police work to his professional colleague. This, too, is in the tradition of the gifted amateur sleuth, whose greatest asset is his intelligence. But Rowlands is no mere dilettante. A self-educated man from a working-class background, he has a natural authority that allows him to move effortlessly between different levels of society, in pursuit of those who have broken its laws. His on–off romance with the alluring Lady Celia, which is carried on over the series, is one illustration of this. Here, and in other narrative strands running throughout the books, Koning aims to capture something of the social fluidity of the period between the wars, as well as its political turmoil.

JILL PATON WALSH (1920s and 1950s Britain)

If you're a Dorothy Sayers fan who has been obliged to read the books featuring her aristocratic sleuth Lord Peter Wimsey again and again in order to feed your habit, help is at hand: Sayers' heir apparent, Jill Paton Walsh (who has already written some much-acclaimed continuations of Wimsey's adventures), has provided us with his first case, *The Attenbury Emeralds* – and Wimsey fans will be pleased to hear that it is an absolute treat: civilised, intelligent and spellbinding. When Walsh (a considerable novelist in her own right) first had the opportunity to complete an unfinished book by her celebrated crime-writing predecessor, she approached the task with trepidation: Sayers was, of course, a hard act to follow. But that book, *Thrones, Dominations*, was a triumph – with crime queens PD James and Ruth Rendell (both Sayers aficionados) marvelling at Walsh's adroit assumption of the earlier writer's mantle. *A Presumption of Death* followed, again utilising Sayers' characters (the source here was 'The Wimsey Papers', published in *The Spectator* in 1939 and 1940). And now, thankfully, we can enjoy another journey into Wimsey's world of good manners and ruthless murder. The war has left its mark on Peter Wimsey, and in 1921 he is recovering from shell shock. His privileged background has not fitted him for employment, but he is craving mental distraction from the horrors that haunt him. Solving the case of the loss of an emerald belonging to Lord Attenbury is to become Wimsey's first triumph as a detective, launching him on a sleuthing career. By the time of the Festival of Britain, Wimsey is 60 and enjoying life with his wife, novelist Harriet Vane, when the emerald once again enters his life. The young Lord Attenbury, strapped for cash, needs to sell it – and asks Peter to look into its provenance. But a different stone is in the bank – and Wimsey finds himself in a maelstrom of duplicity and death that has stalked several generations of one family. Channelling all the authority that Sayers employed right up to her final Wimsey books *Gaudy Night* and *Busman's Honeymoon*, Walsh again shows that she has the full measure of the imperishable Lord Peter and the hyper-intelligent Harriet Vane. Sayers, of course, tired of the superficial, clichéd aspects of her hero, and transformed him into a real, three-dimensional human being – an achievement Walsh is equally keen to maintain in this clever mystery.

TOM FRANKLIN and BETH ANN FENNELLY (1920s America)

Sometimes a crime writer comes along who shakes the genre so that all the clichés come rattling out like loose nails, leaving something clean and spare. Tom Franklin proved to be such a writer with *Crooked Letter, Crooked Letter*, an atmospheric crime offering set in rural Mississippi. But is Franklin even a crime writer at all? Or is he, like his great predecessor William Faulkner (a clear influence), using the trappings of the crime novel for literary ends? So authoritative was the earlier (solo) book that the heart sinks when seeing that he has enlisted his wife (a poet) as co-writer for *The Tilted World*, but this unruly tale set against the historic flooding of the Mississippi River is even more impressive than *Crooked Letter*. Two incorruptible Prohibition-era federal agents are sent to investigate the disappearance of two colleagues who had been closing in on a local bootlegger. Gritty yet cerebral fare.

JEFFERY DEAVER (1930s New York and Berlin)

Like so many lawyers, Jeffery Deaver decided to abandon one already lucrative profession for an even more remunerative one – that of the bestselling thriller writer. And Deaver swiftly built up a considerable following for his Lincoln Rhyme crime novels, highly adroit thrillers featuring a quadriplegic investigator assisted by a young policewoman, Amelia Sachs, who takes on most of the danger. What makes the Rhyme books so individual is Deaver's moulding of a unique protagonist: Rhyme's physical incapacity is hardly unique for brilliant detective figures, but it's rarely been handled with such panache. But while some authors are happy to plough the same furrow for most of their careers, Deaver struck off in another direction with *Garden of Beasts*, a period-set thriller that is among his most accomplished work. Set in New York in the 1930s, the central character here is hitman Paul Schumann, who is grabbed by the police when a hit goes belly-up. Schumann is offered a choice: travel to Berlin to murder Hitler associate Reinhard Ernst or be tossed into jail, with the key thrown away. There would, of course, be no novel if Schumann didn't take the first option! His lethal hunt through a brilliantly realised Berlin, in chaos as preparations for the Olympics are under way, delivers the requisite tension – particularly as an implacable and resourceful German cop is on his tail (not to mention the assembled might of the Third Reich). This 'garden of beasts' is not a comfortable place to be – exactly what thriller aficionados want, in fact – with Schumann a strong antihero. On the strength of this, some postulated that Deaver need never go back to his Lincoln Rhyme books. But he did.

DJ TAYLOR (1930s Britain)

It doesn't do justice to Taylor's diverting novel *At the Chime of a City Clock* to describe it as a pastiche: it's something more than that, but there is no question that the author has considerable skill at channelling such London writers of an earlier era as Patrick Hamilton. Set in a sultry Bayswater of the 1930s, Taylor's protagonist, James Ross, is a struggling writer. Unable to sell his work and struggling to come up with the rent for his nagging landlady, his life suddenly changes when he encounters the seductive Suzi and her mysterious boss, Mr Rasmussen – who seems concerned with the disused premises above a jeweller's shop. As with his earlier *Kept: A Victorian Mystery*, Taylor has a knack for recreating the past with the richness and detail that can bring it to life for the modern reader. *At the Chime of a City Clock* is effortlessly entertaining.

DOLORES GORDON-SMITH (World War One and 1920s England)

The British writer Dolores Gordon-Smith is most celebrated for writing a series featuring the canny Jack Haldean. The inaugural book in the sequence, the punningly titled *A Fête Worse than Death*, appeared in 2007. Gordon-Smith's chosen place and time is England in the 1920s, and nine books have followed the well-received opener. The author has also produced a World War One-set standalone historical novel, *Frankie's Letter*.

WILLIAM RYAN (Stalinist Russia)

Russia, under the iron rule of Joseph Stalin. For the ordinary citizen, mistrust and paranoia are a way of life – make the wrong enemies, and you might end up denounced and sentenced to a living death in a gulag. Or you may – as millions did – simply disappear. In this society, a young policeman is able to do his job only by a queasy accommodation with the state – but he soon finds that everything he has committed himself to may be as dangerous to him as to those he tracks down. Does the above sound like the award-winning novel *Child 44* by Tom Rob Smith? In fact, it is also the premise of William Ryan's crime debut, *The Holy Thief* – and, after all, there's no reason why a strong concept shouldn't do service more than once. In fact, the idea of an honourable copper at the service of a corrupt Soviet state had already fuelled Martin Cruz Smith's *Gorky Park*, so this latest riff on the notion can either stand or fall on just how well it's done. And Ryan's book has an authority that belies its first-novel status. Moscow 1936, and Captain Alexei Korolev is making his mark with the Criminal Investigation Division. The mutilated body of a young woman is discovered on the altar of a deconsecrated church, and Alexei is assigned to investigate the killing. But the woman is an American citizen, and the much-loathed NKVD starts to muscle in; Alexei finds that both he and his investigation are under a microscope. He is aware that a wrong move may propel him into the frigid wasteland of the far north, so he tries a risky strategy: he infiltrates the dangerous world of Moscow's criminal classes. Bodies begin to accumulate, and Alexei finds that not just his life but his political and religious ideals are on the line. Ryan demonstrates considerable skill in evoking this benighted period, along with a deftness at ringing the changes on familiar crime plotting moves. Along with his tense narrative, Ryan (an ex-lawyer) deals intelligently with issues of faith in a society where being a believer is distinctly unhealthy. His hero,

Alexei, is more lightly sketched than those of Martin Cruz Smith and Tom Rob Smith, but he is an intriguing protagonist, and the auguries for the rest of the series (of which *The Holy Thief* is the first book) are very promising indeed. Life is not easy for an honest policeman in the Soviet Russia of the 1930s, but the intuitive Alexei wins the day and is acclaimed as a shining example for the Soviet people – he is even decorated – rather than ending up dead or imprisoned, which he is constantly expecting.

Soviet citizens of this era learned to dread the knock at the door in the dead of night, but when Alexei hears that knock on a snowy Moscow night, it is not the catastrophe he fears. In *The Bloody Meadow*, NKVD Security Chief Colonel Rodinov is the nocturnal visitor, asking him to investigate the apparent suicide of a model citizen. Maria Lenskaya has died during the making of a film in the Ukraine, and her death is a matter of great interest to the sinister Ezhov, Commissar for State Security. The film Maria was making, the eponymous *Bloody Meadow*, is still shooting, and when Alexei arrives on the fraught set, he soon finds himself once again in a dangerous situation, with something unsayable – the failure of the Revolution – a key to the mystery. Authors live in some fear of the second book in a sequence these days, so commonplace are examples of underperformance. The dread of authors and their publishers springs from that familiar refrain from readers: 'That first book was so good... what went wrong?' But nobody asked that question about *The Bloody Meadow*, which is every bit as darkly compelling as its predecessor, with all the elements that made *The Holy Thief* so successful: razor-sharp plotting, an evocative sense of locale (here, historical Ukraine, the scene of endless battles), and – most winning of all – the human (and vulnerable) Alexei Korolev making a nuisance of himself. Ryan's first book was shortlisted for various awards.

🎤 Interview: William Ryan

My first three novels were set in Soviet Russia featuring a detective called Captain Korolev, while my fourth was *The Constant Soldier*, a standalone thriller set in the dying days of Nazi Germany. It's not that I have a fascination with totalitarian states (although I do) – in both cases, I wanted to tell a story about an ordinary person trying to survive and keep their morality intact in the most difficult of circumstances. In Soviet Russia, truth and justice were concepts that were severely skewed and had a tendency to change at a moment's notice, so writing a detective novel where a detective's determination to do his job is itself an act of resistance was tempting. And it wasn't hard to add tension and drama in a place and time where one false move could mean arrest – not only for Korolev but for his friends and family as well. *The Constant Soldier*, on the other hand, features an invalided German soldier who is given the chance to atone for his involvement in the atrocities perpetrated by the Nazi regime. It's a bit more complex morally, as he has been involved in the Nazis' crimes, at least peripherally, but, as with the Korolev novels, and all good historical crime, it's about an ordinary person in an extraordinary time and place and how they cope with it.

You asked what other novelists have been an influence and it would be churlish not to mention Philip Kerr and Martin Cruz Smith – but I think I'd also have to tip the nod to Jason Goodwin, Arturo Pérez-Reverte, Marek Krajewski and Boris Akunin. All of them immerse their readers in the time and place they write about – and tell cracking stories at the same time. That seems to be what the best historical crime is all about.

DAVID ROBERTS (1930s England)

In *Sweet Poison*, David Roberts virtually created – or should that be recreated? – a genre: the elegantly retrospective mystery novel with a period setting and ill-matched period heroes, but with the whole thing shot through with a wry modern sensibility. *Bones of the Buried* is a typical mystery for Lord Edward Corinth and Verity Browne and is a delight – for several reasons. While Roberts plays fair with the reader in his recreation of 1930s England (the historical paraphernalia and character mores are as sharply observed as one could wish), he doesn't introduce elements that would seem extraneous at best and anachronistic at worst: sex, for instance, is subtly handled, although the relationship between the two principals has all the requisite spark. Returning from a sojourn in New York, Lord Edward Corinth finds his friend, journalist Verity Browne, up to her old sleuthing tricks and pulling him into the investigation of a murder in Spain. But the year is 1936, and civil war looms. Verity's lover in the Communist Party has been convicted of murder, and although she asks for Edward's help, she is fully aware that the two men are rivals for her affections. The plotting is quite as idiosyncratic as we have come to expect from Roberts, though it's the irresistible interplay between the main characters that makes *Bones of the Buried* such a pleasurable experience.

Other key books: *Hollow Crown*, *The Quality of Mercy*.

TV: CITY OF ANGELS (various directors)

Riffing on the Polanski film *Chinatown*, this colourful and unusual series is set in Los Angles during the Depression. Its relatively short run still allowed for the utilisation of several real-life crimes for its scenarios, including a conspiracy little-known in Britain, the 'Business Plot', an attempted coup to end the political reign of President Roosevelt. Similarly, the real-life brothel the T&M Studio, with its 'fantasy prostitutes', was featured – an establishment that later appeared in *L.A. Confidential* under another name.

Film: CHINATOWN (Roman Polanski, director)

Given that the premise of this book is the study of period-set crime drama produced by artists from a later era, Roman Polanski's classic 1974 film (from a superb Robert Towne screenplay) undoubtedly fits the bill, with its loving recreation – in colour and widescreen – of the great days of monochrome film noir, and with a compromised private detective played by the hottest actor of the day, Jack Nicholson. The film was an instant classic, and it has not dated an iota. The exemplary production design is matched by the felicities of playing, the jazz-inflected orchestral score (Jerry Goldsmith) and impeccable direction.

TV: BOARDWALK EMPIRE (various directors)

Starting with a considerable flourish (the pilot episode was directed by cinema giant Martin Scorsese), *Boardwalk Empire* may not have gained the popular acclaim of *Breaking Bad* or *The Sopranos* – and it is not in the class of those shows – but it is one of the most ambitious, multi-layered television dramas of recent years. After five seasons, the fifty-sixth and final episode, 'Eldorado', was aired in the UK on 1 November 2014, and the unsparing finale brought some satisfying resolutions. The central character of the series was Enoch 'Nucky' Thompson (a fictionalised version of Atlantic City malefactor Enoch L Johnson), played with characteristic bravura by Steve Buscemi. By hiring the actor, showrunner Terence Winter – one of the creators behind *The Sopranos* – along with executive producer Martin Scorsese showed that they realised they were creating an unorthodox figure that required an actor with considerable presence.

10: World War Two and the Post-war Period

DAVID STUART DAVIES (1940s London)

David Stuart Davies, Britain's premier expert on Sherlock Holmes, has produced some cherishable Holmesiana – both analytical, including *The Sherlock Holmes Book* (co-edited with this writer), and in the nature of ingenious continuing adventures for the Great Detective. His 1940s adventures for private dick Johnny One Eye (such as the very readable *Forests of the Night*) demonstrate that his talents extend beyond Baker Street: this is idiomatic, tightly plotted stuff, full of solid era-specific trappings.

🎙 **Interview: David Stuart Davies**

I have to confess that my novels set in London during World War Two were not particularly inspired by any fiction that I have read but by old movies, especially black and white ones, set in this grim period. The double threat of invasion and bombing combined with the increase in crime during the war years make it a fascinating period for a crime writer. The book that most inspired the Johnny Hawke series was the non-fiction volume *The Underworld at War* by Donald Thomas, which is a brilliant detailed exposé of the range of dirty deeds that blossomed during this period. My two favourite books of my own from this series are *Without Conscience*, which has an incredibly ruthless villain who has echoes of Grahame Greene's Pinky from *Brighton Rock*, and *Requiem for a Dummy*, which features a radio ventriloquist (think Edgar Bergen or Peter Brough) who receives death threats by telephone in the voice of his dummy. Crimes set in the past allow the writer to concentrate on the human elements involved in the drama rather than dealing with the technical and scientific paraphernalia so prevalent in modern novels. No DNA need apply!

SAM EASTLAND (World War Two Russia)

In September 1939, the German army (in Sam Eastland's *Siberian Red*) is laying waste to Poland and on the point of invading Russia. For Stalin, the treasure of Tsar Nicholas would be extremely useful. In order to obtain his freedom, a prisoner in a gulag is prepared to reveal the location of Colonel Kolchak, the man who knows exactly where the Tsar's gold is hidden. But Stalin discovers that the informant has been murdered, and calls upon his most trusted investigator, Pekkala, to journey to the Kremlin in order to crack the mystery. Pekkala takes on the role of a prisoner in the grim and dangerous gulag of Borodok in Siberia, and his new assignment for the man who will soon be the murderous dictator of Russia becomes ever more pressing. As a tale of survival in the face of insuperable odds, this is absolutely splendid stuff, crammed with all the atmosphere that is the hallmark of Sam Eastland's writing.

PHILIP KERR (World War Two and Post-war Germany)

When Scott Fitzgerald said there were no second acts in American lives, he provided a thousand writers with the opportunity to refute that assertion. But had he said it about British lives, it would still be untrue – as the example of Philip Kerr attests. There was a time when Kerr was riding high with a series of high-concept thrillers, not to mention his more serious Berlin Noir trilogy featuring the German wartime detective Bernie Gunther. Inevitably, Hollywood came calling, and Kerr relocated to sunnier climes, working on a variety of projects that were stillborn, although he was handsomely compensated for this work. But just as disappointed readers were beginning to mutter 'Whatever happened to Philip Kerr?', he returned to these shores and began producing new work, once again featuring his dogged German sleuth. Any fears that his creative fires might have been extinguished by his Hollywood sojourn were quickly allayed; not only were the new books as powerfully involving as his earlier work, but more complex moral dilemmas were freighted in for his hero, struggling to retain his soul in a malign society.

In *A Man Without Breath*, the year is 1943. Bernie has a new job at the German War Crimes Bureau in Berlin. There are unsettling reports of a mass grave in a forest near Smolensk, rumours that are validated when a wolf unearths human remains. Polish officers killed by the Russians? This would play into the hands of the regime: a propaganda victory over the Russians. And there is one man who will be able to discern the truth: Bernie Gunther. But Bernie is to find – as so often before – that the truth is not always a welcome commodity. An earlier outing for his compromised hero was *Field Grey*, in which Bernie's wartime record is put under an unforgiving spotlight (as a member of the SS, he killed partisans who were killing German soldiers), and that book took on a level of moral queasiness rarely found in the crime genre. If *A Man Without Breath* rows back from these darker implications, it still makes life satisfyingly difficult for Bernie. It might be argued that there is now a body of work that could be called a genre in itself: the good detective trying to do his best within a corrupt regime (Martin Cruz Smith's *Gorky Park* is another cogent example), but it can safely be said that few writers have tackled the theme with the rigour of Philip Kerr. If *A Man Without Breath* is not as subtly disturbing as *Field Grey*, it still firmly enmeshes the reader in its 500-odd pages – and reminds us that Hollywood's loss is Britain's gain.

🎤 Interview: Philip Kerr

I'm not sure I chose to write about Germany under the Nazis, or if that period chose me. Certainly as a postgraduate student of German law and philosophy I was already very much interested in the whole intellectual and cultural background of Nazi Germany. In the beginning I only wanted to write a novel about Berlin and it took me a while to realise that there was so little information about life for ordinary Germans during the 1930s that I began to feel like a detective looking for clues. It was this experience that persuaded me it might be best to write about a detective, that I could use a detective to answer certain questions I had for myself about why it was that Germany allowed itself to be hijacked by these gangsters. You might say I came into crime writing sideways and through the back door. It wasn't as if I'd read many crime novels. Still haven't, if the truth be told. So I can't point to any influences other than Chandler and Hammett. I don't read many of my contemporaries; that's not because I don't like their work but because I have to do a lot of reading in my research and more often I am reading not for pleasure but for work. This is a shame. I can't therefore claim any insightful overview of the genre if there is indeed such a thing. I think if you ask most of the crime writers I know – Val McDermid, Ian Rankin – they will just agree with me that we don't think of ourselves as working within a genre, but as novelists pure and simple.

The book of mine I am most satisfied with is always the most recent; if only because I can more easily remember how much work went into it. Equally, I don't yet feel I have written my best book. That seems to me the best reason to keep writing. To try to improve upon what I have already done. The few honours I have enjoyed in writing have come from the world of crime writing and for these I am very grateful. But I sometimes think that when people talk about the rules of the genre they don't know what they are talking about. The only rule is to make your writing as good as it can be. This has been my guiding principle for 30 years. I am lucky still to be published. Perhaps now more than ever.

MICHAEL GILBERT (World War Two Italy)

Lincolnshire-born Michael Gilbert spent time as a prisoner of war, which inspired his *Death in Captivity*, possibly the only murder mystery set in a PoW camp. A man suspected of being an informer is discovered dead in a collapsed tunnel in a camp in Italy. In order to protect the tunnel, the body is moved to another one that has already been abandoned. But when the Fascist captors declare the death a murder, an investigation is undertaken by Captain Henry Goyles, ex-headmaster and amateur sleuth. The highly unusual scenario is tackled with real gusto here. Gilbert's settings stretch far and wide and he tended to avoid continuing characters, although he produced a series of novels featuring Inspector Hazlerigg of New Scotland Yard and another with the multilingual policeman Patrick Petrella.

MICHAEL RIDPATH (World War Two Europe)

The versatile British novelist Michael Ridpath has ventured with success into a variety of genres, initially drawing on his experience in the world of finance. In terms of historical crime, his *Shadows of War* is set in a pitch-perfect 1939. Conrad de Lancey was one of those who came very close to assassinating Hitler, but now the British Secret Service enlist him to return to Europe and contact a cadre of German officers planning a coup. In the 'phoney' war, loyalties are fluid and human life cheap when the stakes are so very high. As well as financial thrillers, Ridpath's diverse earlier specialities have included ventures into Nordic noir territory, but *Shadows of War* suggests that the historical thriller is his real métier.

🎙 **Interview: Michael Ridpath**

Like many historical novelists I read history at university and loved it. But what frustrated me was the way that academic historians denied the importance of individuals in history, and of moral decisions. Of course, that's what novels are all about.

It seems to me that the period when such individual moral decisions were particularly relevant was Europe in the late 1930s, when two questions took on enormous importance. How could you be a good and loyal German when your country was fighting a war but was led by an evil dictator? And how could you be a good Briton when you believed that war itself was the ultimate evil and yet someone had to stand up to Germany? My two spy novels, *Traitor's Gate* and *Shadows of War*, examine both of these issues. They feature two friends who studied together at Oxford: one British and one German. The first book is about a German plot to get rid of Hitler in 1938, and the second is about a British plot to get rid of Churchill in 1940. It really is difficult in these novels, as it was in reality, to work out who is on whose side.

I was careful not to read any novels about the period written after 1945, and I tried to forget what I had read, especially John le Carré and Ian Fleming. I was wary of the strong influence that Bond and Smiley in particular have had on the modern reader's view of spying. My reading of the history suggests that spies in the 1930s were incompetent amateurs, who thought themselves terribly clever but weren't. However, I did read lots of contemporary novels – in particular Waugh, Powell and Greene – as well as memoirs and biographies, to give me a feel for how the people of the time spoke, thought and felt.

The late 1930s was a dark time when the stakes for individuals and the world as a whole have never been higher. The perfect time in which to set a thriller.

JAMES HOLLAND (World War Two Europe)

Having demonstrated his considerable skill at conjuring up recent history in a series of splendidly involving novels, Holland moved into fresh territory by introducing a new series character, Sergeant Jack Tanner, encountering danger in the days of Nazi Germany. In *Darkest Hour*, Tanner is posted to a training camp in south-east England in 1940, but the camp has severe problems. Two Polish refugees have died under mysterious circumstances. At the same time, the Germans have launched their blitzkrieg. This is pulse-racing stuff.

RENNIE AIRTH (World War Two Britain)

Rennie Airth has commanded a following with his intriguing combination of storytelling nous and heavy-duty characterisation. A good example of his art is *The Dead of Winter*, although both *Rivers of Darkness* and *The Blood-Dimmed Tide* (the first two books in the series) might also be adduced. The narrative has moved on in time from the 1920s and 1930s, and we rejoin Airth's troubled copper John Madden during World War Two. It is the time of Churchill's radio broadcasts, the blackout and the ever-present threat of V2 bombs. Near the British Museum in London, a young woman refugee from war-torn Poland is killed. She had been engaged as a land girl on a farm where she had won the affection of the farmer and his wife – and that farmer is John Madden, no longer utilising his detection skills for Scotland Yard. But he is prepared to aid his ex-comrades in this disturbing situation, and utilises his still keen expertise to dig into the murder. Madden becomes aware that the killer is almost certainly a professional hitman. Why did he murder his Polish victim? It's up to Madden to construct a plausible case from a slender assortment of clues – and, what's more, in the face of considerable personal danger. Rarely has the wartime ethos been so strongly depicted as in Airth's work.

JOHN LAWTON (World War Two and Post-war Britain)

American-born, English-resident John Lawton is a producer/director in television who was named in a Parliamentary Bill in the House of Lords as an offender against taste – a badge of honour for any artist. In 1995, his first Frederick Troy novel, *Black Out*, bagged him the

WH Smith Fresh Talent Award, and in 2008 he was one of only half a dozen living English writers to be named in the *Daily Telegraph*'s '50 Crime Writers to Read before You Die'. He has also edited the poetry of DH Lawrence and the stories of Joseph Conrad. His protagonist, Fred Troy, is the son of a wealthy émigré who left Russia to start a publishing empire in Britain. To the bemusement of his family, Fred opts to join the police, and when war is declared, he becomes part of the Murder Squad, under the auspices of Superintendent Stanley Onions. In Lawton's busy narratives, real-life walk-ons include Attlee, Gaitskell, Khrushchev, Beaverbrook, Churchill, Hess, Eisenhower and Oppenheimer. A strong entry in the series? *A Lily of the Field*.

Other key books: *Second Violin*, *Riptide*, *A Little White Death*.

RHYS BOWEN (World War Two Britain)

Rhys Bowen's *In Farleigh Field* is a measure of her accomplishment in the historical field. The war is making its mark at Farleigh Place, the ancestral home of Lord Westerham and his five daughters, when a soldier with a failed parachute falls to his death on the estate. After his uniform and possessions raise suspicions, MI5 operative and family friend Ben Cresswell is covertly tasked with determining whether the man was a German spy. Lee Child was an early extoller of the book's virtues, echoed by several subsequent critics.

CARLO LUCARELLI (1940s Italy)

Lucarelli's Inspector De Luca sequence of novels is an unusual series set between 1945 and 1948, from the height of Italy's Fascist regime to the end of the tumultuous post-war period, with De Luca investigating crimes in the city of Bologna and along the Adriatic coast. With little or no regard for those in power, whoever they happen to be, his solitary, uncompromising character often lands him in trouble, but his respect is reserved for truth and justice alone. While working on his thesis on the history of law enforcement during the Fascist period in Italy, Carlo Lucarelli interviewed a man who had been an officer in the Italian police force for 40 years. He had started as a member of the Fascist political police, but, towards the end of World War Two, when the Fascists were on the run, he answered to partisan formations then in control of the country. His job? To investigate the Fascist hierarchy, his former employers. After the war, when regular elections were held and a government formed, he was employed by the Italian Republic. Part of his job was again to investigate and arrest his former employers, this time the partisans. Carlo Lucarelli, however, never finished his doctoral thesis. Instead, Commissario De Luca was born, and overnight his creator became one of Italy's most acclaimed crime authors.

The De Luca trilogy (in splendid translations by Michael Reynolds) starts with *Carte Blanche*, set in April 1945, the final frenetic days of the Salò Republic. A brutal murder on the good side of town lands De Luca in the middle of a hornet's nest where the rich and powerful mix drugs, sex, money and murder. It is followed by *The Damned Season*, in which De Luca is on the run under an assumed identity to avoid reprisals for the role he played during the Fascist dictatorship. Blackmailed by a member of the partisan police, De Luca is obliged to investigate a series of murders, becoming a reluctant player in Italy's post-war power struggle. The final novel, *Via delle Oche*, won the Scerbanenco Prize. The time is 1948, with the country's fate soon to be decided in bitterly contested national elections. A corpse surfaces in a brothel at the heart of Bologna's red light district, and De Luca finds himself unwilling to look the other way when evidence points to prominent local power brokers. The novels (whose tone often veers alarmingly between the sardonic and the massively cynical) are built around one key thesis: the deforming effect of Italy's compromised, slippery politics on every individual, not least the pragmatic but beleaguered De Luca.

TV: INSPECTOR DE LUCA (Antonio Frazzi, director)
In the four TV movies of the series inspired by the novels of bestselling writer Carlo Lucarelli, police detective De Luca always ultimately gets to the bottom of his cases, though what he finds often leaves a bitter aftertaste. The series starts with an original story, *Unauthorised Investigation*, which serves as a prequel, before tackling Lucarelli's trilogy. Alessandro Preziosi is an apposite casting choice in the title role.

RICHARD ZIMLER (1940s Warsaw, Sixteenth-century Lisbon)

Many books have attempted to pull off the remarkable trick of embedding a highly compulsive historical thriller within the context of a serious literary novel, and Richard Zimler's *The Last Kabbalist of Lisbon* is an intriguing contribution to this fascinating sub-genre. Set among Jewish communities living clandestinely in Lisbon in the sixteenth century, Zimler begins his narrative with Abraham Zarco found dead with a naked girl by his side. Zarco is a renowned kabbalist, a practitioner of the arcane mysteries of the Jewish tradition at a time when the Jews of Lisbon have been forced to convert to Christianity.

That earlier book functioned principally as a compelling and atmospheric thriller, and was also a stinging study of intolerance, couched in prose of elegance and gritty strength that overcame some familiar elements. *The Warsaw Anagrams* shares some of those elements, but in essentially different territory. In 1940, the Nazis have sealed thousands of Jews inside a restricted area of the Polish capital. The aging psychiatrist Erik Cohen is forced to move into a cramped apartment with his niece and nine-year-old nephew Adam. But Adam disappears, and his body is later found in the barbed wire of the ghetto, his leg severed. Subsequently, a young girl's body is found, the hand removed. The elderly Erik is obliged to confront evil in the heart of Nazi-occupied Warsaw. Zimler's canny utilisation here of a protagonist far removed from the vigorous heroes of most fiction is a masterstroke and adds a new dimension to a novel that incorporates thoughtfulness and the tragedy of history within the exigencies of a mesmerising thriller-oriented narrative.

LEN DEIGHTON (World War Two Alternative History Britain)

It's difficult in the twenty-first century to remember quite what an impact Len Deighton's espionage sequence (beginning with *The Ipcress File*) had in the 1960s; their remarkable reinvention of the genre (along with similar excavations by John le Carré) remains influential to this day. Of course, one of the elements that made his books so successful was Deighton's attention to detail, and it was that – along with his sardonic wit and considerable knowledge of and enthusiasm for history – that led to the creation of one of the most celebrated of alternative history novels, *SS-GB*. Other writers, both before and since, have imagined a world in which the Nazis won World War Two, but this particular book remains sui generis, not least for its utterly plausible picture of Britain under the heel of the Gestapo. It's a moot point whether alternative histories such as this belong in a book called *Historical Noir*, but it seems to be essential that it at least receives a namecheck.

ALY MONROE (1940s Spain, USA and London)

Aly Monroe is an insightful and deft practitioner of the genre. In *The Maze of Cadiz*, British Intelligence dispatches agent Peter Cotton to Cadiz to track down a rogue spy. The year is 1944, and Cotton is anticipating a none-too-demanding assignment, as the conflict in Europe is reaching its end. But this, in fact, is a very fraught time – and Cotton finds that his arrival in Cadiz seems to be a matter of great interest to a great many people. What Cotton had decided might be a quotidian job turns out to have the highest possible stakes. This is the first in the Peter Cotton series by Aly Monroe, and the good auguries prove fully justified in subsequent books.

Interview: Aly Monroe

I chose this period first because I was still able to listen to people who had lived through the war and its immediate aftermath, and because I was interested in the construction of the 'national narrative' around the dismantling of what had been the British Empire – which still affects how we think now. All official national narratives are an editing of history – encapsulated in Operation Legacy, which consisted of rewriting, burning or giving deep sea burial to documents from the colonies that would have shown the British in a bad light. The rise of the spy genre post-war can be viewed as a reaction to Britain's decline as a world power. Spy fiction offered a kind of vicarious travel, a sensation of freedom and excitement – and perhaps an illusion of control. From the post-war exoticism of James Bond (avocados and luscious, willing women) to the Tiresian wisdom of George Smiley in the 1960s and 1970s, in a world that no longer included the UK as a superpower, the British could at least take comfort and pride in being a very special power. The spy genre is a peculiarly British national construct. My own historically based intelligence novels don't tend to be either as positive or as fantastic. Instead, they aim to be a more realistic and researched account of a process. I am always pleased when readers get in touch to confirm that I got something or somebody right, as in the reorganisation of the intelligence agencies in 1945 in *Washington Shadow*, and the grim winter of 1946–47 in *Icelight*. That's the living link. Of course I am writing fiction. But as the genre-breaking Spanish writer Javier Marías puts it: 'Everything in real life can be contradicted or denied. Not in fiction.' My own interest is in revealing the constructions and workings of real history being accommodated to myth – in an entertaining way. Among the writers who have moved the historical intelligence novel on, I read and admire John Lawton, Andrew Williams, William Ryan and Jason Hewitt. I am also fond of Henry James – especially his portrayal of corruption behind civilised manners, a more thoroughgoing look at John Buchan's 'thin veneer of civilisation'; and I admire Eric Ambler, particularly for his ability to show all races and parts of society making shift as they can in tough circumstances.

ALAN FURST (1930s and 1940s Europe)

Generally speaking, authors hate categorisation – they like to think that they're writing novels that don't lend themselves to easy labels. Conversely, bookshops like categorisation – after all, booksellers have to file all these damned books somewhere. But what about readers? To categorise or not to categorise? If the truth be told, most of us like a little guidance, particularly with a writer new to us. So where do we file the American writer Alan Furst? Literary novel? Espionage? Historical fiction? Furst's *Kingdom of Shadows* invoked glowing comparisons with Graham Greene; his idiosyncratic recreation of 1930s Europe just before World War Two has the richness and authenticity that only the best writers can boast. That novel deals with the growing tide of Fascism in Europe, and displays a new vigour in the espionage tale. *Blood of Victory* has the same trenchant scene setting and felicitous grasp of character as its predecessor. The setting is once again wartime Europe, and it's the territory to which Furst returns in *The Foreign Correspondent*; the author's cheeky appropriation of a famous Hitchcock title is misleading – this is a far darker piece than Hitch's *jeu d'esprit*. In fact, the book is set in the feverish period just before World War Two; the eponymous foreign correspondent is Carlo Weisz of Reuters, covering the final campaign of the Spanish Civil War. But a double death at a Paris hotel (a favourite spot for clandestine sexual liaisons) propels him into a new job. The victims are the editor of émigré newspaper *Liberazione* and his lover – both have been murdered by OVRA, the secret police of Mussolini's Fascist regime. Carlo, seduced by the laudable ideology and the romance of the idea, unwisely agrees to take over editorship of the paper – and puts himself in a dangerous position. And it's equally dangerous to rekindle an old affair in Berlin with intriguing Christa, now married to a rich older man. As Carlo becomes the target of the murderous agents of OVRA, the French Sûreté and even British Intelligence, political imperatives assume second place to the task of simply staying alive.

Furst is an American author who considers himself European, and his lineage as a writer stretches back to Joseph Conrad – although he can, disappointingly, deal in national stereotypes (a Hooray Henry Englishman called Geoffrey Sparrow, given to 'toothy har-hars', is a reminder that we're not reading Greene, who would have balanced the character with other Englishmen presented in more rounded fashion). But *The Foreign Correspondent* is a reminder that the espionage novel – if that's what we're going to call this – can still be a vehicle for fine writing, and Furst's audacious reinvention of the genre is a constant delight.

LUKE MCCALLIN (Post-war Berlin)

Let's not mince words: historical thrillers don't come any better than *The Ashes of Berlin*. Oxford-born, Africa-educated Luke McCallin is one of the most ambitious and accomplished writers in the genre, and this follow-up to the much-acclaimed *The Man from Berlin* has a panoramic sweep to match its laser-sharp characterisation. Humane German intelligence officer Captain Gregor Reinhardt has returned to a broken Berlin after the end of the war to serve in the civilian police force, but finds that divisions and hatreds still reign in the city. A serial killer is on the loose, and one of his victims is the brother of a Nazi scientist. Reinhardt's investigations propel him into the dangerous company of those for whom the war is not over. This is peerless stuff, written with authority, and Reinhardt is a multifaceted protagonist.

🎤 Interview: Luke McCallin

It may sound clichéd, but Gregor Reinhardt walked into my dreams one night. A skilled detective, but still an ordinary man in extraordinary times trying to behave and believe in what makes sense. Painfully aware of his own fears and limitations, but knowing what is right and what is wrong. He waited years for me to find the time and courage to start writing his story. I was working in Bosnia as a UN peacekeeper. Bosnia is a historical and cultural crossroads. It's contested. It defies simple explanation. I learned that the raw edges to life are closer to us than we like to think. Not only that, but a person can be undone and brought to nothing – or worse, can be warped away from who that person might have been. I had one of the most amazing childhoods imaginable. My father worked for UNHCR in Africa, my mother worked with child soldiers. Their vocation became mine. I joined the UN. I went to Chechnya, to Mali, and then to Bosnia. I've been further since, and although not everything I saw and did was worthy of remembrance, somewhere along the line, two things – my work and my writing – began to merge. Bosnia inspired *The Man from Berlin* and *The Pale House*, both set in World War Two Sarajevo, and *The Ashes of Berlin*, set after the war in occupied Germany. Those times fascinate me, when the ability of individuals to decide their fates was cast into the fire. Trying to understand the human condition in that – and in a place and time that's a byword for intrigue and treachery – is what inspires me to write. That, and the sheer pleasure of creation and sharing.

RUTH RENDELL (1940s England)

The late Ruth Rendell's novels featuring her long-term protagonist Inspector Wexford were much loved, but Rendell usually reserved her most cutting-edge writing for her non-Wexford books, with more psychologically acute narratives written as her alter ego, Barbara Vine. One key novel imports all those elements into a story that begins in a typically macabre fashion: *A Dark-Adapted Eye*, with its investigation of a dusty 1940s mystery, is a particular favourite of Vine/Rendell fans.

BEN FERGUSSON (1940s Germany)

If reviews are any guide to the quality of crime novels (and one fervently hopes they are) then Ben Fergusson must have been pleased about the notices that his novel *The Spring of Kasper Meier* received; notices that marked him out as a writer of genuine accomplishment. The novel is set in Berlin in 1946, with the city destroyed and the local population struggling to survive by whatever clandestine means are possible. Kasper Meier trades on the black market, putting food on the table for himself and his ageing father, and will find anything for a price. But then a young woman arrives at his door seeking the whereabouts of a British pilot. Saying yes to this assignment will put Kasper in considerable danger.

BARBARA NADEL (World War Two London)

Barbara Nadel is noted for her distinctive Istanbul-set series of Inspector Ikmen thrillers, with such books as *Belshazzar's Daughter* and *A Chemical Prison* dovetailing exuberant scene setting with deliciously tortuous plots – the resourceful Ikmen is always struggling against seemingly intractable cases. But it is her historical sequence with an undertaker called Francis Hancock that earns her a place in this study. Hancock is also adept at solving crimes, and the four books in the sequence – *Last Rights*, *After the Mourning*, *Ashes to Ashes* and *Sure and Certain Death* – marry the excellent plotting of her Ikmen books with impeccable 1940s scene setting in the East End of London.

🎙 Interview: Barbara Nadel

My historical noir series featuring crime-solving undertaker Francis Hancock is set in the 1940s in the East End of London, with four books in the series. My aim in writing these books was to present a slightly different take on the traditional 'London Blitz' narrative. My own ancestors lived through that time and, largely due to their poverty, had a much more hard-edged view of what happened and why. Also, given their very mixed background, much of what they experienced was interpreted by them in terms of religion and magic. If I had to pick one book that reflects this most powerfully I think it would have to be *After the Mourning*. This is set largely around a community of gypsies who travel in Epping Forest and on the margins of the East End.

Probably my favourite historical noir authors at the moment are William Ryan and Nicola Upson. Bill Ryan's Captain Korolev books set in 1930s Moscow evoke Stalin's terror with chilling accuracy and Nicola's Josephine Tey books are just addictive. I'm about to start *A Rising Man* by Abir Mukherjee, which is set in 1920s British India. I think that at the moment we're witnessing an explosion in historical noir. Almost every period and location imaginable is covered by someone. I find this very exciting. Although still no Albanian noir under King Zog – but then I think I may well have to claim that for myself.

LAURA WILSON (World War Two, 1940s and 1950s Britain)

Just how much comfort does it offer Laura Wilson – while poring over her enthusiastic reviews – to know that she is regarded as one of the country's most acute psychological novelists working in what might loosely be described as the crime genre? Such books as *The Lover* and *A Thousand Lies* glean all the requisite critical plaudits and prize nominations but, despite achieving respectable sales, largely remain caviar to the general, never quite breaking through into the megasales arena that is clearly Wilson's due. It must rankle with her that many a far less talented writer is able to buy a French cottage with the proceeds of workaday writing. Wilson is damned good; take *Stratton's War*, for instance. This hefty novel (weighing in at nearly 500 pages) is one of Wilson's most ambitious, and that ambitiousness adds layers of achievement in a variety of fashions. For a start, there is the setting: London in the dangerous days of the Blitz. Then there's the extensive *dramatis personae*, from caddish upper-crust seducers to Cockney film actresses, Jewish gangsters and vulnerable working-class gay men (when being gay was illegal). But at the centre of the sprawling narrative are two very solidly realised characters, who recur in subsequent books in the series. There is the tenacious Detective Inspector Ted Stratton, a copper whose principal trait is neither alcoholism nor anti-establishment bolshiness. Wilson studiously avoids cliché with Stratton – as well as making him a fully realised figure with subtly understated characteristics, she always ensures plausibility: unlike certain poetry-loving coppers, for instance, Stratton can't get on with Evelyn Waugh ('he could see that the thing was well written, and some of it made him laugh, but the characters were such a shower that you wished you could knock their heads together'). And Wilson's female protagonist is the vulnerable tyro MI5 agent Diana Calthrop, prone to a series of ill-advised judgements about men. Again, Wilson avoids cliché: Diana is no proto-feminist – when she is accused of inviting a rape scenario after a sexual encounter, her response is not a modern one, but one in keeping with 1940s sensibilities. In June 1940, the body of Mabel Morgan, a silent film actress, is discovered impaled on railings in Fitzrovia. Stratton is not persuaded by the coroner's verdict of suicide, and discovers that one of Soho's most notorious gangsters is involved. At the same time, MI5 inductee Diana Calthrop is infiltrating a right-wing group of well-bred Hitler sympathisers – but her job is complicated by a seductive and saturnine male colleague, Claude, who interferes with her composure as much as with her underwear. Needless to say, both Stratton and Calthrop ultimately find that their investigations coincide, and Wilson allows a certain frisson to develop between them. There are echoes here of one of Wilson's favourite novelists, Patrick Hamilton, in the luminous and richly detailed conjuring of period London, although the constraints of the crime genre do not allow her the assiduous psychological strip-mining of the characters that was Hamilton's métier.

In *A Willing Victim*, it is 1956 – a year of seismic changes, with nuclear brinkmanship between the US and the Soviet Union and the Suez Crisis. People sought comfort from the Christian evangelist Billy Graham, who converted many to his brand of unnuanced belief. The appeal of religious demagogues is one of the themes in this outing for Wilson's copper Stratton, as he moves from the World War Two setting of the earlier books to the 1950s. As well as being a slow-burning but accomplished murder mystery, *A Willing Victim* is also a disquisition on the seductive attractions of unquestioning faith. And the word 'seductive' is key here: a femme fatale at a religious commune trades in carnality as much as the state of grace. On a November day in 1956, DI Ted Stratton is at a murder scene in Soho, the victim a solitary individual obsessed with esoteric religions.

Stratton's investigations take him back to what was once his home turf, Suffolk, and a house commonly believed to be haunted. It is now the headquarters of a cult, the Foundation for Spiritual Understanding. Stratton's probings into the life of murdered loner Jeremy Lloyd lead to an encounter with a 12-year-old boy who has been announced as the current incarnation on Earth of Christ and Buddha; there are those at the commune who claim that he is the product of immaculate conception, but the woman reputed to be his mother (whose photograph was in the possession of the dead man) has vanished. Wilson's beguiling book evokes the memory of other authors: the picture of an ill-fated religious commune destabilised by the sexual impulse suggests Iris Murdoch's *The Bell.* But where Wilson really excels is in the passages of unforced poetic description, unusual in a crime narrative – such as the detective's musings on the threat of a bomb-devastated world: 'He imagined the roiling iron-dark winter sky exploding, spreadeagled, into a mushroom cloud. He thought of the Pathé newsreels he'd seen of the tests at Bikini Atoll, suspended skeins of cloud like the skirts of a gigantic ballerina, the air all around dying in the sunless glare.' If there is something of a change of gears when such passages appear amid the crime solving, few will complain – Wilson is as adroit at the straightforward mechanics of the crime mystery as she is at fashioning evocative prose shot through with a keen sense of the past.

🎙 Interview: Laura Wilson

One very good thing about writing a crime novel set at any time in the past is that you are immediately free from the shackles of such developments as mobile phones, the internet and DNA profiling, all of which can really mess up a decent plot.

I'm particularly drawn to the recent past, particularly the 1940s and 1950s, and I think this is because of the inherent contradiction that, although in some respects these two decades seem close enough to be the metaphorical hand stretching out to clasp one's own, in other respects they are more remote than the Dark Ages. Another part of the attraction is that an examination of the recent past is a good way to put one's own life and times in context – and I'm repeatedly astonished by quite how topical it often turns out to be. I'm not convinced by LP Hartley's assertion that the past is a foreign country where they do things differently; the sense I get when I research and write a historical crime novel is one of *plus ça change, plus c'est la même chose* – human beings have a terrible habit of making the same mistakes over and over again.

BEN PASTOR (1940s Italy)

Pastor's *Liar Moon* is set in 1943. Italy is a divided country, pulled apart by its shift of allegiance. The Italian government has disowned its former allies and declared war on Germany, and while the north of the country remains under the control of the Fascists, the south is gradually being liberated by the Allies. Fertile territory, indeed, for the accomplished historical novelist – and Ben Pastor is incontrovertibly that. Despite the first name, Pastor is female and – although born in Italy – has lived for three decades in the United States. On her last visit to this country she cut a distinctive figure: fiercely intelligent and sporting a very British sense of irony (as well as a miniature cowboy hat suggesting an eccentric quality that is also to be found in her highly individual novels). In *Liar Moon*, her aristocratic protagonist, Wehrmacht Major Martin Bora, stationed in Italy, is handed a difficult task: to investigate the death of a local Fascist. This particular murder, however, has some troubling ramifications for the regime, and the wrong result in the case may cause embarrassment. In the frame for the murder is the victim's young widow Clara. At the same time, Sandro Guidi, the local police inspector, is on the trail of a serial killer (the term may not have existed in 1943, but the syndrome did), and it is politic that the two men work together. Bora labours under a disadvantage; he has made clear his objections to the ruthless SS initiatives in Russia. He has to tread carefully, even as all around him anti-partisan conflict and growing realisation of the horrors of the Holocaust create a mire in which both men find themselves sinking deeper. In Pastor's previous book featuring Martin Bora, the much-acclaimed *Lumen*, the author demonstrated an unusual skill: to destabilise reader expectations as to what kind of novel they were reading. Was this literary historical fiction? Certainly, few serious writers could so adroitly conjure up such a peerless sense of time and place. What's more, her carefully wrought, often poetic prose helped her bag the Premio Zaragoza for historical fiction. But the real surprise was the fact that this was a crime novel quite as cunningly orchestrated as the best genre product. The dual identities of the book fuse perfectly, with no sense of shifting gears between serious historical novel and crime thriller. If the second outing for Ben Pastor's sympathetic Wehrmacht Major lacks the sheer authority of its predecessor, it is still at times a hauntingly sad piece that will have readers impatient to spend more time in the company of its melancholic German protagonist.

Other key books: *The Water Thief*, *The Fire Walker* (both featuring Aelius Spartianus, historian to Emperor Diocletian, in early fourth-century Rome).

TV: FOYLE'S WAR (various directors)

The creation of the screenwriter and author Anthony Horowitz (responsible for the TV adaptation of *Midsomer Murders*), *Foyle's War* was commissioned by ITV after the seemingly indestructible *Inspector Morse* was finally terminated in 2000. *Foyle's War* is a detective series set during and shortly after World War Two. After its first showing on ITV in October 2002, ITV's Director of Programmes Simon Shaps cancelled the Horowitz drama in 2007. But the public was having none of this, and Peter Fincham (who replaced Shaps) brought back the show. Writing and direction have made the show a success, but the key element is perhaps the casting of the impeccable Michael Kitchen in the title role. The last episode was aired on 18 January 2015, after eight acclaimed series.

11: The Late 1940s and the 1950s

GORDON FERRIS (1940s Glasgow)

The Hanging Shed was a massive success even before its print incarnation hit the bookshops, proving that new technology cannot be ignored even in the still technophobic world of books: the Kilmarnock-born writer's fourth novel became one of the most downloaded books in Britain after being released on Kindle. Ironically, this success via modern means was granted to what is essentially a traditional piece. The setting is Glasgow in 1946, and the author's delineation of the immediate post-war years has a bristling immediacy. As Ferris has noted, the war years and the rock 'n' roll era of the 1950s have been exhaustively mined by writers, but the mid-1940s remain somewhat underused. The author is particularly sharp on the burgeoning crime of the period, including black market enterprise and violent street gangs. Ferris's tough protagonist Douglas Brodie is an ex-policeman who finds himself forced to save his childhood friend Hugh Donovan from hanging. The latter was shot down over Dresden and has returned to Glasgow in a grimly unrecognisable condition. Scarred and mutilated, he turns to heroin. Donovan makes everyone around him uncomfortable, and when a local boy is discovered raped and murdered, the drug-addicted loner is the perfect fit for the crime. But Brodie distrusts the mass of evidence that points to Donovan's guilt, and – with the aid of local advocate Samantha Campbell – begins a daunting odyssey through the dangerous backstreets of the Gorbals, obstructed by both bent coppers and murderous razor gangs. Ferris is a writer of real authority, immersing the reader into his Celtic nightmare world with a brand of scabrous writing reminiscent of William McIlvanney's *Laidlaw*. If the notion of the sparring male/

female duo at the centre of *The Hanging Shed* has a warmed-over quality, everything else here speaks of an original voice. The book deserved – and achieved – quite as many readers in its hard copy form as it had already gleaned in its electronic version.

🎤 Interview: Gordon Ferris

At its simplest, setting my novels in the late 1940s allowed me to sidestep all the distractions of mobile phones, DNA forensics and CCTV, and concentrate on the story. More importantly, post-war Britain was a cauldron of change and upheaval. The country was broke, its empire disintegrating, and a million men, demobbed after six years in uniform, were fighting for jobs and a new role in society. Their estranged womenfolk had found a taste for independence and wage earning. Rationing was worsening. Spivs and wide boys ruled the roost. Corruption was endemic. A perfect crucible to test a hero.

I grew up devouring novels by Robert Louis Stevenson and Daniel Defoe, Graham Greene and Mary Renault, Patrick O'Brian and John le Carré – an extravagant mix of great writing, inspirational protagonists and fabulous settings. My final catalyst was Willie McIlvanney, a fellow Kilmarnock man. Willie blazed the trail for me and every Scottish crime writer since.

In the late 1940s we still had capital punishment, otherwise there would have been no *Hanging Shed*, the first of the Douglas Brodie books. But we also had the worst winter in memory and a huge influx of Jewish refugees, all providing a perfect backcloth for the Glasgow Quartet, starring my lone hero watching over a mean city, in a mean time. These were harsher times, but more honest. An era when character and principle mattered more than money. My stories are about the wee folk, the ones who quietly made the best of it, despite rationing and deprivation. And who sometimes needed one of their own to step forward and shield them from villainy.

CAY RADEMACHER (1947 Hamburg)

In Cay Rademacher's *The Murderer in Ruins* (as translated from the German by Peter Millar), Hamburg in 1947 is a devastated city occupied by the British who bombed it. It is experiencing its coldest winter in living memory, and the black market is all-powerful – and there is a killer on the loose. Frank Stave is a career policeman dealing with both this external threat and a tragedy in his past. The reputation of this remarkable novel has grown by leaps and bounds, and it proves to be well worth the attention it has received, particularly in this sympathetic translation. It is historical crime writing of a distinguished order.

TOM ROB SMITH (Soviet Russia)

Much enthusiasm was occasioned by the appearance of Tom Rob Smith's *Child 44*, with rave reviews preceded by lively word of mouth on the book. The setting is the Soviet Union in the year 1953; Stalin's reign of terror is at its height, and those who stand up against the might of the state vanish into the labour camps – or vanish altogether. With this background, it is an audacious move on Tom Rob Smith's part to put his hero right at the heart of this hideous regime, as an officer in the brutal Ministry of State Security. Leo Demidov is, basically, an instrument of the state – by no means a villain, but one who tries to look not too closely into the repressive work he does. His superiors remind him that there is no crime in the Soviet Union, and he is somehow able to maintain this fiction in his mind even as he tracks down and punishes miscreants. The body of a young boy is found on the railway tracks in Moscow, and Demidov is quickly informed that there is nothing to the case. He soon realises that something unpleasant is being covered up, but he is forced to obey his orders. However, things begin to unravel and this ex-hero of the state suddenly finds himself in disgrace, exiled with his wife Raisa to a town in the Ural Mountains. And things will get worse for him – not only the murder of another child, but the life and safety of Raisa. Tom Rob Smith cleverly makes the reader wait for his conflicted hero to turn against his totalitarian state, as we know he will at some point. It's a superb debut.

Film: CHILD 44 (Daniel Espinosa, director)

Filmmakers never seem to learn – when attempting to set a piece abroad, they sometimes make the actors adopt cod foreign accents (usually ladled on with a trowel) to suggest a sense of place. It's usually deeply counterproductive, the most egregious example being the woeful film of *Captain Corelli's Mandolin* with its Chico Marx Italian accents. Running it a close second is this adaptation of Tom Rob Smith's 2008 novel, transformed into a stodgy film with the multinational cast speaking in English but utilising comically heavy Russian accents. Tom Hardy plays national hero Leo Demidov in his most monumental style – imposing enough, but resolutely one-dimensional, as is Daniel Espinosa's direction.

NATASHA WALTER (1950s Britain)

What would you expect of the first novel by the feminist writer Natasha Walter? Surely the author of such books as *Living Dolls: The Return of Sexism* and *The New Feminism* might reasonably be expected to grind a few ideological axes in her fiction debut? A twenty-first-century take, perhaps, on Marilyn French's *The Women's Room*? Those expecting such fare from Walter will be in for a surprise – if there is one genre *A Quiet Life* moves in, it's the very different territory of the espionage novel with its attendant betrayals. But just how successful is this change of gears? The novel is inspired by the life of Melinda Marling, the American-born wife of Cambridge spy Donald Maclean, but it inhabits a different universe from that of such writers as John le Carré. For Walter, the most stimulating aspect of the story is not so much the tensions of the Cold War but a determined woman's survival. In her earlier work, Walter addressed the battles that women have fought – and still fight – for equality, but this is an era when such battles were nascent, and her heroine has to deal with something on a far grander scale than the petty perfidies of the war between the sexes. Laura Leverett is living a ghost-like existence in Geneva with her daughter, attempting to come to terms with the disappearance of her duplicitous husband in 1951. Outwardly, she is an unexceptional middle-class woman with no hint of the dark secret she is harbouring. When Laura arrived in London in 1939, she became involved with Communist cells and found herself buffeted between her upper-crust English associates and those seeking to overhaul British society via a radical new order. She fell in love with a man she met at a party – charismatic, attractive and seemingly at ease in both of her contrasting worlds. But the incendiary areas of trust and betrayal that he led her into changed her life irrevocably as she moved from Washington in the grip of McCarthyism to the apparent tranquillity of the English countryside. And in the present,

Laura realises that the repercussions of her youthful idealism and misplaced love will be fateful indeed. Eschewing the apparatus of an espionage narrative, Walter concentrates on the conflicts within her heroine – and it is in the characterisation of the multifaceted Laura that the novel really sings. Feminist points are made about the sacrifices women make for men, but never in unsubtle fashion – Walter is too nuanced a writer for that.

ELIZABETH WILSON (1940s Britain)

The Twilight Hour by Elizabeth Wilson is set in London during the freezing winter of 1947. In the bomb-damaged city, socialite Dinah Wentworth becomes involved in a Fitzrovian scandal when she stumbles on the corpse of the Surrealist artist Mavor. Trying to keep her involvement with him secret, she does not report the crime. But Colin, a friend of her husband, is arrested on suspicion of murder, and Dinah realises that unless she can track down the real murderer, Colin will be hanged. At the more literary end of the crime/espionage genre, one of the most accomplished writers is Elizabeth Wilson, whose *War Damage* and *The Girl in Berlin* combined glittering, dark-hued prose with levels of penetrating psychological insight the equal of her great predecessors in the field. Wilson's upwards trajectory continues here; the author is an academic with a speciality in popular culture, so it's no surprise that her storytelling ethos is so peerless. The picture of an earlier era of austerity Britain has the usual confident sweep.

DAVID LAGERCRANTZ (1950s Britain)

Who is David Lagercrantz? And should we care? Actually, the answer to the latter question is yes, as the Swedish author took on a massively popular publishing franchise, writing further books in the Millennium sequence with everybody's favourite Goth hacker Lisbeth Salander back in the pain business. Inevitably, any writer with the temerity to take up the pen of the late Stieg Larsson (particularly with an unfinished fourth book by Larsson himself squirrelled away somewhere) is making themselves a hostage to fortune. Initially, Lagercrantz seems a surprising choice, given that his book about a footballer, *I Am Zlatan Ibrahimović*, seems a million miles away from Nordic noir

– except that it shares the genre's keen social concerns. However, before the appearance of *The Girl in the Spider's Web*, readers had a chance to assess Lagercrantz's skill in something closer to the crime field with his novel *Fall of Man in Wilmslow* (translated by George Goulding) – and a very curious hybrid it is, though a winning one. This is an amalgam of crime narrative, psychology and science; the strapline reads 'The Death and Life of Alan Turing'. Lagercrantz channels an interest in the mathematician who helped crack the Enigma code in a novel set in 1954, beginning with Turing found dead at his house in Wilmslow. He appears to have created his own unusual method of suicide: a poisoned apple. Assigned to the case, Detective Leonard Corell learns that Turing has been convicted of homosexual offences (in reality, Turing was forced by the judiciary into chemical castration because of his sexuality – he was retrospectively exonerated by Gordon Brown). The verdict of suicide is complicated by the veil of secrecy drawn over the mathematician's war record, and the security services have decided that Turing's illegal sexuality might have made him a target for Soviet spies. But as Corell gets closer to the top-secret work at Bletchley, he finds himself the target of the same individuals who destroyed the dead man. As a Swedish writer attempting to capture an English idiom for this most English of subjects, Lagercrantz shows undoubted chutzpah, but he unerringly finds the correct phrasing (although we do not know what finessing his translator George Goulding has wrought). Perhaps the most signal achievement of the book is its clever melding of two narrative forms: a sympathetic biography of a real-life historical figure treated appallingly by the establishment, and a police procedural in which a dogged copper tries to crack a mystery in the teeth of bloody-minded intransigence. Inevitably, the sections on the detective's own tangled psychology cannot exert the fascination of the dead mathematician. But what really energises Lagercrantz is his passionate distaste for those who brought down Turing – when we hear praise in the book from English authorities for Senator McCarthy's attacks on communists and homosexuals, we know exactly what to think of them. And Lagercrantz is perceptive in his treatment of the tragic Turing.

BENJAMIN BLACK (1950s Ireland)

When John Banville compared himself to a sheep venturing among wolves, there were those who felt he was being a touch disingenuous. Banville was referring to a controversial appearance he had made at the Harrogate crime writing festival wearing his 'Benjamin Black' hat: i.e. as the writer of a historical crime fiction series rather than as the heavyweight literary novelist responsible for the Man Booker Prize-winning *The Sea*. Banville/Black's comments generated quite a furore at the festival – one that enjoyed much subsequent coverage in the press. Banville's offence? In front of an audience of crime writers and aficionados of the genre, he was widely perceived to have suggested that he did not grant his crime novels the same level of seriousness as his literary work; the former were mere *jeux d'esprit* to be dispatched quickly, while the latter – his *real* achievement – required far more time and attention. Banville seemed surprised at the various noses he had put out of joint with this apparent disparaging of the popular writer's trade – did this sheep among wolves have no idea that his remarks would create such a negative impression? The crime writing fraternity is famously prickly about its lack of respectability. However, Banville overlooked another factor in the brouhaha – the way in which his Benjamin Black novels are received among many crime fiction practitioners. Just a few pages of *A Death in Summer* (featuring his pathologist protagonist Quirke) demonstrate just what a stylist he is; a writer whose use of English can create an almost sensuous frisson in the reader. The bloody shotgun murder of a newspaper magnate has Quirke on the trail of a killer, and the Dublin evoked here has a richness reminiscent of the city's greatest chronicler, James Joyce, while the 1950s are evoked with pinpoint precision. But then we come to the sticking point – and the reason why crime writers were grumbling in the wine bars of Harrogate after the perceived slight: Black's plotting. As ever, everything is supremely functional but seems utilitarian rather than inspired. The mechanics of the crime investigation will be familiar to the avid consumer of the genre: the apparent suicide quickly nailed by the sleuth as murder; the array of suspects who might want an unpopular man dead; the divided family; the misdirection – all are present and correct, but are comprehensively the least interesting things about the novel. Raymond Chandler, too, spent little time on his plots – and though that writer would fall into the 'genre' category (by Black's lights) rather than 'serious writer', his genius was to reinvent the tropes of detective fiction so consummately that readers barely noticed the rickety narrative structure. But despite his descriptive skills, Black's use of such legerdemain is less sure. In the final analysis, however, and putting such reservations aside, *A Death in Summer* is still a highly professional and engaging piece of work – and that pellucid use of language will make most readers forget the author's casual downgrading of his own calling.

Holy Orders (overfamiliar title apart) – clocking in at an economical 300-odd pages – is one of the most persuasive in the Quirke series, with a strong vein of melancholy. Previous virtues – notably the stunning picture of mid-century Dublin – are here married to a new rigour in plotting, and the greater focus pays dividends. A body is discovered in the canal, and Detective Inspector Hackett once more inveigles his pathologist friend Quirke to help in the investigation (in fact, Quirke knew the victim, a journalist). With a murderer on the loose, the two men begin to discern that the solution to the case lies at the heart of an institution which is all-powerful in Dublin – the Catholic Church. From James Joyce onwards (with his description of Ireland as a 'priest-ridden country'), the Church, with its immense wealth and political clout, has been a useful lodestone for novelists, and is, inevitably, even more so with the *scheissesturm* that has enveloped it in recent years because of the many abuse scandals. The latter shame is reflected here in a reminiscence of Quirke's own childhood in an orphanage run by priests, and there is a genuine sense of outrage powering *Holy Orders*. Black has always ensured that the Quirke books are beautifully written, but cogent storytelling is a newly added ingredient, with the once rather one-note pathologist now a multifaceted character. The Gabriel Byrne TV series notwithstanding, it's clear that the literary incarnation of Quirke is going from strength to strength.

As Benjamin Black, John Banville has also written standalone crime novels, including *Prague Nights*. In 1599, a young doctor newly arrived in the city is tasked with tracking down the murderer of the Emperor's mistress.

🎤 Interview: Benjamin Black

Unusually, I can remember the exact moment when the idea for *Prague Nights* came to me. I was walking my dog on Howth Head, outside Dublin, where I live, when for no reason I can think of the name 'Christian Stern' sprang into my mind, and within about 15 minutes I had the outlines of a plot, set in Prague around 1600, a period I knew a little about because I had set my novel *Kepler* in the same place and in the same period. I'm afraid none of my books achieved anything even close to what I had hoped for from them. But I keep trying.

I greatly admire Marguerite Yourcenar, and while I haven't reread it for some years now, her novel on alchemy and related matters, *The Abyss*, was in the back of my mind while I was writing *Prague Nights*. Of course, her masterpiece is *Memoirs of Hadrian*, a long and intricate novel distinguished by being without a single line of dialogue. Historical fiction is an extremely difficult genre, especially if one writes of actual historical figures, and tries to stick, more or less, to the facts. How to avoid the snigger-provoking 'I say, Beethoven, isn't that young Mozart over there?' syndrome is a constant preoccupation. And why is it almost impossible to inject humour into historical fiction, unless one is writing a Fielding-esque romp? – and nobody can do that successfully save Fielding. Odd to think that almost all the great Victorian novels were historical, from *War and Peace* downwards. I suppose it's that, in the nineteenth century, no one was expected to be 'relevant'. Ah, those happy days of yore.

🎬 TV: QUIRKE (various directors)

When the Irish actor Gabriel Byrne filmed the BBC adaptation of Benjamin Black's *Quirke*, the mid-1950s time frame and Dublin setting coincided with the actor's own boyhood – which clearly added a level of verisimilitude. Quirke (whose first name we never learn) is the intuitive pathologist at the centre of the mysteries penned by the Booker Prize-winning novelist John Banville under the pseudonym of Benjamin Black. The series was occasionally criticised for its Stygian gloom, but the visuals captured a sense of Black's prose.

STEPHEN L CARTER (1950s America)

Stephen Carter's thriller writing is ambitious and vibrant. *Palace Council* is set in the summer of 1952; 20 influential men meet clandestinely to forge a scheme to influence the actions of the President of the United States. Shortly afterwards, Eddie Wesley, a writer, is at a party and comes across the body of a dead man who is clutching a gold cross in his hands. As Eddie struggles to find out who is behind the death, his sister June becomes involved with an underground group and disappears. Needless to say, her fate is linked to the secret plot discussed at the eponymous – and dangerous – Palace Council.

CRAIG RUSSELL (1950s Glasgow)

Craig Russell is the author of the critically acclaimed Jan Fabel series of thrillers set in modern Hamburg and also writes non-crime fiction under the name Christopher Galt. The fourth in Russell's Lennox series, *Dead Men and Broken Hearts*, is set in November 1956 with the world in turmoil because of the Suez Crisis, the Hungarian Uprising and other turbulence. The book's picture of a dangerous Glasgow underworld of the 1950s is evoked with considerable skill.

JAMES ELLROY (Mid-twentieth-century America)

The Black Dahlia by James Ellroy concerns the 1947 murder and vicious mutilation of Elizabeth Short in Los Angeles, California. The case resulted in the exposure of a major police corruption scandal and had a personal resonance for Ellroy, reflecting as it did the violent death of his own mother. Utilising real individuals and events, Ellroy's novel provides a solution to the unsolved murder. James Ellroy is one of the great American crime writers, with each new book keenly awaited (this was particularly the case with his Underworld USA trilogy); in his work, we are given an amazingly ambitious synthesis of crime and political chicanery, with the social mores of the day forensically examined. And all of this is delivered with the gusto we have come to expect from one of the world's most accomplished novelists.

> **Film: THE BLACK DAHLIA (Brian De Palma, director)**
>
> Who better than Brian De Palma, director of Al Pacino's *Scarface*, to help this 2006 version of James Ellroy's dark novel, a fictionalised version of the murder of Elizabeth Short? In the event, De Palma's sure touch with the crime film scenario appeared to desert him here, as evinced by the unimpressive performances coaxed from the usually reliable Josh Hartnett, Aaron Eckhart and Scarlett Johansson. The plot (in which two detectives watch their personal and professional lives destroyed by the ramifications of the Black Dahlia murder investigation – see also *Who Is the Black Dahlia?* below) is handled with efficiency, but no panache.

MEGAN ABBOTT (1950s America)

Although the talented American Megan Abbott seems to have moved to the contemporary era with her more recent novels, which all display a close and nuanced attention to the psychology of her characters, she has also demonstrated a penchant for the period-set thriller. *Bury Me Deep* (set in 1931) and *The Song Is You* (1951) are both inspired by real-life cases, while *Queenpin* and *Die a Little* are modern takes on the 1950s hardboiled crime novel.

MARK MILLS (1950s Italy, 1930s France)

Is your taste for the literary novel of feeling, in which atmospheric evocations of locale and nuanced descriptions of character are couched in delicate prose? Or do you prefer the stronger meat of crime fiction, in which a baffling mystery is cracked while the hero experiences violent pummellings (and, if the writer is feeling generous, graphically described sexual gratification)? Actually, there are many of us given to alternating such pleasures – and with Mark Mills, we have an author who can simultaneously slake both appetites. As *The Whaleboat House* demonstrated, here was a 'crime' author utilising the kind of writing more often found at the bedside of Booker Prize judges. But Mills is also a dab hand at plotting a mystery, and if *The Savage Garden* doesn't quite bring off these dual skills with total panache, it's still a mesmerising piece. Mills' playfulness is evident in his first chapter – 'My God,' the reader is likely to mutter in dismay, 'this is so *badly* written. What's happened to Mark Mills' talent?' But, in fact, this first chapter (we discover) is something written by a girlfriend of the hero, Cambridge student Adam Strickland. When he is invited to give his opinion, we already know he'll have to bite his tongue. Adam is a complaisant young man, just about getting by in the Cambridge of 1958, when he's handed an intriguing assignment: he is to visit and write about the garden of Villa Docci in Tuscany, devised in the sixteenth century by a widower in memory of his wife. Quickly out of his depth, Adam encounters a series of mysteries: what is the secret of the elderly Signora Docci and her family? What is the truth about the killing that took place at the villa during the German occupation? And is the beautiful Antonella everything she appears to be? All of this is handled with brio by Mills, not least the picture of Florence, intensely realised. So iridescent is the prose that one is prepared to forgive the odd assemblage of books that jostle behind the narrative: there's Henry James' *The Aspern Papers* (reclusive elderly woman and her younger female companion to whom the hero makes love); there's John Fowles' *The Magus*, with a seductive young girl leading a mystified protagonist into a secret world (Fowles' *The French Lieutenant's Woman* also springs to mind, with a powerfully erotic coupling halfway through the book); and, considerably lowering the tone of literary allusions, good old Dan Brown, with clues to the solution of the mystery rather schematically laid out like cats' eyes in the road. But Mills is a skilful writer, and braids these disparate strands into a persuasive tapestry.

A variety of metaphorical ghosts haunts the characters in Mark Mills' mesmerising *House of the Hanged*. But there are also ghosts hovering behind the author – not malign ones, but inspirational shades, steering the author to his best work in an already accomplished career. The setting is France in the summer of 1935. Le Rayol may not be the most prestigious part of the Riviera, but it still offers a retreat from the pending war. A motley community of refugees, expats and underachieving artistic types lulls itself into a false sense of security; the group includes Tom Nash, keen to erase a troubled past spent in the secret services. But as anyone who has ever read a novel featuring an ex-spook protagonist will be well aware, the chances of leaving behind a clandestine past are remote – and so it proves with Tom. He has rather a lot to lose, notably his adored goddaughter Lucy. When a nocturnal attempt is made on his life, Tom realises that someone in his circle is dealing in the kind of betrayal that was once his watchword, and self-preservation must be balanced against the drastic cost to someone he loves. Readers of previous Mills novels will not be surprised that the characters here are as mercurial as ever. Tom Nash's past (spying for the British in Russia during the Revolution) has positioned a Damoclean sword above his head, and a tragic love for a woman during this turbulent period has left him damaged and vulnerable. Tom's struggles to identify who he can and cannot trust among his well-oiled coterie of American, Russian, German and British refugees are fascinatingly handled, with the various dalliances, games of tennis and copiously alcoholic dinner parties the perfect backdrop to the intrigue. But the reader familiar with the great literary figures of the past may discern other hands on Mark Mills' shoulders: the picture of indolent expats in seductive foreign climates echoes Scott Fitzgerald. And there is also a heavyweight Anglo-Polish ghost here who has clearly energised Mills' literary batteries: the terrible cost of the betrayals of the espionage worlds and the Manichaean struggle between elemental forces suggests that a novel or two by Joseph Conrad permanently reside in the author's luggage. If this talented young British writer has some work to do before moving further up the Parnassian slopes towards the writers who inspired him, there is much evidence on every page of *House of the Hanged* that Mills has everything to play for.

🎤 Interview: Mark Mills

I never set out to write period crime novels; I sort of fell into it with my first book, *Amagansett* (aka *The Whaleboat House*). The cultural backdrop to the murder is the growing tension between the local fishing families of a small Long Island town, many of them resident since the seventeenth century, and the wealthy New Yorkers who adopted the area as their summer playground. For reasons of authenticity, this clash of old and new America demanded a period setting, and I opted for 1947, not appreciating at the time just how much work and research it would entail! After that, I had the bug, and although I've deviated from the period route a couple of times, there's nothing quite like steeping yourself in a place then bringing to life a small patch of its past. I once heard it said that a novel is never finished... at a certain point your editor takes it away from you. That's definitely how I feel. I'm never happy with what I produce. If I'm proud of anything, it's of being a Brit who once wrote an American novel that the Americans took to their hearts.

I suppose the authors who have influenced me most are Evelyn Waugh, Graham Greene and William Boyd. That becomes clearer with every passing novel, as I find myself returning once again to the theme of ordinary people caught up in extraordinary events – often in exotic locales. The world of British crime fiction is in better shape than ever. There's so much fresh talent out there and such a voracious appetite on the part of readers that I can only see the genre proliferating, and possibly splintering into a plethora of sub-genres.

CHARLES ARDAI (1950s America)

Charles Ardai is a man of many accomplishments, including writing, television production and even the creation of the respected crime imprint Hard Case Crime. Starting his writing career (as so many do) in *Ellery Queen's Mystery Magazine* and *Alfred Hitchcock's Mystery Magazine*, his first novel, *Little Girl Lost*, written as 'Richard Aleas', appeared in 2004 and was nominated for an Edgar. *Fifty-to-One*, which celebrates the achievements of the imprint, is a clever, self-referential piece set in 1950 that utilises elements from many of the books that Ardai has published.

MARTIN CRUZ SMITH (Cold War Russia)

You've heard it before. Several times. 'It's Martin Cruz Smith's best book since *Gorky Park*!' The fact that Smith's publishers – and, in perfect collusion, the books pages of newspapers – have felt obliged to trot out this refrain for each new Russian-set novel featuring dogged investigator Arkady Renko begs at least one question: why do we need to hear this? Surely each outing for Renko since that wonderfully atmospheric and brilliantly plotted first Renko novel of 1981 has been impressive? Well, up to a point; all have been imaginative and diverting, making full capital out of the novelty of having a Russian detective in strikingly realised Cold War Russian settings – even when the novelty was no more. But only one, *Polar Star* (which has Renko encountering mayhem aboard a huge fishing ship), had the same mesmerising power of that first book. Smith's publishers know that fact as well as readers; hence the talking-up of each new Renko. One thing is inarguable: Smith's second career as a crime novelist (since initiating the Renko series) is far more consistent than his first; when a slew of earlier, non-Renko books were re-released in the wake of *Gorky Park*'s massive success, readers were disappointed to discover how ordinary these were compared with the incandescence of his breakthrough novel. Although these earlier thrillers had enjoyed some success, they were far less complex and interesting than the later series, and now look like an apprenticeship for a subsequent golden age for the writer. (*Gorky Park* was indifferently filmed with William Hurt as Renko in 1983.)

TV: WHO IS THE BLACK DAHLIA? (Joseph Pevney, director)

The murder and mutilation of the unsuccessful actress Elizabeth Short has long been a source of fascination for crime fiction practitioners, most notably James Ellroy, and this difficult-to-see television film stars Lucie Arnaz as Short. The 'lost week' that preceded the actress's gruesome death is the subject here, and Pevney's film is (to date) the only one that puts the luckless Short at the centre of the narrative, rather than using her as a character on the sidelines or as the reason for a murder investigation.

Film: MULHOLLAND FALLS (Lee Tamahori, director)

No, not David Lynch's *Mulholland Drive*, but a Pete Dexter screenplay starring Nick Nolte and a remarkable ensemble cast. Nolte leads a crack team of four 1950s LAPD detectives who are ruthless in their pursuit of criminals. The group is based on the real-life 'Hat Squad', and the film is powerfully made.

Film: HOLLYWOODLAND (Allen Coulter, director)

This 2006 drama features a well-judged and understated performance by the talented Ben Affleck as George Reeves, the ill-fated actor who played Superman on American television in the 1950s. This fictionalised version of his life and death has a private detective investigating Reeves' association with some dangerous people. It's a subtle and intelligent piece.

TV: CRIMES OF PASSION (various directors)

Crimes of Passion is markedly different crime drama from the dark, moody Scandicrime that has characterised the genre for so long. But this sunny, unclouded mystery series was seeded in a different way from *The Killing* or *The Bridge*. Its creator (in the novels on which the series is based) was one of the earlier writers in Swedish crime fiction, Maria Lang (whose real name was Dagmar Lange, and who was writing in the 1940s and 1950s). She was part of the old guard that younger, more socially committed Scandinavian crime writers felt the need to react against, despite the considerable success she enjoyed in her day with such books as *The Murderer Does Not Tell Lies Alone*. Lang's inspiration was – unsurprisingly – the English crime queen Agatha Christie, and Lang's books are undoubtedly enjoyed by many readers – like Christie, she presents a rather unrealistic picture of her country, where crime is not the deeply destabilising force it is for later writers. The adaptations in the series *Crime of Passion* inhabit a Christie-like 1950s Sweden, with the unlikely trio of Puck (played by Tuva Novotny) and her fiancé Eje (Linus Wahlgren) plus friend and policeman Christer Wijk (Ola Rapace) solving various crimes. The series offers relaxing entertainment and attractive locations, and it deserves attention alongside the edgier fare.

12: The 1960s and 1970s

ROBERT HARRIS (1960s Alternative History Germany, Ancient Rome)

Nazi Germany in 1964. The murdered body of an old man is discovered, and an investigation is undertaken by a dogged Berlin copper. But when he finds that the much-loathed Gestapo is in the mix, his own life is soon on the line. The breakthrough novel for Robert Harris – the work that established him as one of the UK's key novelists – was, of course, *Fatherland* in 1992, and even though the concept (Germany winning World War Two) was not original, the treatment was astonishingly assured. Following that novel, a slew of distinctive books flowed from Harris's desk, including *Enigma*, *Archangel* and the *roman-à-clef The Ghost*. All demonstrated the author's reluctance to be typecast in any one field. The thriller may be his preferred habitat, but he has shown a keen readiness to deal with historical subjects and the past: one of his most acclaimed books was the sprawling and ambitious *Pompeii*. Robert Harris is at his considerable best when evoking the ancient past with a vividness that few of his contemporaries can match.

TV: FATHERLAND (Christopher Menaul, director)

While Philip K Dick and Len Deighton have both penned 'alternative histories' in which Germany is the victor in World War Two, Robert Harris's *Fatherland* is perhaps the most influential entry in this sub-genre. Christopher Menaul's adaptation is set in Berlin 20 years after Germany's win, with an SS detective and an American journalist exposing a grim secret of the Third Reich. Strongly cast, with Rutger Hauer, Michael Kitchen and Miranda Richardson (who received a

Golden Globe Award in 1995 for Best Performance by an Actress in a TV Supporting Role), the world building of Harris's novel is cleverly approximated, if not quite as unerringly as the novelist achieved.

REGGIE NADELSON (1960s New York)

The modern-day Artie Cohen novels of Reggie Nadelson customarily furnish sardonic, idiosyncratic reads, but *Manhattan 62* has bigger fish to fry. In 1962, a young Cuban is discovered on a railway, grotesquely mutilated, the second murder in New York that has left its victim with a tattoo of a worm and the words 'Cuba Libre'. Irish NYPD detective Pat Wynne has a politically sensitive case on his hands with espionage a possible element – and minds are concentrated by the fact that Cuban missiles are trained on America; the tension is palpable. Nadelson is fascinated by the atmosphere of political paranoia of the period, but there is also a loving celebration of early 1960s New York in which discussion and debate are endemic. As ever with this writer, the sense of place is crucial, but what really energises the narrative here is the political turmoil, ever present in both the characters' minds and the reader's.

DAVID PEACE (1970s Britain, 1940s Japan)

David Peace's *Occupied City*, the second part of his celebrated Tokyo trilogy, builds on the success of the first book, *Tokyo Year Zero*. That book sported a massive historical canvas and a tough crime narrative. In the second book, the time and place are Tokyo, January 1948. The city is occupied, and a man arrives at a bank talking of a dysentery outbreak that he has been sent to treat. Members of the bank staff are given a liquid which, he says, will save them from the outbreak – but within minutes they are dead. The murderer robs the bank, and a massive manhunt begins. However, Peace's magnum opus was the celebrated and influential Red Riding Quartet, beginning with the caustic *Nineteen Seventy Four* and *Nineteen Seventy Seven* and continuing with *Nineteen Eighty* and *Nineteen Eighty Three*. The quartet deals with the corruption that was so common in the police force in that period, and his antiheroes traverse a society where justice is elusive. Peace's youth in Ossett during the hunt for the

Yorkshire Ripper was drawn on by the author as the basis for the Red Riding Quartet.

TV: RED RIDING TRILOGY (Julian Jarrold, James Marsh and Anand Tucker, directors)

TV broadcasts emphasised the dark visuals of this much-acclaimed series of adaptations of David Peace's scarifying Yorkshire-set crime novels; subsequent DVD issues render detail far more clearly and accessibly. Scripted by Tony Grisoni and directed by Julian Jarrold, James Marsh and Anand Tucker, *Red Riding* is a grim but utterly forceful trilogy of films built around the six-year police investigation of the Yorkshire Ripper, folded in with other fictitious crimes. The reworking of the novels by David Peace (*Nineteen Seventy Four*, *Nineteen Eighty* and *Nineteen Eighty Three*) is handled with assurance, although this is deeply uncomfortable viewing. It's perhaps a legitimate point to make that the treatment of the West Yorkshire Police – while consummately acted and directed – has something in common with Mel Gibson's treatment of the British in such movies as *The Patriot*: they are presented as brutal Nazi stormtroopers, utterly corrupt and beyond any law. But there is no gainsaying the skilfulness of the realisation here. The powerful, resolutely unconsoling dramas are bolstered with remarkable performances from a stellar cast including Sean Bean, Andrew Garfield, Paddy Considine, Warren Clarke, Peter Mullan, David Morrissey, Maxine Peake, Rebecca Hall and Mark Addy.

EOIN MCNAMEE (1960s Northern Ireland)

How legitimate is it to plunder real-life crime as grist for a crime fiction writer's mill? And how long an interval should be left before picking over the bones of murder from the past? With equally scabrous results, two celebrated crime novelists have transmuted grim real-life crimes into deeply uncompromising books: James Ellroy, fictionally dealing with Elizabeth Short's murder in *The Black Dahlia*; and, in this country, David Peace's controversial use of the Yorkshire Ripper's reign of terror in the Red Riding Quartet. Eoin McNamee steps aggressively into this dangerous territory with *Orchid Blue* – less visceral than these famous predecessors, but equally provocative, dealing with the last hanging on Northern Irish soil. The source of McNamee's dispassionate but disturbing novel is the case of Robert McGladdery, who was charged with the brutal murder of 19-year-old Pearl Gamble near the town of Newry on a cold January night in 1961. Later the same year, McGladdery was hanged in Crumlin Road Gaol. The judge in the case, Lancelot Curran, was the youngest attorney general at Stormont, centre of the Unionist establishment. Of this charismatic figure, McNamee has said: 'I've been writing about him for years. Now I'm not sure if I'm the pursuer or the pursued.' Nine years earlier, Curran had been in the news when his own daughter Patricia, also 19 years old, had been murdered. What was Lancelot Curran's involvement in the murder of his daughter – and was an innocent man subsequently sent to the gallows? A similar real-life miscarriage of justice was rewritten in novel form by Laura Wilson in her book *A Capital Crime*, which focused on a calculating older man and a naïve, younger 'sacrificial lamb' (in Wilson's case, John Christie and the educationally subnormal Timothy Evans), but the historical antecedents there were less contentious – and Wilson changed the names of those involved. McNamee's source material may be as recent as the 1960s, but it is far less familiar than the Rillington Place murders, and he is able to fashion a genuinely unnerving fiction out of this once-notorious murder case. His real skill here, apart from his unhurried creation of a dark potpourri of homicide and revenge, is to invent a dirt-digging protagonist, Detective Eddie McCrink, and to insert him in the murky scenario. McCrink, hardboiled and bloody-minded, has returned to Northern Ireland policing from London, and becomes deeply involved in the case. Swiftly, in the teeth of official disapproval, he becomes convinced that powerful people are using the system for their own ends, and that the hapless McGladdery is unlikely to be given a fair hearing. The word of a judge – particularly in the 1960s – was law. In *Resurrection Man*, McNamee detailed the bloodletting of the UVF gang the Shankill Butchers, and his hard-edged novel *The Blue Tango* (a Booker Prize nominee) was another journey into the benighted soul of his native country. If *Orchid Blue* lacks the cold fury of these earlier books, it is still harshly compelling.

JAMES RUNCIE (1960s Cambridge)

If you're from an ecclesiastical bloodline, is there a temptation to rebel against family traditions? After all, Ingmar Bergman, son of a fiercely devout pastor, made films about the futility of faith in the modern world, while Nietzsche's priestly father provoked the philosopher's pronouncement 'God is dead'. And so thorough was the rejection of piety in Freud and Voltaire that both even suggested they were foundlings set down in religious families. With James Runcie's background (son of an Archbishop of Canterbury), one might have thought that when he turned to crime writing he would opt to defy family shibboleths and write gritty, uncompromising novels about alcoholic coppers in urban Britain, but his continuing series of Grantchester mysteries featuring Canon Sidney Chambers (a linear descendant of Chesterton's Father Brown) would have made for a perfectly relaxing read over a cup of Earl Grey for his famous father (after a hard day at the coal face struggling with gay and women priests). But if Runcie *fils*' books are resolutely – even defiantly – old-fashioned, that doesn't mean that they are not subtly and insidiously pleasurable (if, that is, you prefer Alexander McCall Smith to Ian Rankin). *Sidney Chambers and the Problem of Evil*, the third in the series, is as entertaining as its predecessors. Once again couched in the form of separate novellas, we are accorded both persuasive scene setting and a rounded picture of church society. Sidney Chambers' fellow priests in 1960s Cambridgeshire represent a microcosm of the Church of England itself – from an intense biblical scholar to an effète lay reader in suede shoes who is too evangelical for Sidney's taste. Runcie channels a touch of the vitriol to be found in Anthony Trollope's ecclesiastical novels and throughout the sequence he has created a detailed portrait of the era in which the various books are set. In the 1960s, Sidney and his new German wife live in a city with a notionally sedate surface, but we are reminded that political unrest is at large in the world; on the Home Service, Sidney hears that Soviet ships are warily observing US nuclear testing at Christmas Island. Nevertheless, Britain is still very much a Christian country – although the eponymous 'problem of evil' persists. Sidney, returning from church with his wife, finds a pair of dead doves on their doorstep. Sidney prays for their souls (do birds have souls? Sidney is clearly an unorthodox theologian), but does nothing – he has bowed to his wife's firm injunction that he takes no more part in the crime-solving activities in the company of his friend Inspector Keating that we have seen in earlier books. But then fellow priests begin to be murdered, and Sidney finds he can no longer be hors de combat – he might even be next on a ruthless killer's list. The other tales here pose equally pleasurable bafflement for Sidney – and for the reader. And there are modern touches too: Chesterton would never have touched repressed homosexuality.

TV: GRANTCHESTER (various directors)

Does the TV *Grantchester* fall firmly within the 'cosy crime' orbit? After all, a crime-solving vicar is never going to be cutting-edge stuff; you can have Catholic superheroes such as Daredevil, but a certain amount of head busting is de rigueur in the latter. Not as toe-curlingly comforting as the recent TV incarnation of Chesterton's Father Brown, *Grantchester* at least makes an effort to add a little grit to its unthreatening stories, with, for instance, Sidney Chambers' dog-collar-wearing predecessor in disgrace after covering up child abuse. The casting (as Chambers) of the very presentable James Norton assures a following as much for heart-throb reasons as for anything else. Robson Green, as Chambers' police associate, is... Robson Green.

WILLIAM SHAW (1960s London)

William Shaw's Breen and Tozer sequence gleams with its vigorous picture of 1960s London, and the author addresses some edgy themes, including the historic effects of colonialism and the controversies surrounding the new permissiveness of the time. Shaw demonstrates a consummate use of language and can also incorporate the key imperative of the thriller – a page-turning story – which makes this series a cause for celebration. Apart from the literary/ thriller binary, *Sympathy for the Devil* marries the police procedural with the subterfuges of the espionage genre. A murdered prostitute called 'Julie Teenager' had a client book featuring the well-placed and influential. Detective Cathal Breen and colleague Helen Tozer notice that the crime scene has been tampered with, and suspect that there is more than meets the eye to this brutal slaying. Things become very personal for the protagonists, and Breen finds that he is obliged to resist feeling 'sympathy for the devil'. Perhaps longer than it needs to be, this is still psychological crime writing of a singular order.

🎤 Interview: William Shaw

My period's the late 1960s – the era in which London felt like the epicentre of this amazing, dangerous new culture. I'm interested in shocking the readers not just with murder, but with how different the 1960s really were. It makes the key figures of the era so much more heroic when you realise how most of Britain was still stuck in the 1940s and 1950s. I was particularly proud of *A House of Knives* because of the way it drew on the art world that surrounded The Beatles and The Rolling Stones, particularly the art dealer the late Robert Fraser. Fraser was the genius who was responsible for commissioning both the *Sgt Pepper* sleeve and the *White Album*, and he's the one who brought Yoko to the UK first. But he was also a terrible smack addict, at the centre of the vortex of abuse that almost destroyed the Stones. I work hard to make people like that plausible, so it was wonderful when Pace Gallery recently did a retrospective of artists championed by Fraser, and someone asked the curators – who'd both known Fraser well – what was he like? They answered: you should read *A House of Knives* – that's what he was like.

For about ten years before I wrote *A Song from Dead Lips*, I'd been in a writers' group with CJ Sansom. I've been watching him grow from the first draft of *Dissolution* – so I've been learning from a master. I was fascinated not just by how brilliantly he creates a world, but by how he makes Shardlake our interpreter of it. The trick in historical fiction is that you need someone who acts as a bridge between the past and the present, someone who's a misfit in their own time. In my books it's Helen Tozer; she loves the 1960s but she's already way, way ahead of it.

LAURA LIPPMAN (1960s and 1970s Baltimore)

An Arcadian past was the subject of Laura Lippman's much-lauded novel *The Innocents*; the past in *After I'm Gone*, however, is not just a different country but a dangerous one. In prose that is rich and complex, Lippman shows that the crime genre can be infinitely flexible in tackling its basic concerns (and a few new ones). The disparate time periods here would have been quicksand for lesser writers, but they are skilfully negotiated by Lippman, as she describes the lives of five women whose happiness has been destroyed by Felix Brewer, a white-collar crook and adulterer who vanishes in 1976, leaving chaos in his wake. The women are his wife Bambi, his mistress Julie and his three daughters, all of whom are strikingly characterised – as is Detective Sandy Sanchez, investigating Julie's murder in the present day. Sanchez, a retired detective, uncovers a web of criminality, jealousy and avarice stretching over several decades and affecting the lives of these very different women. And even though so much time has passed, the missing conman is still crucial to the women's existence. But a reckoning – for everyone – is in the offing. Anatomising a murky criminal past is meat and drink to writers of crime fiction, but few do it as well as Laura Lippman – and as well as conjuring the individual dilemmas of the women at the centre of *After I'm Gone*, she is particularly adroit at evoking a period when women were only starting to enjoy some autonomy. The locale, too, is powerfully evoked: Lippman's own city of Baltimore. At times she draws us into a modern take on the dark atmosphere of one of her favourite writers who resided in the city, Edgar Allan Poe (Lippman has admitted to obsessively haunting Poe's old stamping grounds). But all of this would count for nothing if the plotting were not as rigorous and impressive as it is here: as Sandy draws ever closer to the truth behind the businessman and the murder of his lover, it will be a very seasoned crime reader indeed who will be able to see the twists coming before they spring out.

The fraught territory of childhood has preoccupied novelists from Charles Dickens to JD Salinger, and clearly remains fertile ground for many current writers – even in the crime field. Stephen King produced one of his most affecting pieces with *The Body* (filmed as *Stand By Me*), in which a dark childhood secret is to throw a shadow over the adult lives of the protagonists, and there are echoes of that book in Laura Lippman's impressive *The Innocents*, which is subtly different from the detective novels with which she made her name. This is a more allusive piece, couched in carefully wrought language that manages to support the grandiose comparisons on the book jacket to Lionel Shriver and Megan Abbott. Dickeyville is a suburb of Baltimore, and the Arcadian past evoked here is the perfect setting for *The Innocents*. Five children, including the tomboyish Mickey and the three energetic Halloran brothers, spend the summer months exploring their territory and – almost as a matter of course – disregarding their parents' instructions to steer clear of the overgrown, wilder areas of the region. The children (of whom Gordon Halloran, known as 'Go-Go', is the youngest) have the kind of childhood adventures that most of us wish we'd had, and begin the process of growing up. But the dream of prelapsarian innocence is shattered one summer during a hurricane, when a rundown cottage is the setting for a terrible event. Three decades pass, and the once cheerful 'Go-Go' is dead – perhaps by accident, perhaps by his own hand. His life has not been a happy one, and its many vicissitudes are well known within the Halloran family. All the now grown-up children present during that fateful summer bear the scars of the traumatic events of the past, and it is the death of their comrade that brings them together for some painful revelations. In *The Innocents* (perhaps not coincidentally also the title chosen by Jack Clayton for his film of Henry James' *The Turn of the Screw* – another picture of ruined childhood), Laura Lippman is nothing if not ambitious in characterising her substantial cast of children and adults (the latter mostly conforming to the Philip Larkin school of childrearing). Another writer who comes to mind in the novel's creation of a vulnerable childhood is Harper Lee, as well as the now largely forgotten American master JR Salamanca. The steady, unhurried pace of Lippman's narrative is justified in every sentence; she is a writer who appears to get better from book to book. If the final revelation does not possess the full thrill of horror that Lippman appears to be building towards, that's a small reservation in the context of this luminous book.

MIKE RIPLEY (1969 Britain)

Although his sardonically entertaining series of Angel modern crime novels might not lead one to think so, the protean Mike Ripley has turned out to be an apposite heir apparent for the great Margery Allingham, with his novels featuring the tenacious Albert Campion (such as *Mr Campion's Farewell* – a title, thankfully, that proved inaccurate) affording a rich blend of affectionate recreation and memorable writing. It's hard to imagine a contemporary writer with a more instinctual feel for the correct idiom here, and if we are to have Allingham at several removes, this is the way to go. Eschewing his customary sardonic wit of the Angel novels – or, to be more precise, holding it in check – Ripley provides us with more diverting cases for Albert Campion along with several characters from the canon. Whether or not you are a worshipper at the shrine of one of the greatest female writers of Britain's Golden Age, Ripley's new outings for her sleuth are most definitely worth your attention.

NICCOLÒ AMMANITI (1970s Italy)

Two books by Niccolò Ammaniti, *I'm Not Scared* and his later novel *The Crossroads*, can be read as companion pieces on the complex relationship between father and son, a theme that clearly fascinates the author – before making his name as a thriller writer, he collaborated with his father (a professor in psychopathology) on an essay on the problems of adolescence entitled 'In the Name of the Son'. *I'm Not Scared* is set in the blisteringly hot summer of 1978. While the adults who live in the few houses that make up Aqua Traverse stay indoors, the children roam the countryside on their bikes. And on one of their excursions, in an abandoned farmhouse, Michele discovers a terrible secret. Ammaniti manages to walk a tightrope between writing from the point of view of the nine-year-old Michele and providing enough information (largely through the voice of the narrator, an older Michele) so that we, the reader, are soon able to connect Michele's fateful discovery with the arrival of a mysterious stranger and the tension pervading the village. Not only is this a gripping, unputdownable thriller, Ammaniti's realistic portrayal of his young hero – and Michele's relationship with his friends and family – makes it a compelling coming-of-age drama. In *The Crossroads*, the lead character, Cristiano, is slightly older – 13. At the centre of the narrative is the complex, loving, but occasionally violent relationship between Cristiano and his father Rino, an alcoholic right-wing extremist who is fighting social services to keep his son. Rino and his two friends – a man who blames himself for the death of his daughter, and a dreamer who was strange even before he electrocuted himself – come up with a plan to solve all their problems: they'll ramraid an ATM machine. But instead of a standard robbery-gone-wrong plot, Ammaniti gives us a series of coincidences and twists that, although totally unbelievable, keep the novel hurtling along. Unlike the earlier *I'm Not Scared*, with its sense of unease and suspense, this is a full-blown black comedy, shocking in its descriptions of violence and human stupidity. The popularity of Ammaniti's books in his native Italy is evidenced by the fact that both these novels have been made into films by Gabriele Salvatores, the director of *Mediterraneo*.

Film: I'M NOT SCARED / IO NON HO PAURA (Gabriele Salvatores, director)

Nine-year-old Michele is playing outdoors and discovers another boy, Filippo, who has been imprisoned in a hole in the ground; the unhappy prisoner is chained. Michele spots an unpleasant criminal in the vicinity and realises that something bad is happening but he is not sure who to inform; he finally chooses his closest friend. This is one of the director's most efficiently made films, and the performance by Giuseppe Cristiano as the boy caught up in a dangerous situation demonstrates that Salvatores' lengthy search through hundreds of children paid off handsomely. Despite its menacing accoutrements, this is essentially a coming-of-age tale with the world seen through Michele's eyes. The community in which the boy lives is in an economically deprived part of southern Italy; it is a hardscrabble life in which the principal lesson to be learned is how difficult it is to survive under these harsh conditions. *I'm Not Scared* demonstrates that the country's long tradition of committed filmmaking is in good health.

NATHAN ENGLANDER (1970s Buenos Aires)

To say that there were high expectations for Nathan Englander's first novel, *The Ministry of Special Cases*, is something of an understatement. Englander is a New Yorker who won the PEN/

Malamud Award for his debut collection of short stories, *For the Relief of Unbearable Urges*. Certainly, that book seemed to signal an astringent, sardonic new voice, with its off-kilter synthesis of Isaac Bashevis Singer and Woody Allen. When it was announced that he was working on a novel, admirers were betting that Englander would be a new shining light in the Saul Bellow/Philip Roth school of modern Jewish novelists. All of this, of course, suggests that Englander might have been in danger of being promoted beyond reasonable expectations. So, does *The Ministry of Special Cases* deliver? The book is set in Buenos Aires in the 1970s, with a pending military coup destabilising society. Englander's antihero is Kaddish Poznan, who has carved out a precarious niche for himself by erasing names from gravestones, stripping away traces of embarrassing ancestors for his Jewish clients. He has a fractious relationship with his wife Lillian and son Pato, and the latter nurses a hatred for his father as he is dragged on nocturnal tombstone-chipping expeditions. In fact, Pato is more socially committed than his father, with political activities likely to upset the authorities. The first section of the book is an exercise in corrosive black comedy – but then, as his parents feared, Pato vanishes, spirited away by the authorities for his indiscretions. Kaddish and his wife begin a frantic attempt to save him – and one of their ports of call is the eponymous Ministry of Special Cases. It is Kaddish's surrealistic, disturbing and often grimly funny dealings with this monolithic department that invite comparisons with one of the author's great forebears, Kafka (although Englander has explicitly – and perhaps disingenuously – disavowed such comparisons). But even if he isn't comfortable with the adjective 'Kafkaesque', there's no denying the panache with which Englander reinvents the tropes of *The Trial*. The other Jewish antecedent of the book's protagonist is, of course, James Joyce's Leopold Bloom in *Ulysses* – and there the comparisons are less flattering to Englander. While Bloom, in search (like Kaddish) of his 'lost son', is ineluctably Jewish in his endlessly philosophical and bleakly fatalistic turn of mind, he remains an everyman to whom every reader (Jewish or goyim) can relate. Kaddish is a much more specific figure, set against less universal parameters; while Joyce's 1904 Dublin to readers today seems like present-day London, Englander's 1970s Buenos Aires remains stubbornly 1970s Buenos Aires. On its own highly individual terms, however, the novel proves that Englander has gone some way to justifying the euphoria his name evokes.

GAUTE HEIVOLL (1970s Norway)

Gaute Heivoll's novel *Before I Burn* arrived on UK shores weighed down with encomiums. One of the chorus of praise is the writer Karin Fossum, and Heivoll's publisher is canny to emblazon the jacket with her quote ('One of the best books I have ever read') as she is acclaimed as the finest wielder of language in the Nordic noir field. Certainly, this luminously written novel qualifies as 'literature' (particularly in Don Bartlett's sympathetic translation), but for all its playing with shifting timeframes and self-reflexivity (Heivoll makes himself part of the narrative), the book still has at its centre a dangerous criminal. In the 1970s, a cloistered community in rural Norway experiences a daily terror as a pyromaniac appears set on destroying the town. Civic panic is the order of the day – as is a large dose of paranoia. Neighbour regards neighbour suspiciously, wondering who is behind the arson, while one woman in particular finds her life torn apart, as she slowly realises that the fire starter is her son. The Norwegian author has under his belt some charming children's books and poetry, none of which prepares the reader for the deeply unsettling experience on offer here. Heivoll is particularly adroit at conveying the growing unease of a community under siege, and his description of the conflagrations is shot through with a kind of poetic imagery that removes the book from the parameters of crime fiction. More problematic is the risky strategy that Heivoll adopts of running his own childhood in parallel with the narrative. The author clearly feels a kind of psychic link to the arsonist, and finds his own youth transformed by the town's trauma, with the inevitable separation of parent from child a central metaphor. Although elegantly written, *Before I Burn* is a book full of pain: the destruction of lives, the narrator's father dying of cancer, and an unsparing examination of the darker recesses of the human psyche. But if Heivoll draws back from explaining the mental processes of his murderous doppelgänger, any frustration on the part of the reader (in that we are granted no closure), is a small price to pay: treating the final mystery of human evil as an unknowable thing gives the book a resonance that lives beyond its pages. Those seeking the more immediate pleasures of a crime narrative should look elsewhere, but Heivoll's unhurried prose satisfyingly addresses the mysteries of memory and the precariousness of human existence.

TV: THE GREAT TRAIN ROBBERY (Julian Jarrold and James Strong, directors)

Written by Chris Chibnall (creator of the much-acclaimed *Broadchurch*), *The Great Train Robbery* is a British television film in two parts (not to be confused with the Peter Yates film of the same events, *Robbery*), which was initially broadcast on BBC One in December 2013. The film is a retelling of the events of the Great Train Robbery on 8 August 1963, told first from the perspective of the robbers, and then from that of the police. The show is well written, but without the richness of characterisation of the more complex *Broadchurch*.

13: And Finally...

ANDREW TAYLOR

In theology, the Four Last Things are Death, Judgement, Heaven and Hell. In the sequence that established his reputation, Andrew Taylor cannily utilises this as the perfect foundation for a crime novel. The Roth Trilogy triumphantly demonstrates that crime novels can try to deal with serious themes and use innovative literary techniques. But this was just the start for the industrious Taylor, whose books have been set in Restoration England, eighteenth-century England and America, Regency England, 1930s London and the 1950s Welsh Borders. There was a time when barely a week seemed to pass without the author tucking another award under his belt for such books as *The American Boy*, which invents a secret history of Edgar Allan Poe's childhood, concentrating on an episode in 1819 (Poe lived in England from 1815 to 1820). Taylor's book reflects as accurately as possible the manners and mores of the period. He researched how people spoke and thought and acted in late Regency England, from the mansions of Mayfair to the slums of St Giles and Seven Dials, from the leafy village of Stoke Newington (where Poe went to school) to a country estate in Gloucestershire. It's a formidable, epic achievement.

But while readers might have thought that Taylor's massive *The American Boy* was his magnum opus, a later book (set in a vibrantly evoked Restoration England) suggests otherwise. *The Ashes of London* has the same sprawling reach, but also presents as breathtakingly ambitious a picture of an era as any that we have seen in the genre. As the Great Fire devastates London in 1666, James Marwood, a young Whitehall clerk, is tasked with finding a brutal killer. Catherine Lovett, resisting an arranged marriage, is dreaming of becoming an architect, but her future is clouded by the fact that her father is on the run from Charles II, who in turn is tracking down those who ordered the execution of the old king. The multiple narrative strands – all equally forceful – are drawn together in a brilliantly orchestrated finale. Taylor has won the Crime Writers' Association Historical Dagger on several occasions; it might be an idea for him to continue clearing more spaces on his mantelpiece.

🎙 Interview: Andrew Taylor

I have never felt that I have chosen a particular historical period for a crime novel. It's more the other way round. And it's not one period, either. History is something of a flirt. For example, my Lydmouth series is set in the 1950s, chosen mainly because I wanted an excuse to look at this oddly invisible decade as a whole. *The American Boy*, on the other hand, is set in Regency England. It came from an interest in Poe and Jane Austen, and the unlikely fact that they could have encountered each other in the same London street. Then came *Bleeding Heart Square*, set in 1930s England, followed by three set in the late eighteenth century; one of which, *The Scent of Death*, took place in New York, the others mainly in England.

Now I'm in the seventeenth century and writing about Restoration England with *The Ashes of London*, and one or more sequels yet to come. With the whole of history to play with, I find it hard to restrict myself to a single period. The one thing all my historical crime novels have in common is this: they are set in times and places that interest me – I wrote them partly to have an excuse to find out more. It's a form of self-indulgence that actually pays the bills.

Historical novelists I admire include Patrick O'Brian and Hilary Mantel. The list of historical crime novelists would include John Lawton, CJ Sansom and Laura Wilson. And many others.

Historical crime novels aren't easy to write. True, you can avoid many of the tiresome restrictions that modern technology and bureaucracy place on fiction, but you have to produce something that works both as crime and as history. You have a double chance of failure. And a double pleasure if you get them both right.

You could say that we have invented the past only relatively recently. In 1985, the late Julian Symons published the revised edition of *Bloody Murder*, his critical account of the crime novel's development. His last chapter discusses both existing and emerging trends in the genre. There is nothing about the 'history mystery', or crime novels set in the past. Historical crime novels had existed before the 1980s, of course – among them, John Dickson Carr's *Fire, Burn!* and *The Devil in Velvet* are well worth revisiting – but there were surprisingly few of them. You could call Josephine Tey's *The Daughter of Time* a history mystery, but only if the label is more elastic than usual. About 20 years ago, however, the landscape of the genre began to change. On both sides of the Atlantic, crime fiction was gathering confidence, experimenting and expanding in all sorts of directions. One event nudged an exploratory tendril towards the past, towards the history mystery. This was the enormous worldwide success of Umberto Eco's *The Name of the Rose* in the early 1980s.

My own preference, as a reader, is for history mysteries that work their setting subtly into the fabric of the narrative rather than embroider it garishly in the most visible places. You know the sort of thing – 'How do, Sir Isaac, is that an apple in your hand? You're working on one of your theories, I'll be bound.' A sense of history is rather like having an ear for music. You can understand musical theory but you may not be able to hear the difference between a B flat and a C. A good historical novel of any type is not solely dependent on knowledge, though most of them have that too. It also depends on the author having a feeling of what is fitting, what suits the context and what doesn't. Yes, a good historical novel is a pack of lies, but some lies are more plausible than others. Some lies even achieve their own truth. I came to write historical crime novels by accident. Many of my earlier novels had hinterlands in the past, which probably reflected my own interest in history and a fascination with the way the past and present interact. If nothing else, a historical novel may give us a better idea of the baggage that we ourselves carry in the present.

TV: FALLEN ANGEL (David Drury, director)

Andrew Taylor's success is not due to luck but to his nonpareil writing skills – and the same might be said for his numerous awards. But perhaps casting played a part in the acclaim that greeted the television adaptation of his Roth Trilogy, which bore the title *Fallen*

Angel. The impeccable players included Charles Dance (now firmly ensconced in character parts) and Emilia Fox, along with an equally strong supporting cast. *Fallen Angel* drew from Taylor's trilogy the notion of the plot travelling backwards in time, showing the clandestine history of a murderer from effects to causes. While many of the novels' nuances were elided, it was a creditable piece of work.

ROBERT GODDARD

Publishers have long touted other writers as the world's great storytellers, but that term really belongs to the accomplished Robert Goddard, whose very English novels tackle a wide variety of idioms, periods and locales. The hero of his first book, *Past Caring*, is a historian, and Goddard's own interest in that field becomes more and more evident throughout his work. Two novels in particular feature strong evocations of the past, *Painting the Darkness* and *The Ways of the World* (the first instalment of the Wide World trilogy). The former, set in in 1882, is a particularly formidable achievement. Goddard's protagonist William Trenchard receives an unexpected visitor one autumn afternoon, blissfully unaware that this stranger will bring about the destruction of all that he holds dear. The visitor's name is James Norton, and he claims to be the man to whom William's wife Constance was once engaged – and who was said to have committed suicide over a decade ago. Trenchard fears the loss of his wife's affection, but that proves to be the very least of his problems. What is so satisfying here – as with Goddard's other historical novels – is the marriage of his ironclad storytelling skills with an unforced abundance of epochal indicators, never shoehorned into the narrative but always perfectly at the service of the story.

🎙 **Interview: Robert Goddard**

I've never wanted to tie myself down to one historical period. I always suspected, even before becoming a writer, that there would be ideas to be mined from the present day, the recent past, and, come to that, the not-so-recent past. The plots my imagination supplies often tend to involve the past influencing the present, so a historical element is more or less inescapable. Not that I've ever wanted to escape it. I approach a contemporary setting in much the same way as a period setting, looking for a sense of time and place for the characters to explore the story in. Everything's history really. That's why there are so many stories to be told.

The structure of a story is as important as the idea itself in determining whether it will truly satisfy as well as entertain. In terms of historical noir, I think those two features came together to particularly good effect in *Caught in the Light*, *Sight Unseen*, *Long Time Coming*, *Fault Line* and my recently concluded Wide World trilogy.

The two writers who really inspired me before I started writing were Wilkie Collins and John Fowles. Collins is unsurpassed – probably unsurpassable – for sheer plot-making energy. Maybe the laudanum had something to do with it, but the style and originality of *The Woman in White* in particular, given that it was written way back in the 1850s, are just breathtaking. And I think you can see in many writers, including me, the influence of what he achieved. Is historical noir a genre or simply a portmanteau phrase for crime and mystery thrillers set in the past? In the end, it doesn't really matter. It encompasses a wide range of fascinating stories and storytellers. Who can ask for more?

Appendix

THE ELLIS PETERS/CWA ENDEAVOUR HISTORICAL DAGGER

Endeavour
2017: *A Rising Man* by Abir Mukherjee
2016: *Stasi Child* by David Young
2015: *The Seeker* by SG MacLean
2014: *The Devil in the Marshalsea* by Antonia Hodgson

Ellis Peters
2013: *The Scent of Death* by Andrew Taylor
2012: *Icelight* by Aly Monroe
2011: *The Somme Stations* by Andrew Martin
2010: *Revenger* by Rory Clements
2009: *If the Dead Rise Not* by Philip Kerr
2008: *Stratton's War* by Laura Wilson
2007: *Mistress of the Art of Death* by Ariana Franklin
2006: *Red Sky Lament* by Edward Wright
2005: *Dark Fire* by CJ Sansom
2004: *The Damascened Blade* by Barbara Cleverly
2003: *The American Boy* by Andrew Taylor
2002: *Fingersmith* by Sarah Waters
2001: *The Office of the Dead* by Andrew Taylor
2000: *Absent Friends* by Gillian Linscott
1999: *Two for the Lions* by Lindsey Davis

Acknowledgements

Firstly, I'd like to thank all the novelists who allowed me to interview them for these pages. And as with this book's predecessor, *American Noir*, I owe a debt of gratitude to *The Rap Sheet*'s knowledgeable J Kingston Pierce, whose advice was extremely useful. As was that of ace practitioners of the genre Imogen Robertson and Andrew Taylor. The customary nods go to Kim Newman and Ayo Onatade, my colleagues at No Exit Press and Judith Forshaw.

Index

About Us

In addition to Pocket Essentials, Oldcastle Books has a number of other imprints, including Kamera Books, Creative Essentials, Pulp! The Classics, No Exit Press and High Stakes Publishing > oldcastlebooks.co.uk

For more information about Crime Books go to > crimetime.co.uk

Check out the kamera film salon for independent, arthouse and world cinema > kamera.co.uk

For more information, media enquiries and review copies please contact marketing > marketing@oldcastlebooks.co.uk